triumphlearning™

English Language Arts

5

Coach®

Contents

CHAPTER

Reading Literature

1 Diagnostic Assessment

Read the passage and answer the questions that follow.

Life on a Houseboat

Declan was working on his report for school. It was about the Illinois and Michigan Canal. Declan had made good progress so far. Normally, he got distracted by something halfway through. But not this time!

The canal connected Chicago and the southern tip of Lake Michigan with the upper Illinois River valley. Before the canal was built, the northern part of Illinois was a frontier area with few people living in it. After the canal was built, farms, stores, and factories started appearing in this part of the state. They supplied the people of Chicago with many things. Boats carrying people and goods traveled through the canal until the late 1890s. In its later years, it was used more for pleasure than business.

Declan stopped reading. He got up from his desk and paced around his room. He had learned a great deal about the canal. But now he was thinking about something else. While doing research for his report, he had read about houseboats. They're just like houses, except they're boats that people live on. Some are kept moored at a dock and don't go anywhere. Some have engines and travel across lakes, rivers, or canals.

Imagine living on a houseboat, thought Declan. *You could travel over water, right from where you live.* The more he thought about it, the more fun it seemed. He decided he wanted to learn more about houseboats. He went online and started doing more research.

One of the first things Declan learned was that people live in houseboats all over the world. They're extremely common in Holland, especially in the city of

Amsterdam. This city has many canals, and there are houseboats moored all along them. In fact, there are about 2,400 houseboats tied up along Amsterdam's canals. There are even houseboats that are hotels. And one is a flower market.

Shaking himself out of his daydreams, Declan decided to see where in the United States people live on houseboats. He soon found out that people live on houseboats all over the country. Houseboats are very popular in Seattle, Washington, where there are about 500 of them. They're also popular in Sausalito, California. There are houseboats there owned by famous musicians, film stars, and authors.

Declan stopped reading again. He imagined steering his own houseboat to a dock and mooring it next to a houseboat owned by a movie star. That would be fun!

What he read next surprised Declan. In some places, boats are just like stores. There's a floating bank in Virginia. There's even a floating post office in Alaska.

Will I ever get to live on a houseboat? Declan wondered. What he read next made him think he might, if only for a short time. There are lakes and rivers where people can rent houseboats by the week or month.

Declan began to get an idea. Would his mom and dad consider going there on vacation this summer? If they did, would they be willing to rent a houseboat? The more Declan thought about it, the more excited he became. He could see himself on the boat, cruising down the river with trees standing tall against the sky on the shore.

"Declan! Time for dinner!" his mom called out.

Declan ran to wash his hands and went into the kitchen. His mom and dad were sitting at the table, waiting for him. Declan's smile was like a torch, right there in the dining room.

"How are you doing on your report?" his dad asked.

Suddenly, Declan's smile faded, as he realized what had happened. He'd never finish his report now.

"Is something wrong?" his mom asked.

"No…not really…," he said, as he thought about what was going to happen next. He wouldn't finish the report. He'd get points taken off. He'd get a bad grade on the paper. And then…the houseboat trip? Not a chance.

"Well, actually…I think I might need some help," he said. His dad had helped him before, and hopefully he would help him again.

"Let me guess," his dad said. "Hmm… This isn't about your report, is it?"

"How'd you guess?" said Declan.

"You seemed way too cheerful to be thinking about your homework," said his dad, grinning.

1. This passage is written from which point of view?

   A. first-person

   B. second-person

   C. third-person omniscient

   D. third-person limited

2. Which sentence from the passage BEST helps you identify the setting?

   A. "Declan was working on his report for school."

   B. "They supplied the people of Chicago with many things."

   C. "He got up from his desk and paced around his room."

   D. "They're also popular in Sausalito, California."

3. Declan can BEST be described as

   A. practical.

   B. focused.

   C. easily distracted.

   D. disagreeable.

4. What does the following sentence mean?

   Declan's smile was like a torch, right there in the dining room.

   A. Declan was very warm.

   B. Declan was smart and bright.

   C. Declan's smile cheered up the room.

   D. Declan's smile made him sweat.

5. Based on the passage, what can you infer about houseboats?

_____

_____

_____

_____

_____

_____

Read the passage and answer the questions that follow.

Grounded Plans

(Setting: *As the curtain goes up, Audrey is sitting on a couch next to a cat. The couch is facing stage right. Under the girl's feet is a plush carpet. There is a bay window in the room, and light flows from it onto the pale yellow walls. On the coffee table there is a soda can, chips, and magazines. Audrey is tapping her foot on the edge of the coffee table as she types on her cell phone with great speed. The cat is cleaning itself.*)

AUDREY: (*hears her mother's footsteps*) Oh great.

(*Audrey removes her foot from the coffee table. Audrey's mother turns the doorknob.*)

MOTHER: Well, I really wish you would've told me.

(*The cat jumps off the couch.*)

AUDREY: (*without looking up from her phone*) Told you what?

MOTHER: Could you please take your eyes off the phone for a second?

(*Audrey takes a moment before looking up.*)

MOTHER: Your teacher just called. She's concerned. Your report's a week late.

AUDREY: I can explain!

MOTHER: Explain what? You had over two weeks to work on that report. What exactly were you doing last weekend?

AUDREY: Research.

MOTHER: Into what?

AUDREY: For my report!

MOTHER: Really? That's the truth? Sometimes you're as deaf as a stone wall. I tell you not to make up things, but you don't listen. Your younger sister told me...

AUDREY: (*face turning red*) Brianna's not telling you the whole story.

MOTHER: (*crosses arms*) Brianna said you were at the mall instead of working at the library. So I called Shawna's mother, and she confirmed that you were at the mall.

AUDREY: I'm telling you she doesn't understand.

MOTHER: (*places hands on hips*) What doesn't she understand?

AUDREY: (*goes back to looking at her phone*) Shawna and I started out at the library. And then, when we realized—

MOTHER: Realized you were bored?

AUDREY: No, when we realized we didn't have the books we needed, we decided to go to the bookstore in the mall. How many books on houseboats do you think the library has?

MOTHER: So you went to the bookstore, and went back to the library?

AUDREY: Well… Not exactly.

MOTHER: I thought so.

AUDREY: But I needed new shoes!

MOTHER: You've got seven pairs already.

AUDREY: But—

MOTHER: Your report's due at the end of this week. No mall, no shoes, no TV, and no phone until it's done!

AUDREY: (*dejected*) Fine…

6. The conflict in this passage is between

   A. Audrey and her mother.

   B. Audrey and Brianna.

   C. Audrey and Shawna.

   D. Brianna and Shawna.

7. What is the theme of the passage?

   A. It is easy to get away with lying.

   B. Sometimes you have to tell lies to get what you want.

   C. Lying can get you out of trouble.

   D. Lying can get you in trouble.

8. What does the following sentence mean?

   Sometimes you're as deaf as a stone wall.

   A. I can't see through you.

   B. I can't get through to you.

   C. You are not nice.

   D. You are very strong.

9. According to the description of the setting, Audrey and her mother are

   A. at the mall.

   B. on vacation.

   C. in their living room.

   D. going to Shawna's house.

10. How are Declan from "Life on a Houseboat" and Audrey from "Grounded Plans" alike? How are they different?

_____

_____

_____

_____

_____

1 Support Your Ideas

Getting the Idea

Sometimes you make generalizations about what you read. A **generalization** is a broad statement. You make this statement based on the text and your own experience. Quoting a phrase or sentence from a passage is a good way to support a generalization. Read the paragraph below.

> Tables and chairs had been set up in the school gym for the big checkers tournament. The gym was packed with students talking excitedly as they waited to see whom they would be paired with. Suddenly, Steve walked into the gym. The students stopped talking and stared. A few began to bite their fingernails. Most of them hoped they would not have to face Steve in the first round.

What generalizations can you make from this paragraph? One generalization would be that checkers is important at this school. The paragraph also supports the generalization that the students fear and respect Steve's skill as a checkers player. Generalizations must be supported by the text. In the example above, you could support your generalization by quoting from the passage. You could say, for instance, that the gym was "packed with students talking excitedly." This would indicate that checkers is important at the school. If you mentioned that the students "stared" at Steve when he entered, this quote would support the generalization that they fear and respect his skills.

You will mainly support your generalizations about texts with **details**, such as names of characters, lines of dialogue, or descriptive sentences. On the next page are some examples of details you might encounter.

Types of Details	Examples
names of characters	Ramona Quimby has a great imagination.
description of the environment	The rain whipped across the deck.
names of places	Jimmy lives in Lexington, Kentucky.
dates and times	Keegan was born at 7:00 a.m. on May 21, 1999.
the things that the narrator tells you	Frank wanted to be rich when he grew up.
the things that characters say and do	Gary told Lewis, "Everybody loves a clown."

There are many other types of details not listed in the chart. As you read, pay attention to all of the details in the text. The better you understand a story or poem, the easier it will be to form ideas and make statements about what you read.

Sometimes the author of a story does not tell you exactly what is happening. If you don't know what's happening in a story, it's hard to make a broad statement about it. This means that you have to figure things out on your own. When you do this, you make an inference. An **inference** is a decision based on available details. When you make an inference, you must have some form of support to back it up. You will often be asked to cite details from the text that led you to make your inference. You can also use your prior knowledge. **Prior knowledge** is knowledge you have before you read a text. Suppose a writer has a character do the following things: tap his feet, look at his watch, scratch his head, look at his watch, stand up, sit down, and look at his watch again. You can infer from these actions that the character is waiting for someone and is getting impatient. Even if the author doesn't tell you this, you can infer it from the information you have been given.

When you read, you can make inferences about

- a character's personality, interests, or physical appearance
- a character's history
- a character's age
- the history of relationships between characters
- the reasons for a character's specific behaviors
- a character's intentions
- the next action a character will take

Thinking It Through

Read the following paragraph, and then answer the questions that follow.

Manuel had been talking about his birthday for months. He kept reminding his mom and dad about the video games that would make great presents. The week before his birthday, Manuel made sure to finish his homework early and do extra chores around the house. While cleaning out one of the closets, Manuel saw a package wrapped in colorful paper. He looked around to make sure no one was around and carefully peeled off the tape to look inside.

Do you think Manuel is patient or impatient? Which details in the paragraph support your inference?

_____

_____

_____

_____

 Remember, any inference you make must be based on specific details.

DISCUSS Discuss your answer with a classmate. Then tell about a time when you felt impatient about something. What made you feel that way?

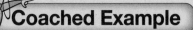

Coached Example

Read the passage and answer the questions.

The Rodriguez family was very involved in their community. When the McDonnells' house was leveled by a tornado, the Rodriguezes got the entire neighborhood to help rebuild the damaged home. Mr. Rodriguez and the other men worked on the roof, while Mrs. Rodriguez worked in the McDonnells' garden with some of the women. Jose Rodriguez and his older sister, Angela, helped paint the walls. Jose tried painting with a roller brush, but he couldn't reach very high. He jumped as high he could and splattered paint all over the windows. Angela shook her head and walked inside the house. Jose looked up and smiled when he saw Angela carrying a footstool. Jose stood on the stool while Angela showed him how to use the roller brush.

1. Based on the passage, you can infer that

   A. the Rodriguezes are selfish.

   B. Jose wants to work in the garden.

   C. Jose is not an experienced painter.

   D. the McDonnells' house was beautiful.

   HINT An inference is a conclusion based on available details.

2. Which detail from the passage does NOT support the idea that Angela is patient?

   A. She helps paint the walls.

   B. She brings a stool for Jose.

   C. She shows Jose how to use the roller brush.

   D. She shakes her head.

   HINT Details from the passage should support any inferences you make.

Lesson Practice

Use the Reading Guide to help you understand the passage.

Reading Guide

Why does Monica smile?

What can you infer about Ebony's character?

What generalization could you make about Ebony's friendship with Monica?

Storming the Castle

Monica and Ebony ran toward the castle door. But as Ebony reached it, she tripped and fell on her face.

"Cut!" Mr. Washington yelled. "Are you okay, Ebony?"

A couple of the other actors helped Ebony up.

"I'm okay," Ebony replied, "Sorry, everyone."

Monica smiled and wiped dust off Ebony's costume. "Wow, Ebony. I can't believe how clumsy you are."

Ebony held back her tears and tried to pretend everything was fine. The students had been practicing for their annual play for weeks. Every day after school, they stayed late to make sure that everything was perfect. This year, the play was about a witch trying to take over a medieval castle. The students wrote the script and even designed the sets and costumes. Everyone learned something new on this project.

Monica and Ebony had been friends since kindergarten. They both tried out for the role of the princess. Ebony won the leading role, even though Monica had taken more acting classes. They had a fight after Ebony got the role, and then they saw less of each other. By this point, they had stopped talking to each other outside of rehearsals.

Monica walked back to her place and waited for the others to take their places. Ebony walked up and stood next to Monica. They looked at each other, as if to ask, "Are you ready to get back to it?" Ebony began to cry. Monica put her arms around Ebony as tears welled up in her eyes, too. Soon, they both began sobbing.

The other students watched the two friends. The rehearsal could wait a few minutes.

Answer the following questions.

1. Based on the passage, you can infer that

    A. Monica is jealous of Ebony.

    B. Monica is clumsy.

    C. Ebony is jealous of Monica.

    D. Ebony is not a good actress.

2. Ebony is PROBABLY

    A. happy that she received the leading role.

    B. happy to be in the play.

    C. looking for attention.

    D. upset that she and Monica are not getting along.

3. Which detail from the passage does NOT support the idea that Monica and Ebony were getting along poorly?

    A. Ebony trips and falls.

    B. Monica does not help Ebony up.

    C. Monica calls Ebony clumsy.

    D. Monica and Ebony cry together.

4. Which sentence from the passage supports the idea that the play is important to the students?

    A. "A couple of the other actors helped Ebony up."

    B. "Every day after school, they stayed late to make sure that everything was perfect."

    C. "This year, the play was about a witch trying to take over a medieval castle."

    D. "The other students watched the two friends."

5. Do you think Monica and Ebony will be friends after the play is over? Which details in the passage support your inference?

    _____

    _____

    _____

    _____

    _____

Use the Reading Guide to help you understand the passage.

How does Randy behave at the start of the passage? What details suggest his mood?

What generalization can you make about how Randy feels about meeting the band after the concert? What details from the story support your generalization?

Backstage Passes

Randy clutched the badge hanging on the lanyard around his neck. It was still secure. Undoubtedly, it was the most amazing prize he'd ever won. And yet, it was the most uncomplicated contest he'd ever entered. All he had to do was answer trivia questions about his favorite band, the band he was going to meet immediately after the concert.

Randy pointed to the badge and said loudly to his friend Pete, "Backstage Passes!"

Pete gave Randy an enthusiastic high-five. Pete was thrilled to join his friend at the concert.

Randy and Pete screamed, clapped, and sang along to every song of the night. By the end of the concert, they were drenched with perspiration.

As the rest of the audience exited the stadium, Pete and Randy sprinted toward a gate adjacent to the stage. When they flashed their badges to the guard, he acknowledged their special privileges by opening the gate.

"I can't believe we're going to meet the band," Randy said. "What do we say to them?"

"You can always recite trivia facts about their songs," Pete joked.

The reception room was jam-packed with people. Randy scanned the crowd. He shifted his weight from one foot to the next and then adjusted his badge.

"There are too many people," Randy said. "What if they're not even here?"

"They're here, somewhere," Pete said.

Pete grabbed Randy's arm and pointed. Randy stared into the crowd. There, not ten feet in front of him, was the lead singer, the man Randy idolized.

Answer the following questions.

6. Use your answer to Part A to answer Part B.

   Part A

   Based on the passage, what can you infer about Randy and Pete?

   A. The boys met recently at school.

   B. The boys have similar interests.

   C. The boys only go to concerts together.

   D. The boys have very different personalities.

   Part B

   Which sentence from the passage BEST supports your answer to Part A?

   A. "Undoubtedly, it was the most amazing prize he'd ever won."

   B. "Pete grabbed Randy's arm and pointed."

   C. "'There are too many people,' Randy said."

   D. "Pete was thrilled to join his friend at the concert."

   E. "By the end of the concert, they were drenched with perspiration."

7. Choose all the words that describe how Randy feels about meeting the band, based on evidence from the text. There is more than one correct choice listed below.

   A. agitated

   B. hurt

   C. eager

   D. embarrassed

   E. indifferent

   F. tense

Use the Reading Guide to help you understand the passage.

Memory Jars

Reading Guide

Why doesn't Felipe listen to Kenzie when she shows her collection?

What can you infer about Felipe's character?

What will Felipe likely do when it is his turn to share his collection?

As Kenzie showed the class her collection of animal figurines, Felipe thought about the small jars buried deep in his backpack. One jar held beach sand from his family's vacation in California. Another jar was filled with tiny pine cones he found when hiking with his grandmother. Other jars held assorted bits and pieces that reminded Felipe of special days or places.

Also in Felipe's backpack was a stack of baseball cards. At one time he had collected them, but he had soon lost interest. A question swam in Felipe's mind. His memory jars or the baseball card collection? Which would he talk about?

Felipe had seen five other baseball card collections, stamps, and shell collections. Right now Simon was showing rocks that he pulled out of his pockets. Felipe smiled and shook his head. He had seen Simon picking up the rocks before the first bell.

"Thank you, Simon," Mr. Talbot said. "Collecting rocks can be an interesting hobby. Maybe you can learn the types of rocks and let us know later!" Simon frowned and stuffed the rocks back into his pockets.

"Lunch time!" said Mr. Talbot. "Felipe, you're up when we get back."

At lunch, Felipe sat with Kamal and Matt. "What did you bring?" Kamal asked Felipe.

Felipe hesitated before answering. "Baseball cards," he said. "What about you?"

"Movie stubs," Kamal said. "I know, strange, right? I've saved the ticket stub for every movie I've ever seen."

"That's awesome!" said Matt. "I wish I had a cool collection. I brought baseball cards like just about everybody else."

"I couldn't decide, so I brought in another collection, too," Felipe said.

Answer the following questions.

8. Based on the first paragraph, you can infer that

    A. Felipe thinks Kenzie's collection is silly.

    B. Felipe collects special memories.

    C. Kenzie is very excited about her collection.

    D. Kenzie wants to impress her classmates.

9. Which detail from the passage does NOT support the idea that Felipe is nervous about showing his collection of jars?

    A. Felipe also brought in a baseball card collection.

    B. Felipe hesitated before answering Kamal.

    C. Felipe had already seen five baseball card collections.

    D. Felipe had the jars buried deep in his backpack.

10. Kamal is PROBABLY

    A. interested in Matt's baseball card collection.

    B. upset that he doesn't have baseball cards.

    C. happy to show his movie stub collection.

    D. nervous to show his movie stub collection.

11. Which detail BEST supports the idea that Simon was not prepared when he got to school that morning?

    A. Simon picked up the rocks before school.

    B. Simon took the rocks out of his pockets.

    C. Felipe smiled when Simon showed his rocks.

    D. Mr. Talbot wants to know the types of rocks he has.

12. Which collection do you think Felipe will show when it is his turn? Which details in the passage support your inference?

_____

_____

_____

_____

2 Plot, Character, and Setting

Getting the Idea

Many elements make up a story. The three main elements are plot, character, and setting. The **plot** is the series of events in a story. The **characters** are the people or animals in a story. **Setting** is the location and time in which a story takes place. As you read, you need to fully understand these elements. There may be more than one setting in a story, and there may often be more than one character. A story may also have more than one plot; there may be a plot developing at the same time as a sub-plot. As you read, learn to compare and contrast characters with each other. Learn to notice how settings change from one part of a story to another.

Sometimes, the setting is stated directly in the story. Look at this example.

> It was a hot summer in the early 1940s. The Stevens'
> house was nestled in rolling green hills that overlooked
> an ocean.

The paragraph shows the reader when and where the story takes place. Sometimes, however, the author does not say directly what the setting is. When this happens, you have to figure out the setting from clues in the story. Longer stories may have different settings for different parts of the plot.

Each story includes at least one character. Every character has at least one **trait**. Character traits are all the qualities that make up a character's personality. For example, the following sentence shows a character trait.

> Sally's backpack was overflowing with wrinkled bunches
> of papers, candy wrappers, and broken pencils.

This sentence shows that messiness is one of the girl's traits. Sometimes, if a character speaks in a certain way, his or her **dialect** may also become one of his or her traits. The way a character looks and dresses might be a trait, as well.

A **motivation** is the reason a character does a certain thing or acts a certain way. A good way to learn about character motivation is to ask yourself, "Why is the character doing this?" or "Why is the character behaving this way?" If you can recognize both traits and motivations, you will have a good understanding of the characters in a story.

Characters and settings are both essential parts of the plot. Setting usually affects the plot, and all of the main characters are somehow involved in the plot. Each event in a story usually affects the event following it.

It's not enough to say that a story has a beginning, a middle, and an end. There is much more to a story than that. One important element is exposition. **Exposition** introduces the reader to the characters and the setting early on in the story. Stories also have conflict. A **conflict** is the struggle between the characters in a story. The plot's conflict could be between two characters who both want the same thing. It could be between two characters who have very different personalities. It might be between a character and his own feelings or wishes. It might also be between people and some aspect of nature, such as bad weather. The conflict often causes a problem that must be solved. The **climax** occurs when the main characters address the conflict directly. The climax is usually the most exciting part of the story. For example, a character might decide to try to solve a problem by having an argument. The argument itself then becomes the climax. The **resolution** is the solving of the story's problem. For instance, if there were a fight in the story, the resolution would tell the reader the outcome of the fight.

Thinking It Through

Read the following paragraph, and then answer the questions that follow.

It was summertime, and all the lawns in the neighborhood had just been mowed. The sky was blue, and smoke reached into the sky from a neighbor's barbeque. On days like these, Jamie could jump rope in the back yard for hours.

What is the setting of the story? How do you know?

_____

_____

_____

_____

 Setting is where and when a story takes place. Check the paragraph for words that give clues to its time and location.

DISCUSS Describe a place you like to visit in the summer. Include details that would help listeners to picture what the place looks like. Share your ideas in a group.

Coached Example

Read the passage and answer the questions.

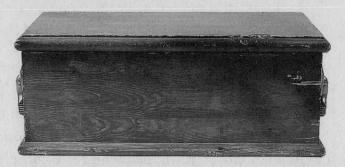

Olivia had been looking forward to the concert for months. Her favorite violinist was playing at the orchestra hall. However, she needed a nice outfit. Her best friend, Hailey, helped her repair an old dress. Hailey was always doing nice things for Olivia. Olivia couldn't wait to show off the dress. Hours before the concert, however, Olivia remembered that she was supposed to clean out the garage before she could leave. She'd promised earlier, and she always kept her promises. When Olivia lifted up an old pile of newspapers, she saw a wooden box. She picked up the box and noticed some strange scribbles on the lid. They looked like they were from some kind of alphabet, but not one she had seen before. It looked like it might be a combination of Chinese and hieroglyphics. As Olivia rubbed the dust and grime off the lid, the box rumbled and the lid flew open. Olivia dropped the box and stood in amazement as a genie appeared before her. "You have one wish and one wish only," the genie said. Olivia smiled.

---

1. What is the conflict of the story?

   A. Olivia wants to make a new dress.

   B. Olivia's mother wants to clean the garage.

   C. Olivia's friend, Hailey, wants to help sew a dress.

   D. Olivia wants to go to the concert but has to clean the garage instead.

   HINT The conflict is the problem that the characters are faced with.

2. What do Hailey and the genie have in common?

   A. They are both human.

   B. They are both superhuman.

   C. They both do favors for Olivia.

   D. They are both related to Olivia.

   HINT Find some actions in the passage that show the genie's and Hailey's character traits.

Lesson Practice

Use the Reading Guide to help you understand the passage.

Reading Guide

What might motivate the speaker to make these statements about facts?

Who are the characters in the passage?

Think about the difference between the schoolmaster and his students as you read.

excerpted and adapted from

Hard Times

by Charles Dickens

"Now, what I really want is facts. Teach these boys and girls nothing but facts. Facts are the only thing anyone wants in life. Only facts will be useful for all people. This is the principle I use to bring up my own children. I will use the same principles to bring up *these* children. Sir, stick to the facts!"

The scene was in a plain, bare, and boring schoolroom. The speaker had a big square forefinger. As he spoke, his finger waved in the air as if to bring emphasis to every sentence. The emphasis was helped by the speaker's square wall of a forehead. His eyebrows made the base of the wall. His eyes were deep in his head, like two dark caves. The emphasis was helped by the speaker's mouth, wide, thin, and hard set. The emphasis was helped by the speaker's hair that bristled on the edges of his bald head. The speaker wore a square coat and he stood on square legs. Lastly, he wore a big tie that looked like it wanted to take him by the throat and make him gasp.

The speaker's presence made his speech sound more serious. "In this life, we want nothing but facts, sir; nothing but facts!"

The speaker, the schoolmaster, and another adult stepped back. They looked at the children. To the speakers, the children looked like empty containers ready to be filled with facts.

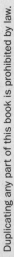

Answer the following questions.

1. The speaker can BEST be described as

   A. a person who has an interesting appearance.

   B. a person who likes to teach art and music.

   C. a person who believes in one way of teaching.

   D. a person who does not like to talk.

2. Which sentence from the passage BEST helps you identify the setting?

   A. "The scene was in a plain, bare, and boring schoolroom."

   B. "The emphasis was helped by the speaker's square wall of a forehead."

   C. "The speaker wore a square coat and he stood on square legs."

   D. "They looked at the children."

3. The conflict in this story is between

   A. the speaker and the schoolmaster.

   B. the speaker and the other adult.

   C. the speaker and the children.

   D. the schoolmaster and the other adult.

4. What will MOST LIKELY be the resolution of the story?

   A. The speaker's tie makes him gasp.

   B. The children are taught facts.

   C. The schoolmaster and the speaker fight.

   D. The speaker teaches facts to his own children.

5. What is one difference between the schoolmaster and the students?

   _____

   _____

   _____

   _____

   _____

Use the Reading Guide to help you understand the passage.

What is the setting of this passage?

What character traits would you use to describe the narrator, Jim?

What is the narrator's motive for jumping from the boat and running?

excerpted and adapted from

Treasure Island
by Robert Louis Stevenson

The captain whipped out of sight in a moment, leaving Long John Silver to arrange the party. It was as plain as day. Silver was the captain, and a mighty rebellious crew he had. The honest hands, and there were some, must have been very stupid fellows.

At last, however, the party was made up. Six fellows were to stay on board, and the remaining thirteen, including Silver, began to embark.

Then it was that there came into my head the first of the mad notions that contributed so much to saving our lives. It occurred to me at once to go ashore. In a jiffy I had slipped over the side and curled up in the bow of the nearest boat, and almost at the same moment she shoved off.

No one took notice of me, only the bow oar saying, "Is that you, Jim? Keep your head down." But Silver, from the other boat, looked sharply over and called out to know if that was me, and from that moment I began to regret what I had done.

The crews raced for the beach, but the boat I was in, having some start and being at once the lighter and the better manned, shot far ahead of the other boat. The bow struck among the shore-side trees, and I caught a branch and swung myself out and plunged into the nearest thicket while Silver and the rest were still a hundred yards behind.

"Jim, Jim!" I heard him shouting.

But you may suppose I paid no heed; jumping, ducking, and breaking through, I ran straight till I could run no longer.

Duplicating any part of this book is prohibited by law.

30 • Chapter 1: Reading Literature

Answer the following questions.

6. Write words from the word boxes to complete the chart. Choose three character traits to describe the narrator, Jim. Then choose three details to support your answer.

Character Traits
confused
comical
cunning
determined
quick-witted

Supporting Details
"…I had slipped over the side and curled up in the bow…"
"…I ran straight till I could run no longer."
"It occurred to me at once to go ashore."
"…must have been very stupid fellows."

Jim

Character Traits	Supporting Details

7. Use your answer to Part A to answer Part B.

Part A

Choose all the words that describe how Jim feels about Silver, based on the text. There is more than one correct choice listed below.

A. admiring

B. annoyed

C. distrustful

D. generous

E. fascinated

F. terrified

Part B

Choose a sentence from the text to support one of your answers to Part A. Write the sentence below.

_____

_____

_____

_____

_____

Use the Reading Guide to help you understand the passage.

Reading Guide

Which words give clues about the setting of the story?

What actions show the character traits of Tessa and Amber?

What is Amber's motive for changing her mind about the water slide?

At the Water Park

Tessa and Amber stood at the entrance to Plunge Water Park, shading their eyes in the hot sun. It was ten o'clock, and Tessa's mom had just dropped them off. The girls paid the entrance fee and scanned the park map.

Tessa wasn't sure where to start, so Amber suggested they go to the splash pad. Tessa agreed, and soon they were playing in the cool spray that shot up from jets in the ground.

"That was just a warm-up," remarked Tessa. "Let's try something more challenging." She pointed to the towering water slide across the park.

The girls made their way to the water slide. Once they stood beside it, Amber realized how enormous it was. To reach the top, they would have to climb a tall, winding staircase. The ride down was on a steep, twisting slide. Some sections went through tunnels.

Amber took a deep breath. She didn't want to spoil Tessa's fun, but she just couldn't imagine taking that intimidating ride. She proposed something a little tamer. "How about the lazy river?" Tessa knew that was a slow-moving water ride on rafts, and it was not very thrilling. But when she saw how anxious her friend was, she went along with Amber's idea.

The girls enjoyed the leisurely ride. "Thanks for riding the lazy river with me, Tessa. Maybe next time I'll feel braver," Amber said.

Then the morning was over, and Tessa's mom picked them up. In the car, the girls planned their return in a few weeks.

The next month, Tessa and Amber went back to the water park. Amber wanted to head straight for the giant water slide. The two friends smiled at each other. Today they were *both* ready for an adventure.

Answer the following questions.

8. What is the setting of the story?

   A. afternoon in the car

   B. morning at the splash pad

   C. morning at Plunge Water Park

   D. summer at the beach

9. Which sentence helps you identify how the setting changes at the end of the story?

   A. "The next month, Tessa and Amber went back to the water park."

   B. "The girls enjoyed the leisurely ride."

   C. "The ride down was on a steep, twisting slide."

   D. "The girls made their way to the water slide."

10. Which character trait BEST describes Tessa?

    A. bossy

    B. daring

    C. timid

    D. selfish

11. What is the conflict in the story?

    A. Tessa does not like challenging rides, but Amber does.

    B. Amber wants to return to the water park, but Tessa does not.

    C. Amber is willing to ride the lazy river, but Tessa is not.

    D. Tessa wants to ride on the water slide, but Amber does not.

12. How is the conflict resolved at the end of the story?

    _____

    _____

    _____

    _____

    _____

3 Theme

Getting the Idea

The **theme** is the central idea or meaning of a story. It is a lesson, moral, or comment on life that an author wants the reader to understand. You can think of theme as the author's message to the reader.

A written work may have a single theme or several themes. Many common themes can be expressed through well-known sayings that you might recognize in the box below.

Common Themes

Patience is a virtue.

Giving is better than receiving.

What's good for one person might not be good for another.

Family and friends are worth more than gold.

People succeed when they work together.

You should treat others the way you would like to be treated.

How do you know what the theme of the story is? The author does not usually tell you the theme of the story. You have to figure it out yourself. To identify themes, the reader must consider the actions, feelings, thoughts, and words of characters in the story. Think about how the characters deal with conflicts. And then think about how these actions are connected to life in the real world. Ask yourself, "What lesson should I learn from this story?" Look at the example below.

> Rebecca and I bought a cookie at the mall. She tried to break the cookie in half, but when she did, one side was bigger than the other. She gave me the bigger half.

Now ask yourself, "What lesson should I take away from this?" Your answer might be, *Think of others before yourself.*

Along with characters' actions, you should also pay attention to characters' feelings, thoughts, and words. Look at the following paragraph.

> Allison became angry while trying to undo the knot in the kite string. "Why must this knot be so difficult?" she thought. Allison threw down the kite. She walked away and returned a few minutes later. Allison told herself to be calm. She took a few deep breaths and returned to the knot. This time, she was able to untie the knot.

A theme for this paragraph might be *Patience is a virtue*. Look at what Allison does before she solves the problem with the string. A character's accomplishments in a story can point to the theme.

Sometimes, finding themes in literature will be more difficult. Some poetry, for example, will not have clear actions and conflicts. In such cases, you need to pay close attention to the speaker's expression of feelings or thoughts about a topic. For example, a poem's speaker might describe the beauty of nature, or the speaker might talk about his or her feelings about war. The speaker's expression of feelings or thoughts about a topic can point to a theme in the poem. Sometimes, summarizing a poem can help you figure out its theme. A **summary** is a retelling of the important points of a story or poem in your own words. Recognizing themes in stories or poems can help you better understand what the author thinks is important or what the author is trying to say.

Thinking It Through

Read the following paragraph, and then answer the question that follows.

Roger saw that his friend Brianna was stooped over and crying. He remembered that the last time he cried, his dad made him feel better. His dad simply made him laugh. He thought the best approach might be to make Brianna laugh. So he walked up to where she was sitting and waited for her to look up and see him. He stood quietly. When Brianna looked up, he began to stagger around, wave his arms, and make crazy faces. Roger crunched up his face, used his fingers to distort his mouth, and stuck out his tongue. Brianna immediately laughed. His trick worked!

What is the theme of this paragraph?

_____

_____

_____

_____

 **HINT** A theme is usually a lesson that applies to the real world. Think of a general statement that the author wants you to learn from the paragraph.

DISCUSS Tell about a personal experience that is similar to the one in the paragraph. What did you learn from the experience?

Coached Example

Read the passage and answer the questions.

The Bragging Traveler
adapted from
a fable by Aesop

A man returned home after traveling around the world. He bragged about the many adventures he had. Among other things, he said that when he was in Greece, he made a huge jump. No man alive, in fact, had ever jumped farther than him. In fact, there were many people in Greece who saw him do it, and he could call witnesses. One of the bystanders interrupted him, and said: "Well, if this is all true, then we don't need witnesses. Pretend we are in Greece right now and jump for us."

1. What is the theme of the passage?

A. Never trust anyone.

B. Seeing is believing.

C. There are liars everywhere.

D. Do not believe people who travel.

HINT Many common themes can be expressed through well-known sayings.

2. Which sentence from the passage BEST supports the theme?

A. "A man returned home after traveling around the world."

B. "He bragged about the many adventures he had."

C. "Among other things, he said that when he was in Greece, he made a huge jump."

D. "Well, if this is all true, then we don't need witnesses."

HINT Think about what the author's message is to the reader.

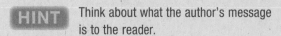

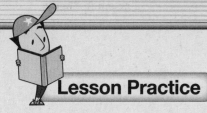

Lesson Practice

Use the Reading Guide to help you understand the poem.

Reading Guide

What is the theme?

Is the theme repeated in the poem?

What events or images help you figure out the theme?

Protection

The mountainside was our home.
It belonged to us,
or maybe we belonged to it.

The mountainside was our shelter
5   from the wind that swept the plains,
from the heavy rain,
from the cruel, burning sun.

The mountainside was our protector.
And we protected the mountainside.

10   Some people wanted to make the mountain theirs,
build homes,
build lives there.
They wanted the mountain,
but we wouldn't give it to them.

15   But we didn't fight. We sang.
Our leaders met, one day in the spring.
They talked as the sun rose.
As the sun set, they were still talking.
As the sun rose the next day,
20   the mountain was still ours.

Answer the following questions.

1. What is a theme of the poem?

   A. Developers need land.

   B. Only worry about yourself and your needs.

   C. Protect what is precious and important to you.

   D. Mountains are good during harsh weather conditions.

2. Which of these lines BEST supports the theme of the poem?

   A. "Some people wanted to make the mountain theirs,"

   B. "But we didn't fight. We sang."

   C. "The mountainside was our home."

   D. "The mountainside was our protector."

3. The speaker's actions tell the reader that

   A. dancing is part of a ritual to protect the land.

   B. wind, rain, and sun are not necessary.

   C. powerful people can be difficult to deal with.

   D. mountains should be developed.

4. What does the author believe about the mountainside?

   A. It can be sold and traded.

   B. It is a place of great beauty.

   C. It is a very ancient place.

   D. It can be destroyed if it is not protected.

5. Write a summary of the poem.

   _____

   _____

   _____

   _____

   _____

   _____

   _____

Use the Reading Guide to help you understand the passage.

Reading Guide

How does Wade react to Brent's news?

What did Wade hope to accomplish by reacting the way he does?

How does Wade feel about Brent? What details from the story support your response?

Life Lessons

Brent observed a group of five classmates standing in a semi-circle in the hall. They seemed somber, even from afar. Brent sprinted over to the group, smacked them all on the backs, and pushed them into one another.

"What are you all so serious and intense about?" asked Brent.

"Karen got injured on the playground," said Wade. "An ambulance just pulled up in the school parking lot and put her on a stretcher."

Brent shrugged his shoulders. After he left, the boys huddled closer together to try to figure out what had happened to Karen.

That night, Wade thought about Brent's reaction. He wondered if Brent cared about anyone but himself, or if it was all an act.

The next day Brent sauntered into the classroom, but he wasn't his aggressive self. Instead, he was quiet and didn't annoy anyone verbally or physically.

"What are you so serious and intense about?" asked Wade.

Brent tried to keep his voice from trembling. "Yesterday, my mom told me she needs surgery. I'm really worried about her."

Wade shrugged his shoulders and pretended to walk away, but then he turned around just in time to see Brent hastily wipe a tear off his face.

Wade felt awful and ashamed of his behavior. "I apologize! I wanted to get you back for how you treated us yesterday. I'm really sorry about your mom."

"I was immature and disrespectful yesterday. I'm sorry, too."

Wade socked Brent's shoulder, trying to do it in a carefree manner, and Brent slugged him back lightly.

Answer the following questions.

6. Use your answer to Part A to answer Part B.

Part A

Which word describes how Wade initially responds to Brent's news about his mom?

A. guarded

B. enthusiastic

C. uninterested

D. sympathetic

Part B

Why does Wade respond this way?

A. He thought Brent was playing a practical joke.

B. He was upset by Brent's response the day before, and he wanted to show Brent how it felt.

C. He felt badly for Brent and wanted him to know that he had a friend.

D. He was disrespectful, and he didn't realize it.

E. He did not like Brent and did not have any interest in him.

---

7. Use your answer to Part A to answer Part B.

Part A

What is a theme of this story?

A. You get what you pay for.

B. Mind your own business.

C. Never take others for granted.

D. Treat others as you want to be treated.

Part B

Which detail from the story BEST supports the answer to Part A?

A. "'What are you all so serious and intense about?' asked Brent."

B. "Wade socked Brent's shoulder, trying to do it in a carefree manner, and Brent slugged him back lightly."

C. "'I'm really worried about her.'"

D. "Brent shrugged his shoulders."

E. "That night, Wade thought about Brent's reaction."

Use the Reading Guide to help you understand the passage.

Reading Guide

How does the narrator introduce the battle?

What words and phrases suggest the narrator's feelings about the battle?

How does the final sentence express the narrator's attitude toward the events of the passage?

Witness to a Battle

The weather was hot on the morning of July 1, 1863. It was the type of weather where the discomfort of the heat far outweighed the beauty of the summer day. Far worse than the heat were the sounds of the rifles and cannon fire. As the sounds of battle drew nearer, my parents remembered the stories they had heard about desperate Confederate soldiers looting houses for food, clothing, and supplies. They decided to send me to a friend's farm, south of the town. My parents stayed behind in Gettysburg to watch over our house and help where they could.

The next morning, I was sent to Mr. Walters' farm. No sooner had I arrived than the Union army began to thunder past on the very same road. Watching the men hurry to battle, we knew that many would not return home. They kept up their courage, though, by shouting and cheering each other on.

By the next day, the fighting had gotten so close we had to move to another farm, farther away. We waited there for most of the day, until the sounds of battle began to fade. When all was quiet, we started back to the Walters's farm.

We returned to find the house filled with casualties from the battle. Army surgeons set up a tent to serve as a makeshift operating room, and we gave them whatever supplies they needed from the house.

Only later did we learn how many Americans on both sides suffered in this single battle of the terrible Civil War. More than 28,000 Confederate soldiers were reported dead, wounded, or missing, and the number of Union casualties amounted to 23,000. Thinking about the death and destruction on both sides, my heart is filled with sorrow.

Answer the following questions.

8. What connection does the narrator make between the weather and the sounds of the battle?

    A. the battle sounds caused more discomfort than the hot weather

    B. the battle sounds caused less discomfort than the hot weather

    C. the hot weather and the battle sounds ruined the beauty of the day

    D. the battle sounds were a distraction from the hot weather

9. Which sentence BEST describes how the narrator felt while watching the men hurry to battle?

    A. The narrator was afraid that the men would loot Gettysburg for food, clothing, and supplies.

    B. The narrator was happy to see the army thundering past on the road to Mr. Walters' farm.

    C. The narrator was surprised that the men were shouting and cheering each other on.

    D. The narrator was sad that many of the men would die and not return home.

10. The theme of "Witness to a Battle" connects to the narrator's experiences during which time period?

    A. The American Revolutionary War

    B. The Civil War in the United States

    C. The fighting in Europe during World War I

    D. The protests against the Vietnam War

11. Which piece of evidence from "Witness to a Battle" best shows the connection between a historical event and the passage's theme?

    A. "My parents stayed behind in Gettysburg to watch over our house and help where they could."

    B. "No sooner had I arrived than the Union army began to thunder past on the very same road."

    C. "When all was quiet, we started back to the Walters's farm."

    D. "Thinking about the death and destruction on both sides, my heart is filled with sorrow."

12. Identify the theme in the passage and three details that support it.

Lesson

4 | Point of View

Getting the Idea

Everything you read is written from a point of view. The **point of view** is the position from which the story is told. Writers commonly use two main points of view: first person and third person.

A story in **first person** is told from the personal point of view of *I* or *we*. The narrator is a character in the story. Look at the following sentences; they are told in first person.

> Cheryl and I went to the party at noon. We stayed for a few hours and then we went home.

The first sentence uses *I* and the second sentence uses *we*. A first-person story can show you a lot about the feelings and thoughts of the narrator. The story may give you this information directly, or it may suggest this information.

A story in **third person** frequently uses *he*, *she*, *they*, or someone's name to narrate or to give information. A third-person story is not told by a character in the story. The following sentences are in third person.

> Cheryl and Finn went to the party at noon. They stayed for a few hours and then they went home.

In a story from a **third-person limited** point of view, the reader finds out what characters say and do, and little else. In a story from a **third-person omniscient** point of view, the reader finds out the thoughts of most of the characters. The example above is in the third-person limited point of view.

Point of view is also the perspective, or attitude, of an author. It is the way an author feels about someone or something in a story. Read the paragraph below.

> Adam liked listening to music with his headphones. Even though he kept the volume at a reasonable level, he began to have alarming problems with his hearing. His mother told him he needed to go to the doctor. The next week, Adam went to the doctor and found out that, unfortunately, the headphones had caused damage to his eardrums. They alone were the reason for his hearing loss.

What is the author's point of view about headphones? To figure out the point of view, look carefully at the author's choice of words. The words *alarming, unfortunately,* and *they alone* show that the author has a negative view of headphones. The author probably feels that people shouldn't listen to them so much.

The author's point of view may affect the overall tone of the writing. Pay attention to not only what the author says, but *how* the author says it. When an author feels particularly strongly about a topic, the tone of the writing may reflect that. For example, the tone may be happy, sad, angry, sarcastic, serious, or humorous. Think about tone as you read this paragraph.

> Warren opened the door of his truck and was struck by the terrible stench. He was disgusted by the damage the oil spill had done. Tar balls covered the sand, broken up by an occasional oil-covered bird or fish. All over the beach, Warren could see the horrible effects of the disaster.

The author's choice of words—*terrible stench, disgusted, horrible*—creates an angry tone.

Thinking It Through

Read the following paragraph, and then answer the question that follows.

Gary had never seen so many people at a movie. He tried to move his popcorn out of the way in time, but it was too late! The older kids in the movie theater pushed right into him. The older kids didn't care about Gary. They cared even less about his popcorn, as they knocked it right out of his hands. Gary knew his dad wouldn't want to buy another bag. He also knew he would probably have to help clean up the mess.

Rewrite the first two sentences of the paragraph using the first-person point of view.

_____

_____

_____

_____

 When you write in first person you use *I*, so the person telling the story does the action.

DISCUSS Tell the rest of the story using the first-person point of view. How does this point of view affect your reading experience? Discuss your ideas with the class.

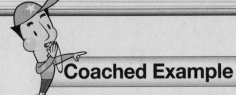

Coached Example

Read the passage and answer the questions.

excerpted and adapted from

The Dragon's Teeth
by Nathaniel Hawthorne

King Agenor had three sons, Cadmus, Phoenix, and Cilix, and a beautiful daughter, Europa. One day, the children were playing together near the seashore. The children wandered far from their parents' palace and found themselves in a green and blooming meadow next to the sea. The sea was sparkling and dimpling in the sunshine. It hummed gently as it lapped against the beach. The three boys were very happy, gathering flowers. They twisted them into garlands to place on Europa. She was seated on the grass and was almost hidden under all the buds and blossoms. Then her rosy face peeped happily out, and Cadmus said that she was the prettiest of all the flowers.

---

1. This passage is written from which point of view?

   A. first-person

   B. third-person limited

   C. third-person omniscient

   D. first- and third-person

   HINT Remember first person uses *I* and *we*. Third person uses *she*, *he*, *it*, and *they*.

2. Which word BEST describes the tone of this passage?

   A. lonely

   B. happy

   C. fearful

   D. humorous

   HINT Think about what the author says and how the author says it. What are the author's word choices?

Lesson Practice

Use the Reading Guide to help you understand the passage.

Reading Guide

Which words tell you what point of view this passage will be in?

Can you tell the author's point of view on the subject?

Taking Care of Josie

Bryan and Marie asked me to look after their horse, Josie, while they were vacationing in Hawaii. I had only looked after horses once or twice before, so I was a bit nervous. But Marie assured me it would be a piece of cake. "Allie," she said, "Josie is a sweetheart. Besides, Josie's trainer, Bruno, will be at the stables most of the time."

Bruno tended to all the horses at the stable, including Josie. Marie told me that he was a good trainer, but every now and then he was hard to find. "Just keep an eye out and make sure he stays on top of things," Marie said.

The first couple of days at the stables were pretty boring. Bruno seemed really nice, but he was always on his cell phone. On the third day, something was bothering the horses. Josie didn't want to get back into her stall. I called for Bruno, but he was already taking care of another horse.

While I struggled to get her inside, she accidentally bumped her head on the doorframe of the stable. Oh, poor thing! As soon as Bruno came, he calmed the horses down. He cleaned Josie up and explained to me how I could handle the horses better. He also said he was sorry he couldn't come sooner.

The next day, Marie called me and I told her what happened. She was upset at first but was glad to hear that the horse was fine. I'm visiting their stable again next week!

Answer the following questions.

1. This passage is written from whose point of view?

   A. Josie's point of view

   B. Allie's point of view

   C. Bryan's point of view

   D. Bruno's point of view

2. Which word in the sentence below indicates the first-person point of view?

   While I struggled to get her inside, she accidentally bumped her head on the doorframe of the stable.

   A. she

   B. her

   C. I

   D. on

3. Which statement BEST describes how the author feels about Bruno?

   A. Bruno is a hard worker.

   B. Bruno is irresponsible.

   C. Bruno likes taking care of horses.

   D. Bruno does not like to talk on the phone.

4. The reader can tell that the author believes that

   A. it is important to leave animals alone.

   B. phones can be distracting for people.

   C. people should take their animals on vacation.

   D. animals should be treated with care.

5. Rewrite the following sentences from Marie's point of view.

   But Marie assured me that it would be a piece of cake. "Allie," she said, "Josie is a sweetheart. Besides, Josie's trainer, Bruno, will be at the stables most of the time."

   _____

   _____

   _____

   _____

   _____

Use the Reading Guide to help you understand the passage.

Reading **Guide**

From what point of view is the narrator telling the story?

What evidence from the text tells you the point of view?

Near the end of the story, something gives Robert an idea. What is Robert's idea?

How will Robert's idea help him solve his problem?

A Solution to a Problem

Robert stared at his crumpled bike lying in the yard. Yesterday, he had carelessly flung his bike in the driveway before dinner. His dad, a firefighter, was called to an emergency during dinner. When he got the call, he ran out the door, put his truck in reverse, and smashed Robert's bike to smithereens. The bike was beyond repair.

His dad was adamantly opposed to buying Robert a new bike. If he wanted a new bike, he would have to buy it himself. But Robert had no money.

As Robert sat on the porch, he saw his neighbor come out of her house. She looked frantic as she tried to juggle her dog's leash, check her cell phone messages, and walk hurriedly in high-heeled shoes.

"Do you need some help?" he asked.

"I'm late for work, but Rosie needs a walk. It's her only exercise of the day."

"I can give her a walk now and later today after lunch," said Robert.

"That'd be great! I can give you five dollars for doing this."

As Robert took Rosie for her walk, he mentally calculated how long it would take to save for a bike at five dollars a day. And as he walked, he began to notice other neighbors in business suits hurriedly walking their dogs. That gave him an idea.

When he got home, he grabbed paints and a sheet of plywood. He made a sign, "Robert's Dog Walking Business," and put it up in the front yard. Then he picked up his bike and carefully placed it in the corner of the garage.

Answer the following questions.

6. Use your answer to Part A to answer Part B.

Part A

What point of view is used in the story?

A. third-person limited

B. first person by Robert

C. third-person omniscient

D. first person by Robert's dad

Part B

Choose the details that BEST support your answer to Part A. There is more than one correct choice listed below.

A. "The bike was beyond repair."

B. "Robert stared at his crumpled bike lying in the yard."

C. "'That'd be great! I can give you five dollars for doing this.'"

D. "As he sat on the porch, he saw his neighbor come out of her house."

E. "'I'm late for work, but Rosie needs a walk.'"

F. "'Do you need some help?' he asked."

_____

7. Read this paragraph from the passage. Revise the paragraph, using a different point of view.

> **Robert stared at his crumpled bike lying in the yard. Yesterday, he had carelessly flung his bike in the driveway before dinner. His dad, a firefighter, was called to an emergency during dinner. When he got the call he ran out the door, put his truck in reverse, and smashed Robert's bike to smithereens. The bike was beyond repair.**

_____

_____

_____

_____

Use the Reading Guide to help you understand the passage.

Reading Guide

Which words help you recognize the point of view in this story?

How does Gail feel about science?

Why does Nicole have a change of heart at the end of the story?

Science Saves the Day

"Who will stay after class to help me set up tomorrow's science lab?" asked Mrs. Lynch. Before the science teacher had finished her question, Gail's hand shot up. Of course she would help Mrs. Lynch. Gail would be happy if every class every day was science. She glanced around the classroom. The other students rolled their eyes. They dreaded coming to science class.

The bell signaled the end of class. As the students filed out, Nicole paused next to Gail. Nicole whispered, "We know you're only helping Mrs. Lynch because you want to get a good grade."

Gail didn't bow her head. She was proud that she was a good science student. The subject was thrilling! Think of how many things in the world had been improved because of science! Gail could go on daydreaming forever, but right now she had to help Mrs. Lynch. In no time, the pair had all the equipment set out for tomorrow's lab.

The next morning at school, Gail found her classmates milling around outside the cafeteria. They were grumbling about missing breakfast.

When Gail got to the cafeteria door, she discovered the problem. The door was locked and the key wouldn't turn. Mr. North, the custodian, had been attempting to open the door for a half hour.

Gail had an inspiration. She asked to borrow a lead pencil and quickly exposed a length of lead. Next, she pushed the lead into the lock and twisted it. Then she asked Mr. North to slide the key in the lock and turn it. After a few rotations and several clicks, the lock opened.

The students cheered and gave Gail high fives as they entered the cafeteria. Nicole smiled at Gail and admitted, "I guess science isn't so bad, after all."

Answer the following questions.

8. What point of view is used in this story?

   A. first-person

   B. third-person omniscient

   C. third-person limited

   D. first- and third-person

9. Which word gives a clue about the point of view in the story?

   A. I

   B. she

   C. me

   D. we

10. Which word BEST describes the tone of the story?

    A. positive

    B. silly

    C. gloomy

    D. amused

11. Which sentence supports the tone you identified?

    A. "The other students rolled their eyes."

    B. "They dreaded coming to science class."

    C. "The subject was thrilling!"

    D. "They were grumbling about missing breakfast."

12. What is the author's point of view on science?

    _____

    _____

    _____

    _____

    _____

    _____

    _____

    _____

    _____

5 Figurative Language

Getting the Idea

Many ideas and feelings are hard to express, so sometimes writers use **figurative language** to add meaning to their writing. Figurative language helps the reader picture parts of the story better—and that makes the text more fun to read. You'll find figurative language most often in poetry and stories. The two most common forms of figurative word use are similes and metaphors.

A **simile** compares two things using *like* or *as*. It uses descriptive language. When you use a simile to make a comparison, you create an image in the reader's mind. That image should connect qualities of the two items you are comparing. Read the sentence below.

> The clouds hung over the horizon.

You know what this means, but it's not an interesting way to say it. Here is another way to say the same thing:

> The clouds hung over the horizon like misty gray curtains.

A simile usually compares two things that are different. Clouds and curtains are different things, but when they are compared, we know what the writer means. Clouds float above the horizon. Curtains look like they are floating above the floor because they are held up by rods.

The comparison drawn in a simile often involves exaggeration. For example:

> The dog was as big as a house!

In this sentence, the size of the dog is compared to the size of a house. In other words, the dog is quite large. However, the dog is not *actually* the size of a house. This is merely an exaggeration to make a point.

Sometimes a writer makes a comparison without using *like* or *as*. This is called a metaphor. A **metaphor** says that one thing *is* another. This suggests that the two things are alike. Writers may also use metaphors to help readers understand an unfamiliar idea or thing. They compare the unfamiliar idea to something they hope the reader will already know. Here is a metaphor:

> The moon is a night watchman.

You know that the moon and a night watchman are two very different things. But the writer is telling you that he feels as if the moon watches him, because he is on Earth, and the moon is up above him, in the sky. Here is another example:

> Barry was a real tiger on the playing field.

In this sentence, the writer states that Barry is a tiger when he's on a playing field. This clearly isn't possible, because a human being can't turn into a tiger. The person writing this sentence means that Barry is brave and strong, much like a tiger might act. By using the metaphor, the writer immediately creates in the reader's mind an image of Barry as a person who is a good athlete.

Some figurative language uses sound to make an impression on the reader. In poetry, **alliteration** occurs when the writer uses words that have the same beginning consonant sound. Alliteration can call attention to a phrase or image. Here is a famous example of alliteration from "Meeting at Night" by Robert Browning.

> The grey sea and the long black land;
> And the yellow half-moon large and low;
> And the startled little waves that leap
> In fiery ringlets from their sleep,
> As I gain the cove with pushing prow,
> And quench its speed i' the slushy sand.

In this poem, the phrases "large and low" and "pushing prow" are examples of alliteration. Readers might pay more attention to these phrases, and what they mean, because of the way they sound.

Thinking It Through

Read the following paragraph, and then answer the questions that follow.

Darcie held her tennis racket tightly. Her heart was pounding like a jackhammer. Her knees were two rubber lumps at this point. She looked ahead and waited for the serve to come. Darcie liked playing tennis, but competing made her nervous. After two hours of playing, the tennis match came down to this last game.

Which sentence from the paragraph includes a simile? What is being compared?

_____

_____

_____

_____

 A simile compares things using *like* or *as*.

DISCUSS Describe something in your classroom using a simile. For example, "the chalk is as white as snow." Share your ideas with a partner.

Coached Example

Read the poem and answer the questions.

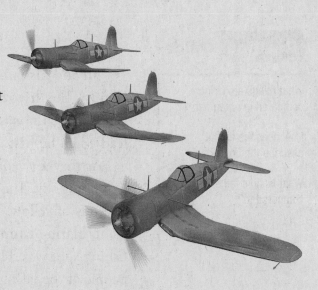

The runway is a pond, black from the night
Little airplanes swarm above it
They buzz in and out, unseen
They nose nearer, then farther away

---

1. Which line from the poem contains a metaphor?

   A. line 4

   B. line 2

   C. line 3

   D. line 1

   HINT Remember, a metaphor makes a comparison without using *like* or *as*.

2. Which phrase from the poem contains alliteration?

   A. "black from the night"

   B. "Little airplanes swarm"

   C. "They nose nearer"

   D. "They buzz in and out"

   HINT Alliteration occurs when two or more words have the same starting sound. Read each answer choice aloud to help answer the question.

Lesson Practice

Use the Reading Guide to help you understand the passage.

Reading Guide

What things are being compared in paragraph 1?

How does the author describe the boats?

What is Jin's father's smile compared to?

Rise and Shine

Jin and his father set out early in the morning to go fishing. The drive to the lake was as slow as molasses. Thankfully, Jin was able to sleep. Jin's eyes felt as heavy as lead when he first woke up. The air was as cold as ice, too.

As they arrived, the stars were becoming ghosts in the lightening sky. The sky was a huge bruise, with purple, blue, and bits of yellow. The sun, as it rose out of the lake, was a giant, blazing lamp. Jin was amazed at how beautiful their fishing spot was. He was surprised to see so many other people at the lake getting ready to fish. The first couple of boats left the shore, and soon other fishing boats began to leave their docks quickly. The boats cut the water like scissors and left a big V-shaped trail behind them.

Jin and his dad were finally on the fishing boat. Jin felt so happy and awake. As his father drove the boat, Jin prepared the fishing poles. He also got out their container of hot tea and poured a cup for each of them. His father smiled as big as the sunrise and took the cup from Jin. Jin sat next to his father with the teacup in his hand. The hot tea in his hands felt like a little burning coal.

Answer the following questions.

1. Which sentence from paragraph 1 does NOT include a simile?

   A. "Thankfully, Jin was able to sleep."

   B. "The drive to the lake was as slow as molasses."

   C. "Jin's eyes felt as heavy as lead when he first woke up."

   D. "The air was as cold as ice, too."

2. What does the following sentence mean?

   The stars were becoming ghosts in the lightening sky.

   A. The stars were hard to see.

   B. The stars were disappearing.

   C. The stars were really a pencil drawing.

   D. Jin wishes to see all the stars in the sky.

3. What does the following sentence mean?

   The sky was a huge bruise, with purple, blue, and bits of yellow.

   A. The sky was hurt.

   B. The sky looked like a bruise because of its colors.

   C. It was really early.

   D. Jin had a bruise he was comparing to the sky.

4. Which sentence from the passage contains a metaphor?

   A. "Jin was amazed at how beautiful their fishing spot was."

   B. "Jin felt so happy and awake."

   C. "The hot tea in his hands felt like a little burning coal."

   D. "The sun, as it rose out of the lake, was a giant, blazing lamp."

5. What does the narrator mean by saying, "His father smiled as big as the sunrise and took the cup from Jin"?

   _____
   _____
   _____
   _____

Use the Reading Guide to help you understand the passage.

Reading Guide

Find an example of a simile in the first verse of the poem. What two things are being compared?

Which line in the poem contains a metaphor? (Remember that a metaphor compares two things but does not use the words *like* or *as*.)

Is line 15 an example of a metaphor or a simile?

A Life on the Ocean Wave
by Epes Sargent

A life on the ocean wave,
A home on the rolling deep,
Where the scattered waters rave,
And the winds their revels[1] keep!
5   Like an eagle caged, I pine[2]
On this dull, unchanging shore:
Oh! Give me the flashing brine,
The spray and the tempest's[3] roar!

Once more on the deck I stand
10   Of my own swift-gliding craft:
Set sail! farewell to the land!
The gale follows fair abaft[4].
We shoot through the sparkling foam
Like an ocean-bird set free;
15   Like the ocean-bird, our home
We'll find far out on the sea.

The land is no longer in view,
The clouds have begun to frown;
But with a stout vessel and crew,
20   We'll say, Let the storm come down!
And the song of our hearts shall be,
While the winds and the waters rave,
A home on the rolling sea!
A life on the ocean wave!

[1] **revels:** noisy festivities
[2] **pine:** grieve, long for
[3] **tempest:** violent windstorm
[4] **abaft:** behind, closer to the back of the boat

6.   Read lines 13–16 from the poem.

> **We shoot through the sparkling foam**
> **Like an ocean-bird set free;**
> **Like the ocean-bird, our home**
> **We'll find far out on the sea.**

Part A

Underline the simile used in these lines.

Part B

Explain the meaning of the simile. What two things are being compared?

_____

_____

_____

7.   Use your answer to Part A to answer Part B.

Part A

Which lines from the poem contain alliteration? There is more than one correct answer choice listed below.

A. "On this dull, unchanging shore:"

B. "The spray and the tempest's roar!"

C. "Set sail! farewell to the land!"

D. "We'll find far out on the sea."

E. "The clouds have begun to frown;"

F. "While the winds and the waters rave,"

Part B

Explain why the lines you chose in Part A are examples of alliteration.

_____

_____

_____

_____

Use the Reading Guide to help you understand the passage.

Reading Guide

Which sentence in the first paragraph contains a simile?

To what things are Hector's life compared?

Why does the author compare Mom's surprising news to music?

Why does the author write that a light bulb went on in Hector's head?

Game Time

Hector had the same routine every day. He got up, ate breakfast, went to school, and came home. Day in, day out, it was always the same. To Hector, his days were as exciting as watching paint dry. Nothing changed.

Then, one afternoon, Mom came home with a surprise. Her voice was light as a feather. She danced into Hector's room, looked around, and shook her head. His room was a disaster area. A towel on the floor was as stiff as a board.

"You'll want to find some clean clothes in a hurry. We're going to the game tonight," Mom said. She held up two basketball tickets.

Mom's news was music to Hector's ears. His favorite basketball team was playing the home team. Instantly, his eyes lit up.

Mom explained that they would be night owls tonight. Since the game started at eight o'clock, they might not get home until eleven or later. Hector didn't mind. The game would be very exciting, and he knew that he would sleep like a baby.

Just before Mom and Hector were about to leave, Gran called. She needed Mom's help to get ready for a doctor's visit the next day. Mom agreed to go to Gran's house right away, but she and Hector had to hatch a new plan. As they tossed ideas back and forth, a light bulb went on in Hector's head. Maybe Gramps would like to go in Mom's place. They called Gramps, and his reply came as quick as lightning. He would love to go to the game! It was smooth sailing now, thought Hector. If only his team could win tonight.

Answer the following questions.

8. Why does the author compare Hector's room to a disaster area?

    A. The room is very messy.

    B. The room looks empty.

    C. The room is too small.

    D. The room needs new paint.

9. Which sentence from the last paragraph is a simile?

    A. "Mom agreed to go to Gran's house right away, but she and Hector had to hatch a new plan."

    B. "As they tossed ideas back and forth, a light bulb went on in Hector's head."

    C. "He would love to go to the game!"

    D. "They called Gramps, and his reply came as quick as lightning."

10. Which sentence from the story contains a metaphor?

    A. "The game would be very exciting, and he knew that he would sleep like a baby."

    B. "Day in, day out, it was always the same."

    C. "Mom's news was music to Hector's ears."

    D. "Her voice was light as a feather."

11. Read this sentence from the passage:

    Mom explained that they would be night owls tonight.

    What does the sentence mean?

    A. They would look for food.

    B. They would stay up late.

    C. They would go to the woods.

    D. They would stay outdoors.

12. Use the space below to explain what the author means by the sentence: "To Hector, his days were as exciting as watching paint dry."

    _____

    _____

    _____

    _____

    _____

6 Story, Drama, and Poem Structure

Getting the Idea

Writers of literature create different types of texts, depending on the type of story they want to tell. Stories, dramas, and poems are all structured differently.

Works of **fiction** are usually novels and short stories, long, made-up works with characters, settings, and plots. Stories are written in sentences and organized into paragraphs. A **paragraph** is a group of sentences that support or explain one main idea. In stories, paragraphs help readers move from one event to another. Paragraphs begin with an indentation. Longer works of fiction, like novels, are broken up into sections called **chapters**. Some stories include pictures or illustrations to help the reader better understand the story. Heavily illustrated stories, such as graphic novels, are presented in comic-strip format.

Poetry is a type of writing which uses figurative language and literary devices to create meaning and invoke emotion in the reader. Poetry is usually easy to recognize because of its structure. It generally takes the form of a series of lines of text, or verses. A **verse** is a line of poetry. Verses may or may not be complete sentences. Poems are also broken up into groups of lines called **stanzas**. Poems have stanzas instead of paragraphs. Look at the following poem.

> The dark skies of autumn
> Cry soft tears falling gently
> On fallen leaves curling on the ground
>
> Inside, kitchen windows fog
> With the kettle's screaming
> Ready to steep tea, dark and gentle.

Pay attention to the structure of poems. Notice how the poem is separated into lines instead of sentences. Also, the poem is structured into stanzas instead of paragraphs. Stanzas can be short or long.

Drama is a type of literature that is written to be performed onstage by actors. All drama uses dialogue. **Dialogue** is a written conversation between two or more characters. A character's dialogue may be written to reflect his or her dialect. **Dialect** is the way language is spoken by a particular group or in a particular region. When you read drama, you are often reading dialogue. Drama has several parts that are key to understanding it.

Element in Drama	Definition
acts	the main sections of a drama
scenes	smaller sections of an act
cast of characters	the people in a drama
stage directions	actions that are performed (often written in italics)

The following is a sample of dramatic literature.

> JACQUES: I hear Monica coming up the stairs.
>
> MOTHER: Quick, hide her birthday present before she comes into the room and sees the paint set.
>
> (*Jacques grabs the paint set and hides it under the bed*.)
>
> (*The door opens and Monica walks in*.)
>
> MONICA: (*smiling*) Are you hiding my birthday present?

The names that are in capital letters are the characters. **Lines** are the words after the character's name and are often spoken aloud.

The setting descriptions are often in italics. This shows the reader who or what is onstage and where and when the play is taking place.

The following is an example of a setting description.

> Setting: *The curtain opens and the light falls upon Alice. She is sitting in a chair knitting. There is a grandfather clock in the far corner. Next to Alice is a small table with a phone, and she sits waiting for the phone to ring.*

Thinking It Through

Read the following poem, and then answer the question that follows.

The girls and boys walked happily
Into the woods and sat on the grass.

Emily brought pears,
Michael brought grapes,
Stacey brought bread,
And the sun brought warmth.

A red checkerboard blanket
Covered the tall grass—
Today, Earth would be their table.

Rewrite the poem into a small story.

_____

_____

_____

_____

 Poems are structured with lines and stanzas, while stories are structured with sentences and paragraphs.

 **DISCUSS**   Read the poem and your brief story aloud. In a group, talk about how they are alike and different. Which structure do you prefer? Why?

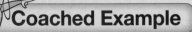

Coached Example

Read the passage and answer the questions.

Bobby loved trains. He could hear the trains whistling during the day from his house near the factories. Sometimes, he and his father would walk down to the railroad tracks to watch the trains go by.

Sometimes they would get to the tracks just in time to see the railroad crossing sign start flashing red. The sign had long, black-and-white striped arms. The arms came down when the lights flashed to prevent cars or bikes from crossing. The flashing red lights and the lowering arms were accompanied by loud ringing bells. The bells warned drivers and bicyclists that it was not safe to cross. Bobby never bothered to plug his ears like some other people. He liked the sounds of the warning bells and whistling trains. The train wheels also screeched, which sometimes sent shivers up his spine.

Bobby liked watching all the colorful cars go past him. He imagined what might be inside some of them. Maybe there were new, shiny motorcycles in them! He wondered if the cars with a lot of holes in the sides were carrying live animals to a new farm.

---

1. What type of passage is this?

    A. fairy tale

    B. poetry

    C. drama

    D. fiction

    HINT Stories are organized by sentences and paragraphs. Poetry is organized by lines and stanzas. Dramas are organized by scenes and acts. What kind of passage is this?

2. What is the purpose of paragraph 3?

    A. to describe what is inside the train cars

    B. to explain how trains work

    C. to show what Bobby thinks about when he watches the trains

    D. to describe the way the train looks

    HINT Think about the reasons authors include visual details in stories.

Lesson Practice

Use the Reading Guide to help you understand the passage.

Reading Guide

How is the passage organized?

Is the passage structured by paragraphs or dialogue?

As you read, pick out the stage directions. These will help you picture the actions meant to take place on stage.

excerpted and adapted from

The Tinker's Wedding

by J.M. Synge

Act 1

Setting: *A village roadside after nightfall. A small fire burns near a ditch by a chapel. Michael is working beside it.*

SARAH CASEY: (*approaching eagerly*) We'll see the priest as he walks home tonight.

MICHAEL BYRNE: (*grimly*) That'll be a great joy!

SARAH: (*sharply*) It'll be small joy for you if you're not ready with my wedding ring. (*She goes over to him.*) Is it almost ready?

MICHAEL: Not really. It's hard making a ring; my hands will be useless if I keep working.

SARAH: (*sitting down beside him and throwing sticks on the fire*) Well, keep working and stop your foolish talking.

MICHAEL: (*slowly and glumly*) You're the one talking foolish, dragging us here by the chapel and talking about marriage. This was all your idea.

(*Sarah turns her back to him and arranges something in the ditch.*)

MICHAEL: (*angrily*) What's wrong now?

SARAH: (*musingly*) Nothing's wrong. I was just thinking.

MICHAEL: Maybe you'll think of some new idea by dawn.

SARAH: (*teasingly*) Maybe by dawn I'll think of having an easier life with Jimmy.

MICHAEL: (*with dismay*) Is that what you're thinking?

SARAH: Yes, Michael Byrne, a fine life with sunny skies and a gentle breeze.

MICHAEL: (*hands her the ring*) Will that fit you now?

Answer the following questions.

1. What type of literature is this passage?

   A. drama

   B. fiction

   C. nonfiction

   D. poetry

2. What is missing from the passage?

   A. lines

   B. stage directions

   C. setting

   D. cast of characters

3. The words in italics are

   A. stanzas.

   B. characters.

   C. stage directions.

   D. dialogue.

4. According to the setting description, Sarah and Michael are

   A. in a chapel.

   B. on a roadside.

   C. with a priest.

   D. under sunny skies.

5. How are stories and dramas structured differently?

   _____

   _____

   _____

   _____

   _____

   _____

   _____

   _____

   _____

   _____

   _____

Use the Reading Guide to help you understand the passage.

Reading Guide

At the beginning of the passage, how does Lisa feel about being in the wedding party?

How does she feel by the end of the passage?

How is the passage structured?

Covered in Pink

Lisa stood in the changing room with all the other bridesmaids in her brother's wedding party. The room looked like a cotton candy machine that had exploded. Ten young women, including her, were dressed from head to toe in pink. The uniform of the day was pink satin dresses with gigantic pink bows, pink high-heeled shoes, and pink headbands. Lisa hated pink, but any shade of pink would have been better than this bubble gum hue.

Everyone else was talking and giggling. All of the other girls were friends of the bride and much older than twelve-year-old Lisa. They exclaimed over their matching earrings, cackled as they compared matching nail polish, and preened in front of the mirror. Lisa wished she could be outside, playing baseball with the boys.

Soon it was time to line up. Lisa was scheduled to be the last of the bridesmaids to walk down the aisle. As Lisa waited her turn, the bride leaned over and whispered, "Thank you so much for being part of our special day. I know how much your brother loves you. It means a lot to him, and to me, that you are part of our wedding party."

Lisa looked up the aisle at her brother, grinning like a happy puppy, and back at her new sister-in-law who was waiting to make her big entrance after the bridesmaids. It was a special day, for both of them and for her family. When it was her turn, she walked proudly down the aisle in her shiny pink dress. Maybe pink wasn't such a bad color to wear, at least for a day!

Answer the following questions.

6. Use your answer to Part A to answer Part B.

   Part A

   What type of literature is this passage?

   A. drama

   B. novel

   C. poem

   D. short story

   Part B

   Which detail about the passage BEST supports the answer to Part A?

   A. It is fiction.

   B. It has dialogue.

   C. It has a cast of characters.

   D. It is organized in paragraphs.

   E. It has rhythm and rhyme.

   _____

7. Rewrite the last two paragraphs of the passage as a poem or a drama. Use the events of the plot and the dialogue to guide your writing.

   _____
   _____
   _____
   _____
   _____
   _____
   _____
   _____
   _____

Use the Reading Guides to help you understand the passages.

Reading Guide

Is the passage structured by paragraphs, dialogue, or stanzas?

What descriptions tell you how the narrator is feeling?

As you read, look for figurative language.

Family Dinner Circus

They say it's good to come together
for peaceful family dinners.
But those who have met my family
know our meals aren't really winners.

5 It's a three-ring dinner circus
when we each take a seat
at our family dinner table
and then attempt to eat.

Marla makes a moat with gravy.
10 Daniel plays around with peas.
And when Theresa tastes tomatoes,
she declares, "I can't eat these!"

Everyone talks at once
about school, work, and sports.
15 I try to concentrate on my plate,
but soon start feeling out of sorts.

Then like the sun on a rainy day
a delicious smell makes me more alert.
This three-ring circus has been worth it,
20 because after dinner comes dessert!

Reading Guide

Where can you find a description of where the passage takes place?

What kind of information does the italic text give you?

How is this passage structured?

The Bear
Act 1

SETTING: *It is nighttime. The interior of a tent is depicted by draped fabric. Two girls are sitting up in sleeping bags, holding flashlights. A rustling and thumping sound is heard offstage.*

LEENA: (*wide-eyed and frightened*) I am telling you, it's a bear!

MAI: (*frantically covering Leena's mouth, speaking in a stage whisper*) Shhhh! Not so loud. It will hear you.

LEENA: (*muffled under Mai's hand*) Sorry.

MAI: (*removing her hand from Leena's mouth and gathering her resolve*) Besides, it's probably not a bear. It's probably . . . (*pausing to think*) the wind or something.

(*Another thump and a crash are heard offstage. Both girls jump.*)

LEENA: (*hysterical*) That is *not* the wind. Oh, if my mom knew there'd be bears on this trip she never would have let me join the Nature Rangers.

MAI: (*taking a big breath*) Okay, so we're Nature Rangers. Bears are part of nature. We can totally handle this. We'll . . . we'll *talk* to the bear!

LEENA: (*incredulous*) Mai, are you completely out of your—

(*A huge crash sounds. Mai and Leena scream. A bearlike shadow is silhouetted behind the tent.*)

CHANDRA: (*offstage*) Mai! Leena! Is that you? Let me in. I lost my flashlight, and I can't find my tent!

MAI and LEENA: (*together as they open the tent flaps for Chandra to enter*) Chandra?

CHANDRA: (*enters wearing a bulky hooded parka*) What's wrong, you two? You look like you've seen a bear!

Answer the following questions.

8. What type of literature is "Family Dinner Circus?"

    A. fiction

    B. nonfiction

    C. poetry

    D. drama

9. The narrator of "Family Dinner Circus" compares family dinnertime to

    A. a three-ring circus.

    B. school, work, and sports.

    C. sun on a rainy day.

    D. dessert.

10. "The Bear" is structured using

    A. verses.

    B. stanzas.

    C. paragraphs.

    D. dialogue.

11. What part of "The Bear" tells how the characters are feeling?

    A. setting

    B. stage directions

    C. figurative language

    D. stanzas

12. Which character is incredulous?

    A. Mai

    B. Leena

    C. the narrator from "Family Dinner Circus"

    D. the bear

13. How are poems and dramas structured differently? Use examples from the passages in your response.

_____

_____

_____

_____

_____

_____

_____

_____

_____

_____

_____

7 Compare and Contrast Literary Works

Getting the Idea

When you **compare** things, you tell how they are alike. When you **contrast** things, you tell how they are different. You can compare and contrast many things when you read different works of literature, including characters, plots, and themes. Sometimes you might compare two characters in the same work. You might also contrast elements in two or more works.

In literature, certain character types appear regularly. For example, many stories and dramas might have heroes and villains, wise or foolish rulers, or honest or dishonest characters. Read the following paragraphs.

Passage 1

King Ferdinand was a strict ruler. When his army had a huge victory, he didn't celebrate. He built a larger army instead. To pay for his army, King Ferdinand created new taxes. Many people protested the new taxes. King Ferdinand placed all the protesters in jail.

Passage 2

In the mountain kingdom of Neverlandia, the farmers and villagers prepared to celebrate the birthday of King Fredo. The past year had been difficult for the farmers and villagers. There had been a large earthquake and a long drought. But King Fredo was wise. He had saved the taxes collected over the past few years. He made sure that hungry people were fed and sick people were nursed back to health.

The two stories both have a king as the main character. But one story's king is a mean, unfair ruler, while the other king treats his people well and is loved by all. Comparing and contrasting across texts helps a reader better understand the characters in each text.

Readers can also compare and contrast plots. Many stories and dramas are based on classic plots. In a quest story, for instance, a character goes on a long journey, usually in search of something that will improve his or her life. In a challenge plot, a character has to perform one or more very difficult tasks. Read the following paragraphs.

Passage 1

Hawaiian legend tells of a boy named Maui who had three older brothers. Their parents were powerful gods. Maui had to perform many heroic acts to gain acceptance from his brothers. Maui fished islands from the sea. He even captured the sun with his snare!

Passage 2

It was Oliver's first week at his new school, and the kids were not very friendly. One day, as Oliver stood on the playground, a basketball rolled by. He picked up the ball, tossed it to one of the boys, and asked if he could play. The boys agreed, and they encouraged him. Soon he was playing better than anyone else.

In both passages, the main characters deal with similar conflicts—feeling alone and unaccepted, and they both go through their own challenges.

Many stories and dramas are based on other classic themes as well, such as good vs. evil and not judging by appearances. For example, in the story of the little red hen, a hen doesn't share the bread that she baked with the other animals because they did not help her. The theme of the story is that you shouldn't expect to receive something if you do nothing to deserve it. This is a familiar theme in modern stories.

Prose stories can be compared with graphic novels. Unlike a prose version, a graphic novel uses detailed illustrations to tell the story. Some panels of a graphic novel use only pictures to tell the story. Other panels may use captions to explain what is happening or speech balloons to show what a character is saying. Read the panel at the right from the story of Maui.

AS HIS OLDER BROTHERS WATCHED IN **AMAZEMENT**, MAUI FISHED ISLANDS FROM THE SEA.

Thinking It Through

Read the following paragraph, and then answer the questions that follow.

Jason and Lamar have been friends since kindergarten. Jason was a gifted athlete; he was good at every sport he ever tried. Lamar was not good at sports, but he was a gifted musician. Luckily, both boys liked humor a lot. When Jason was not at practice, the two friends were always together, cracking jokes and telling stories.

How are Jason and Lamar similar? How are they different?

_____

_____

_____

_____

 Look for similarities and differences before answering the question.

💬 **DISCUSS** Think of two books, stories, or articles you read recently. How were they similar? How were they different? Share your ideas in a group.

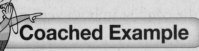

Coached Example

Read the passages and answer the questions.

The Forbidden Room

The newly married princess had just moved into a castle when, after a few weeks, the prince told her that he had to travel to see his father. The prince said, "While I'm away, please make yourself at home. You may go into any room in the castle except for the one room at the top of the stairs."

The princess explored all the rooms of the castle except that one. She had promised, of course, that she would not go into the forbidden room. However, she was very curious about what could possibly be in there. Finally, she could not contain herself any longer; she just had to know what was in the forbidden room. The princess took a deep breath, slowly turned the doorknob, and opened the door. She was shocked at what she saw, and then she hung her head in shame. For there, inside the room, was the prince and his father. "We were wondering how long it would take you to arrive!" the prince exclaimed.

A Big Surprise

1. One way that the graphic novel differs from the first story is that

   A. it includes more characters and scenes.

   B. it takes place over a longer period of time

   C. it shows more details about the setting and characters.

   D. it includes more dialogue for the characters.

   HINT Which version of the story helps you to visualize the castle and the time in which the story takes place?

2. What is the conflict in both versions of the story?

   A. The prince leaves to go and visit his father.

   B. The prince's father does not like the princess.

   C. The princess is not allowed in the forbidden room.

   D. The princess is very curious about what is inside the castle.

   HINT The conflict is a problem that the main character must solve.

3. How do the illustrations of the princess in the graphic novel add to your understanding of her character? Write your answer below.

   _____

   _____

   _____

   _____

   _____

   HINT Look closely at the princess in the panels of the graphic novel. What do her actions and expressions tell you about her?

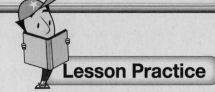

Lesson Practice

Use the Reading Guide to help you understand the passage.

Reading Guide

How does the scene description show you what these characters might have in common or how they might be different?

What is different about the characters' situations?

Shall We Sing?
Act 1
Scene 1

Setting: *It is night. There is one light shining from Mr. Ferguson's apartment window, and all other lights in the building are out. Another light goes on. A woman is using a broom to poke the ceiling to Mr. Ferguson's apartment.*

MR. FERGUSON: (*opens the window and yells*) That's not going to stop me from singing!

MISS HENDERSON: (*muffled yelling*) Keep it down! I have to work in the morning!

MR. FERGUSON: (*singing*) La de da. La la…

MISS HENDERSON: (*throwing her window open and yelling up to Mr. Ferguson*) Do I have to remind you that it's 10:30 P.M?

MR. FERGUSON: Do I have to remind you, Miss Henderson, that not everyone wakes up at dawn? I feel like singing! And I don't have to work tomorrow.

MISS HENDERSON: Well, I do work tomorrow! Can you hold it down?

MR. FERGUSON: I live here too, you know—I should be able to sing if I feel like it.

(*Miss Henderson slams the window closed. She pokes her broom at the ceiling again.*)

MR. FERGUSON: (*at the window*) Here's a nice, soft song for you, Miss Henderson. You can think of it as a lullaby. (*Soft melody plays.*)

(*Miss Henderson's light goes out.*)

Act 1
Scene 2

How does Mr. Ferguson
appear different?

What do these characters
have in common?

Setting: *One week later. Mr. Ferguson is taking out the trash and sees Miss Henderson at the dumpster struggling with her trash.*

MR. FERGUSON: Let me help you with that. It's too heavy.

MISS HENDERSON: No, thank you. (*trying to toss the trash*) I should play loud music late at night! I wonder how you'd like that!

MR. FERGUSON: If you did that, I would sing along.

MISS HENDERSON: I would never do that!

MR. FERGUSON: Why not? (*helping her with the trash*) You might like it…

MISS HENDERSON: (*interrupting*) No.

MR. FERGUSON: (*continuing*) It's an excellent idea! What could be wrong with singing?

MISS HENDERSON: I prefer to sing in the proper place and at the proper time.

MR. FERGUSON: (*following*) How about this? I won't sing in my apartment until you sing with me.

MISS HENDERSON: (*smiling*) Great idea. I'll be quiet for a long time!

(*Miss Henderson goes into her apartment.*)

Answer the following questions.

1. How are Mr. Ferguson and Miss Henderson alike?

   A. They live on the same floor in their apartment building.

   B. They both live alone.

   C. They both get up early to go to work.

   D. They both like to play music late at night.

2. Which of the following BEST describes a difference between settings in scenes 1 and 2?

   A. Scene 1 takes place in both apartments, and scene 2 takes place in Mr. Ferguson's apartment.

   B. Scene 1 takes place in Mr. Ferguson's apartment, and scene 2 takes place by the dumpster.

   C. Scene 1 takes place in Miss Henderson's apartment, and scene 2 takes place outside.

   D. Scene 1 takes place in both of their apartments, and scene 2 takes place outside by the dumpster.

3. How is the conflict similar in both scenes?

   A. Miss Henderson wants it to be quiet, and Mr. Ferguson wants to play music.

   B. Miss Henderson has to work in the morning, and Mr. Ferguson doesn't.

   C. Mr. Ferguson wants to sing with Miss Henderson.

   D. Mr. Ferguson wants to be helpful to Miss Henderson.

4. Which of the following describes an important difference between Mr. Ferguson and Miss Henderson?

   A. Miss Henderson has more trash than Mr. Ferguson.

   B. Miss Henderson is quiet, but her neighbor is not quiet.

   C. Miss Henderson needs lullabies to go to sleep, and Mr. Ferguson doesn't.

   D. Mr. Ferguson wants Miss Henderson to sing with him, and she won't sing.

5. How are the themes in both scenes similar?

   _____

   _____

   _____

Backyard Baseball

Reading Guide

What is Thomas's problem in the story?

What role does Thomas's dad play in the resolution of the problem?

Thomas looked at the crowd as he nervously waited for his turn at bat.

Thomas loved playing baseball, but he hated going up to bat. He struck out every single time. It wasn't that he couldn't hit the ball, but that he couldn't hit the ball when anyone else was watching.

Thomas and his dad had practiced for hours in the backyard. His dad would pitch and Thomas would hit, many times hitting the ball far across the yard. But as soon as anyone was watching, Thomas would become self-conscious and unable to concentrate.

When it was Thomas's turn at bat, he anxiously walked up to the plate. He dug his bat into the dirt, swung his bat, and looked to his dad. When his dad touched his cap brim and nodded, Thomas nodded back.

Before the game, his dad had given him some advice. "When you're standing up at home plate, look for me," his dad said. "When I touch the brim of my cap, that's our secret signal. Pretend I'm on the mound pitching. Pretend there's no one around except you and me in the backyard."

Thomas positioned himself at the plate. He imagined it was only he and his dad in the backyard.

When the pitcher released the ball, Thomas swung just like he did every day during practice. And just like in the backyard, the bat made contact with the ball. It sailed past the pitcher and past the left fielder until it hit the outfield fence and bounced onto the field. Thomas circled the bases, touching the brim of his cap all the way back to home plate.

Reading Guide

Look at these scenes from a graphic novel version of the story. Compare this version with the first story you read.

How does Thomas feel as he steps up to the plate?

What information does the graphic novel convey that the first story does not?

Answer the following questions.

6. Choose all words that describe Thomas right before he goes up to bat, based on evidence from both versions of the story. There is more than one correct choice listed below.

    A. forgetful

    B. animated

    C. anxious

    D. conceited

    E. quiet

    F. enthusiastic

---

7. Use your answer to Part A to answer Part B.

    Part A

    What information do you learn from both versions of the scenes from the story?

    A. Thomas strikes out every single time.

    B. Thomas and his father practice a lot.

    C. Thomas's dad has a solution to the problem.

    D. Thomas hits a home run.

    Part B

    Which detail BEST supports the answer to Part A?

    A. "Thomas and his dad had practiced for hours in the backyard."

    B. "But he and his dad had a plan."

    C. "He struck out every single time."

    D. "Before the game, his dad had pulled him aside to give him some advice."

    E. "Thomas circled the bases, touching the brim of his cap all the way back to home plate."

8. How do the dad's thoughts, as shown in the graphic novel, add to your understanding of his character? Write your answer below.

_____

_____

_____

_____

_____

9. Read the sentence from the prose story in each box on the left. Then match this sentence to its corresponding text from the graphic novel on the right.

A. When it was Thomas's turn at bat, he anxiously walked up to the plate.

1. "I did it!"

2. "Just like at home, Tommy. Just like at home."

B. Thomas circled the bases, touching the brim of his cap all the way back to home plate.

3. Would it work?

C. When his dad touched his cap brim and nodded, Thomas nodded back.

4. Thomas was up at bat, as usual. But he and his dad had a plan. Would it work? Would today be different?

5. Thomas at Bat

Use the Reading Guides to help you understand the passages.

Reading Guide

Why does Ellie ignore Dad's advice about the instruction booklet?

What does Ellie learn after crashing the plane?

The Plane

Two days ago, Aunt Ginger mailed Ellie's birthday present. When Ellie opened the package, she couldn't believe her eyes! It was the remote control plane she wanted. How had Aunt Ginger known? Then Dad had grinned at Ellie, and she realized that Aunt Ginger and Dad had talked.

Dad had advised Ellie to read the instruction booklet carefully, but how hard could flying a plane be? In her excitement, she set aside the booklet without opening it.

Now Ellie and Dad stood in the middle of a large field, away from the trees. The little plane sat on the ground. Ellie held the remote control device in her hands. Then Dad gave the thumbs-up sign. As Ellie pulled back slightly on the control stick, the plane moved slowly along the ground and lifted into the air.

Dad coached Ellie to steer the plane away from the trees. As she worked the control stick to keep the plane in flight, Ellie became more confident. *This is easy*, she thought.

As she pulled harder on the control stick, the plane's nose lifted into the air. The plane was no longer flying level. Its nose rose higher and higher, and then there was silence. The plane had stalled! Without power, the plane fell to the ground.

Dad walked over, shaking his head. "I didn't know what to do when the plane stalled," moaned Ellie.

"Didn't you read the instructions?" asked Dad, as he gazed at the wrecked plane.

Ellie looked down at her shoes and replied sheepishly, "No, I thought I could figure out it out on my own."

Dad said, "Well, I think I can fix this broken wing when we get home . . ."

Ellie interrupted. "I will read all the instructions, Dad, I promise!"

Must-See Movie

Reading Guide

Why does Flor stay with Mom in the museum?

What does Sabina learn about listening to directions?

Sabina hurried up the science museum steps ahead of Flor, her twin sister, and Mom. Sabina had been waiting for months for this visit. There was a special exhibit on volcanoes and a 4-D movie about them.

Once they were inside, Mom said, "Remember, we only have two hours here today. First, we'll *all* go to the dinosaur center that Flor wants to see. Then I want *all* of us to visit the exhibition on the planets. And then we will *all* go to the volcano exhibit." Each time Mom said the word *all*, she looked straight at Sabina.

Sabina looked at Flor with desperation. "Could we go to the volcano exhibit first?" Sabina pleaded.

"We'd better stick with Mom's plan," answered Flor.

Flor examined the museum map and beckoned Mom and Sabina to follow her. Sabina trudged behind. What if they ran out of time for volcanoes?

Just then, Sabina spied an arrow pointing to the volcano exhibit. A digital sign read: *Last movie showing in 5 minutes.* Sabina tried to call out to Mom and Flor, but they were too far ahead. Sabina had to decide quickly. She hurried down the hall toward the movie theater. She would meet up with Mom and Flor later.

Sabina settled into her seat, and the movie began. Just as the narrator was explaining about magma, there was a pause. A voice announced, "Sabina Gomez, please report to the information booth." Sabina's heart sank as she found her way out of the theater.

Mom and Flor looked upset as Sabina explained where she'd been.

"I'm sorry you were worried. I won't do that again," apologized Sabina.

Mom nodded at Flor as she said, "If we hurry, we can go back and catch the end of that volcano movie you want to see."

Answer the following questions.

10. How are Ellie and Sabina alike?

    A. They both spend time in the park.

    B. They both like to fly model planes.

    C. They both like to visit the science museum.

    D. They both fail to follow directions.

11. Which of the following describes an important difference between Sabina and Flor in "Must-See Movie?"

    A. Sabina is interested in volcanoes and Flor is interested in dinosaurs.

    B. Sabina acts in a selfish way and Flor acts in a kind, thoughtful way.

    C. Sabina is the older sister and Flor is the younger sister.

    D. Sabina acts responsibly and Flor acts unreliably.

12. How are the settings in the two stories different?

    A. "The Plane" takes place at a field in a park and "Must-See Movie" takes place at a science museum.

    B. "The Plane" takes place at Aunt Ginger's home and "Must-See Movie" takes place in a museum lobby.

    C. "The Plane" takes place in a forest and "Must-See Movie" takes place in a movie theater.

    D. "The Plane" takes place at Ellie's home and "Must-See Movie" takes place at Sabina's home.

13. How do the actions of the main characters in both stories lead to similar results?

   A. Their actions help others.

   B. Their actions solve a problem.

   C. Their actions lead to a problem.

   D. Their actions go unnoticed.

14. How are the endings of the two stories similar?

   A. Both main characters have to give up on what they wanted to do.

   B. Both main characters get punished for not following directions.

   C. Both main characters fail to learn a lesson from their actions.

   D. Both main characters get a second chance to do what they set out to do.

15. How are the themes in both stories similar?

_____

_____

_____

_____

_____

_____

_____

_____

_____

_____

_____

_____

_____

_____

1 Cumulative Assessment

Read the poem and answer the questions that follow.

The Echoing Green
by William Blake

The sun does arise,
And make happy the skies;
The merry bells ring
To welcome the Spring;
5 The skylark and thrush,
The birds of the bush,
Sing louder around
To the bells' cheerful sound;
While our sports shall be seen
10 On the echoing green.

Old John, with white hair,
Does laugh away care,
Sitting under the oak,
Among the old folk.
15 They laugh at our play,
And soon they all say,
"Such, such were the joys
When we all—girls and boys—
In our youth-time were seen
20 On the echoing green."

Till the little ones, weary,
No more can be merry:
The sun does descend,
And our sports have an end.
25 Round the laps of their mothers
Many sisters and brothers,
Like birds in their nest,
Are ready for rest,
And sport no more seen
30 On the darkening green.

---

1. How many stanzas are in this poem?

A. 1

B. 2

C. 3

D. 4

2. Which line BEST helps you identify the setting?

A. The sun does arise

B. To the bells' cheerful sound

C. Old John, with white hair

D. On the echoing green

3. Which line from the poem includes alliteration?

    A. Many sisters and brothers

    B. The sun does descend

    C. The sun does arise

    D. And our sports have an end

4. What is a theme of the poem?

    A. Nothing lasts forever.

    B. Believe in yourself.

    C. Hard work is always rewarded.

    D. Treat others kindly.

5. Read the following lines from the poem.

> **Many sisters and brothers,**
> **Like birds in their nest,**
> **Are ready for rest,**

What kind of figurative language is in these lines? What is being compared?

_____

_____

_____

_____

_____

_____

_____

_____

_____

_____

_____

_____

_____

_____

Read the passage and answer the questions that follow.

Balloon Trip

When Chandra wrote her essay, she had no idea if she would win a prize. The contest was sponsored by Chandra's favorite radio station. The station asked listeners to write a short essay about why they liked living in Seattle. Chandra wrote about Pike Place Market. A month later, the radio station announced the winners. Chandra was one of them!

According to the contest, each prize would be a surprise. It would arrive in the mail. Chandra waited for two weeks. Finally, her prize arrived.

"It's a gift certificate for a ride in a hot air balloon," her mom told her. "You can take three people with you."

Chandra didn't know if she felt excited or nervous. She had never seen Seattle from the air. That would be fun! But she would be in the air, and she wasn't crazy about heights. She was worried that she might get sick. She thought about telling her mom that she'd rather not go. Then she imagined seeing things she had never seen from the air before. How could she not go?

She would pick her mom and dad, of course. And she would also ask her best friend, Madison.

The day of the balloon ride was sunny with clear skies. When they arrived at the balloon company, Chandra saw the balloon. It was huge and had many different colors. But there was no air in it. It lay on the ground like an enormous melted rainbow. Chandra wondered if something was wrong. She was disappointed, but almost relieved.

Nearby was the pilot. "Does anyone have questions?" he asked them.

"How is the balloon supposed to work? It's flat," said Madison.

"We pump air into the balloon," said the pilot. "The air inside the balloon is warmer than the surrounding air. The warmer air rises, and it takes the balloon with it.

"How do you get air into the balloon? It seems like it would need a lot of it," said Chandra.

"We blow regular air in with a fan. When we want the balloon to rise, we use burners to heat it."

"Is it noisy?" asked Chandra's dad.

"It gets a little noisy when we use the burner. But when the burner is off, it's very quiet. All you'll hear is the wind."

"How high will we go?" Chandra asked. She was still not sure she should do this.

"Most flights go between 1,000 and 3,000 feet up. Sometimes we go higher. Sometimes we're as low as the tops of trees."

The tops of trees weren't too high, but 3,000 feet sounded very high. Chandra was nervous all over again.

"Does the basket sway a lot?" she asked.

"It doesn't," the pilot smiled. "It just moves with the wind."

Chandra wasn't convinced. She really didn't want to get sick.

"I can't wait to go up there!" Madison said with a grin.

Chandra could definitely wait. But then men started pumping the balloon full of air. Soon it wasn't a melted rainbow, but a barrel of color.

"Time to get in," the pilot said.

Everyone took their place. Chandra held on tightly to the basket's edge. The captain used the burner to heat the air in the balloon. The balloon and basket lifted off the ground.

Up, up, up, the balloon rose. Soon it was higher than the trees. Everything on the ground looked smaller and smaller. Chandra was fascinated. She might have been nervous before, but now she was anything but nervous.

Before she knew it, they could see Seattle and the mountains. The city sprawled in all directions.

"There's the Space Needle," said her dad.

"I can see Mt. Rainier," said Madison.

"And there's Mt. Baker!" said Chandra's mom.

In every direction they looked, there was something else to see.

Chandra felt like they were just beginning when the captain said, "We'll have to start back now."

Soon they were back on the ground.

"Did you have a good time?" Chandra's dad asked as they walked back to their car.

"I had a great time!" Chandra answered.

"Do you feel sick?" asked her mom.

Chandra looked up at her mom and smiled. "Sick? No way!"

6. Which sentence from the passage does NOT support the idea that Chandra is easily scared?

   A. "She was worried that she might get sick."

   B. "Chandra could definitely wait."

   C. "Chandra held on tightly to the basket's edge."

   D. "Chandra was fascinated."

7. The reader can tell that the author believes that

   A. flying in a hot air balloon is dangerous.

   B. flying in a hot air balloon is safe.

   C. Chandra is often sick.

   D. Chandra is afraid of everything.

8. What is the conflict in the passage?

   A. Chandra is nervous about being up in the air.

   B. Chandra is annoyed at her parents.

   C. Chandra does not know who to take with her.

   D. Chandra wrote an essay.

9. What is the resolution of the passage?

   A. Chandra sees the balloon for the first time, and she wonders if it will float.

   B. Air is put into the balloon.

   C. Chandra's mom opens an envelope.

   D. Chandra discovers riding in the balloon isn't so bad.

10. What is a similarity between "The Echoing Green" and "Balloon Trip"?

_____

_____

_____

_____

_____

_____

_____

_____

CHAPTER

Informational Texts

Chapter 2: Diagnostic Assessment

Lesson 8: Main Idea and Supporting Details

Lesson 9: Use Factual Details for Support

Lesson 10: Sequence

Lesson 11: Cause and Effect

Lesson 12: Compare and Contrast Informational Texts

Lesson 13: Using Different Sources

Lesson 14: Reasons and Evidence

Lesson 15: Compare and Contrast Texts Across Genres

Chapter 2: Cumulative Assessment

2 Diagnostic Assessment

Read the passage and answer the questions that follow.

The Chicago Public Library

The Beginning

The Chicago Public Library had an odd beginning. It was born after a disaster and thought up by people in London. Chicago was still recovering from the great Chicago Fire of 1871. But then, a man in London decided to help Chicago with an "English Book Donation." He said, "I propose that England should present a Free Library to Chicago. The library is to remain there as a mark of sympathy now and a keepsake and a token of true brotherly kindness forever . . ." The plan carried the support of Thomas Hughes, a prominent Member of Parliament and author. Hughes had visited Chicago in 1870.

Over eight thousand books arrived in Chicago from England. The citizens of Chicago created a petition for a Free Public Library. Before the great Chicago Fire, all of the libraries had been private. You had to pay a fee to become a member. Many people could not afford to pay these fees. The petition led to the Illinois Library Act of 1872. This act ordered cities in Illinois to establish libraries paid for by taxes.

In April 1872, the Chicago City Council established the Chicago Public Library. On January 1, 1873, the library opened its doors. It was located at the southeast corner of LaSalle and Adams Streets. Oddly enough, it was housed in a huge water tank that had survived the fire.

The Library Grows

The library didn't stay in the water tank for long. During the next twenty-four years, the library would move several times. For eleven years it was on the fourth floor of Chicago's City Hall. Then in 1897, the Central Library opened to the public. It was located at Michigan Avenue between Washington and Randolph Streets. The library cost around $2 million to design and build. Remembering the Chicago Fire, the people who created this building designed it to be practically fireproof.

In 1916, Chief Librarian Henry E. Legler presented a bold plan. He called for a wide network of neighborhood libraries throughout Chicago. He wanted "every person in Chicago who can read or wants to use books" to be able to get to a library. The first regional library, the Henry E. Legler Regional Library, was established in 1920.

Beginning in the 1960s, a large number of neighborhood branch libraries were opened. They were built or were established in leased storefronts. By 1985, there were seventy-six such branches throughout the city.

During the seventy-five years of library growth, it became clear that the Chicago Public Library needed to grow even more. It had outgrown its Central Library on Michigan Avenue. Chicago Mayor Harold Washington and civic leaders planned for a new Central Library. The chosen site for the new Central Library was 400 S. State Street, a one-and-one-half block tract in the South Loop. The Library Board decided that the new Central Library would be named after the late mayor. Harold Washington was the city's first African American mayor. He was a great lover of books and a great supporter of the Chicago Public Library.

The Chicago Public Library has grown steadily. In 1991, the city's newest central library, the Harold Washington Library Center, opened. At the time, it was the world's largest city public library.

The Library Today

The Chicago Public Library has come a long way since the 1800s. Today it has a total of seventy-nine locations. It is the largest library system in the Midwestern United States. With over ten million volumes, it is one of the largest public library systems in the country.

1. This passage is MAINLY about
   A. the Chicago Fire of 1871.
   B. the beginning and growth of the Chicago Public Library.
   C. librarians with large plans.
   D. the generosity of London patrons.

2. What happened AFTER the Henry E. Legler Regional Library was established?
   A. Over eight thousand books were sent from England.
   B. The library moved to Michigan Avenue.
   C. The Harold Washington Library Center opened.
   D. The library moved to City Hall.

The Washington Monument

The Washington Monument was built to honor our first president, George Washington. This monument is an obelisk—a four-sided pillar that gradually narrows as it rises and ends in a pyramid at the top. Made of marble, granite, and sandstone, it is located near the west end of the National Mall in Washington, D.C. It is the tallest obelisk in the world. It is also the tallest stone structure in the world.

There were two stages in its construction. One occurred between 1848 and 1856; the other lasted from 1876 to 1878. The pause occurred for several reasons. There was not enough money available to continue construction. The political conflict within the country, as well, got in the way of construction. In 1783, Congress made its first proposal for the monument: a statue of George Washington. Although the proposal was approved, and a site was even chosen for it in 1791, construction would not begin for many years. After Washington's death in 1799, there was a rebirth of interest in creating a public monument. Again, funds were not available for the construction. Soon, a group called the Washington National Monument Society was started. The society sponsored a contest for the monument's design. Robert Mills won the contest; he suggested an obelisk surrounded by pillars. A statue of Washington in a chariot was supposed to sit on top of the obelisk.

In 1848, construction finally started. The construction was completed in 1884. The cornerstone was laid in place on July 4, 1848, in an ornate ceremony. Gathering funds for the construction was a steady problem, and work halted in 1856. When the Civil War broke out in 1861, raising funds became even harder. By the time work resumed in 1876, the design had developed considerably. The new design was much simpler, just an obelisk with a pyramid-shaped top. The U.S. Army Corps of Engineers managed the construction to its end. The monument became open to the public on October 9, 1888.

The Washington Monument weighs 81,120 tons and is 555 feet and 5 1/8 inches tall. At the monument's base, its walls are 15 feet thick. Near the top, the walls are 18 inches thick. The white marble blocks that compose the walls came from Maryland and Massachusetts. At the 150-foot point, you can see a slight color change; this was where construction slowed in 1854. A total of 193 memorial stones were placed in the interior walls. These stones came from countries, states, cities, groups, and individual donors around the globe.

The hollow monument contains 896 steps inside it, supported by an iron framework. An elevator runs up through the monument's center, taking tourists to the observation level. The pyramid windows at this level offer nice views of the city. When the monument was built, it was the world's tallest structure. In 1889, however, the Eiffel Tower in Paris was completed, which was taller.

The monument has been closed twice, both times for repairs. It was closed from late 1997 to mid-2000, and then from December 2000 to February 2002. Fixing the monument's exterior cost about $10 million. Repairs also included rebuilding the elevator system; replacing the heating, electrical, and air-conditioning systems; and increasing the size of the observation areas.

---

3. This passage is MAINLY about

   A. George Washington and his legacy.

   B. political problems in the nineteenth century.

   C. renovations made to the Washington Monument.

   D. the history of the Washington Monument.

4. How are the stories of the two structures different?

   A. The Washington Monument was built quickly, while the Chicago Public Library ran into many problems.

   B. The Washington Monument ran into many problems before opening, while the Chicago Public Library continued to grow.

   C. Only the Chicago Public Library was opened quickly and needed renovations.

   D. The Chicago Public Library had trouble with funding because of political problems.

---

5. How are the two passages similar?

_____

_____

_____

_____

Read the passage and answer the questions that follow.

You Can Say That Again!

Despite my reservations, I was pleasantly surprised by Darlene Drake's latest movie, *You Can Say That Again!* It is her best film yet. Drake is fantastically funny in this picture! And, well, we all know that Drake's movies in the past haven't exactly been funny. Plenty of times, this young actress has played roles that weren't right for her. In her newest film, she is playing a more complicated role. It is quite refreshing to see her play a role where she wasn't miscast.

I found *What Does That Have To Do With Anything?*, her last film, dull. Drake just didn't seem right for the part of a babysitter. The character was annoying at best, babysitting, managing her home life, and playing sports at the same time. And frankly, Drake just seems too mature to be playing the role of babysitter. In the movie, she looks like she could be at least twenty or twenty-one years old, which is too old to be playing a babysitter. Her lines didn't sound natural, and her fake laugh was irritating.

The movie released before the babysitter movie, *It Happened Again*, was a humorless mess that was trying too hard to be funny. Some reviewers said the movie was "like torture." And I would not have disagreed. Drake played the sidekick role unsteadily. At times she took over the screen, and other times she was too silent. In fact, I was starting to think Drake didn't have too much talent. However, I'm happy to say that this time I feel very differently. Now that I know how well Drake can do, I don't think she'll be playing the sidekick anymore. She displayed her ability to be a wonderful actress. She will probably be getting some big roles in the future.

In her latest film, *You Can Say That Again!*, Drake is a scream! She plays a hopeful scientist. Finally, Drake got to play an adult role. And a scientist, of all things! I was thrilled that she did this movie. Her character, the scientist, is trying to invent a formula that will keep people eternally young. But instead of creating something that will keep people young forever, she stumbles upon something else. She invents a potion that allows a person to know what others are going to say five minutes before they say it.

And if you think you know what happens next, you're wrong. This movie is filled with constant surprises. I mean, just imagine knowing what someone is going to say. It really makes you think about the conversations that we have with people. It's quite an interesting movie, and Drake shows off her terrific timing.

I won't say any more because I don't want to give away surprises. But if this movie is any indication of things to come from Drake, we have a lot to look forward to!

6. Why was the author surprised by Drake's new movie?

   A. The author thought the movie would be bad, like Drake's other movies.

   B. The author thought the movie wasn't funny.

   C. The author doesn't usually like movies about scientists.

   D. The author really liked Drake's other movies.

7. Which of the following sentences BEST states the main idea of paragraph 3?

   A. "The movie released before the babysitter movie, *It Happened Again*, was a humorless mess that was trying too hard to be funny."

   B. "In fact, I was starting to think Drake didn't have too much talent."

   C. "Drake played the sidekick role unsteadily."

   D. "However, I'm happy to say that this time I feel very differently."

8. Which statement BEST expresses the author's argument?

   A. Drake played bad roles very well in the past.

   B. Drake played bad roles poorly in the past.

   C. Drake is a great actress who always plays creative roles.

   D. All of Drake's movies are not very good.

9. If you wanted to learn more about what other movie reviewers think about Drake's new movie, what source would you use?

   A. the Internet

   B. an encyclopedia

   C. a dictionary

   D. an atlas

10. What is MOST LIKELY the author's attitude toward Drake? Which details in the passage support your inference?

_____

_____

_____

8 Main Idea and Supporting Details

Getting the Idea

The **main idea** of a passage is what it is mostly about. **Supporting details** are the facts or other pieces of information that prove the main idea. A detail may be a name, date, place, or action.

Every story and article has a main idea. You can usually find it near the beginning of a passage. Every paragraph has a main idea, too. This is often found in the first sentence of the paragraph, though it might occur later. A main idea is not the same as a topic. A topic is the subject of a passage. For example, the topic of a passage may be "bicycles." The main idea would be a statement about bicycles: "Riding bicycles is good for the environment."

As you read this paragraph, try to identify its main idea and supporting details.

> There are many different kinds of carnivorous plants. Carnivorous plants are plants that get nutrients from trapping and eating insects and spiders. These plants are generally found in locations with poor soil. There are many different ways carnivorous plants trap and eat animals. Pitcher plants have a large cavity, or pitcher, that insects fall into. The Venus flytrap has leaves that close and trap insects.

The main idea of this passage is that there are many different kinds of carnivorous plants. Supporting details include the different ways pitcher plants and Venus flytraps capture and eat animals.

To figure out the main idea of a story, article, or paragraph, look for the idea that stands out as most important. The other ideas are details, and should only support the main idea of the passage. In many nonfiction works, the title is directly connected to the main idea. Looking at the title might help you if the passage doesn't state its main point explicitly.

Also, thinking of a possible title for a passage can help you figure out which parts of it are most important.

In longer articles or essays, there may be more than one main idea. These main ideas will both be about the same topic, but they will cover different aspects of the topic in detail.

Look at the following two paragraphs from a longer passage. The main ideas are underlined. The other sentences provide details about the main ideas.

> <u>Cars are bad for the environment</u>. Cars and trucks emit more than 300 million tons of carbon into the atmosphere each year in the United States. They are responsible for about one-third of our nation's total production of carbon dioxide. Carbon dioxide is one of the greenhouse gases that contributes to global warming. Cars and trucks also consume almost 9 million barrels of oil per day. That is more than 25 percent of the world's total!

> <u>The United States needs to explore different ways of traveling</u>. Alternative transportation causes less pollution. Bicycling and walking are good alternatives for short distances. Trains, buses, and other public transportation should be used whenever possible. If more people use alternative transportation, we can make up for the negative impacts of cars and trucks.

The main idea of the first paragraph is that cars are bad for the environment. They cause pollution and consume a lot of oil. Meanwhile, the main idea of the second paragraph is that people should explore other forms of transportation. What is probably the main idea of the passage? Based on the two paragraphs, the most likely main idea of the passage is that the United States needs to explore transportation alternatives because cars are bad for the environment. Often, when you express the main idea of a passage you have read, you give a summary of its content. A **summary** is a brief restatement of the most important ideas of a passage in your own words.

Thinking It Through

Read the following paragraph, and then answer the question that follows.

John Keats was a famous poet. He was known for his odes and sonnets. His books did not sell very well during his lifetime. However, he is regarded as one of the greatest poets in the English language.

What is the main idea of this paragraph?

_____

_____

_____

_____

 The main idea is the most important idea in the paragraph.

DISCUSS Discuss your answer with the class.

Coached Example

Read the passage and answer the questions.

adapted and excerpted from
"Chanticleer"

from Birds in Town and Village
by W.H. Hudson

That morning, I found myself paying special attention to one rooster. It was about a hundred yards away, or a little more perhaps. All the other birdsongs seemed inferior to it. Its voice was uniquely clear and pure. The last note was very long and seemed to fall at the end. However, it didn't collapse like long notes often do, ending with a little croak, as if the singer had run out of breath. It was perfect in its way, a finished performance. It was artistic, and, by comparison with other songs, brilliant. After I heard this bird, I paid little attention to the others. After each call it made, I counted the seconds until the call came again.

1. Which sentence BEST states the main idea of the passage?

    A. "That morning, I found myself paying special attention to one rooster."

    B. "Its voice was uniquely clear and pure."

    C. "It was perfect in its way, a finished performance."

    D. "The last note was very long and seemed to fall at the end."

    HINT When you are looking for the main idea, look for a broad concept, not specific details.

2. What would make another good title for the passage?

    A. "What Roosters Like to Eat"

    B. "The Rooster's Song"

    C. "Different Birdsongs"

    D. "Common Barnyard Animals"

    HINT The title often gives clues about the main idea.

Lesson Practice

Use the Reading Guide to help you understand the passage.

Reading Guide

What does the title tell you about this passage?

In paragraph 2, what important detail do you learn about slavery?

What is the main subject of paragraph 5?

Making Equality

The right to vote is one of the most important rights and duties of a citizen because everyone didn't always have it.

When the Constitution was written, African Americans did not have the rights of citizens. Instead, they were still enslaved in the United States. The Thirteenth Amendment made slavery illegal. The Fourteenth Amendment made all people born in the United States equal citizens under the law; it gave African Americans citizenship. The next step was to give them the right to vote.

In 1870, when the Fifteenth Amendment passed, women and people under twenty-one were not allowed to vote. With the Fifteenth Amendment, African American men over twenty-one were allowed to vote. In many states, there were other requirements as well, however. In some places, there was a tax on voting, while in others, there were tests voters had to take to prove that they could read.

Other amendments were passed to give citizens more just voting rights. The Nineteenth Amendment, passed in 1920, gave women the right to vote. The Twenty-fourth Amendment ended poll taxes, or taxes charged to vote. The Twenty-sixth Amendment changed the national voting age to eighteen.

Today, any person born in the United States or naturalized as a citizen who is over eighteen can vote. He or she does not have to pay a tax and does not have to have a certain heritage or gender. By making all voters equal, the Constitution makes all citizens equal.

Answer the following questions.

1. This passage is MAINLY about

   A. amendments.

   B. African Americans.

   C. voting rights.

   D. citizenship.

2. Which of the following BEST states the main idea of paragraph 2?

   A. Once, African Americans could not vote.

   B. African Americans gained equality very slowly.

   C. At first, African Americans were citizens.

   D. African Americans had important rights.

3. What is paragraph 4 MAINLY about?

   A. voting rights amendments

   B. women's right to vote

   C. poll taxes

   D. lowering the voting age

4. According to the passage, which amendment gave African American men over twenty-one the right to vote?

   A. Thirteenth Amendment

   B. Fourteenth Amendment

   C. Fifteenth Amendment

   D. Sixteenth Amendment

5. Write a sentence that summarizes the entire passage.

   _____

   _____

   _____

   _____

   _____

   _____

   _____

   _____

Use the Reading Guide to help you understand the passage.

Reading Guide

How does the title give you a clue about the main idea of the passage?

Look for the main idea in each paragraph. Then think about the main idea of the passage as a whole.

What details support the writer's argument?

A Dangerous Intersection

Our neighborhood has a very dangerous crossing at the intersection of Valley Road and Maple Drive. Many minor accidents have happened there already, as well as several close calls when cars narrowly escaped hitting one another. In some cases, pedestrians have been hurt as well. The city needs to put up four stop signs, one on each corner, immediately, before someone gets seriously injured.

At one time, fewer people lived in our neighborhood, and this intersection was relatively safe. There were only a few houses built because most people had large farms, and there was very little traffic. People drove slowly through the intersection and yielded to make sure there were no cars coming. There were hardly ever any cars coming.

Now, more people are driving on our roads. Over the past ten years, many of the farms have been sold and the property divided. Many new houses have been built. Each house has at least two drivers in it. Some people do slow down at the intersection. And they should, because usually another car is coming. But we often hear brakes squealing and horns honking because one driver didn't see the other.

If four stop signs are put up, then all drivers will be required to stop and look. They will be able to see if there is another driver coming from the other road. I believe the signs will solve this problem and prevent people from getting hurt in our neighborhood.

Answer the following questions.

6. Read paragraph 2 from the passage.

> **At one time, fewer people lived in our neighborhood, and this intersection was relatively safe. There were only a few houses built because most people had large farms, and there was very little traffic. People drove slowly through the intersection and yielded to make sure there were no cars coming. There were hardly ever any cars coming.**

Circle the sentence that states the main idea of the paragraph. Underline the details that support the main idea.

7. Read paragraph 3 from the passage.

> **Now, more people are driving on our roads. Over the past ten years, many of the farms have been sold and the property divided. Many new houses have been built. Each house has at least two drivers in it. Some people do slow down at the intersection. And they should, because usually another car is coming. But we often hear brakes squealing and horns honking because one driver didn't see the other.**

Part A

Read each choice in the chart below. Circle the choice that states the correct main idea of paragraph 3.

Main Idea	People drive too fast, which is dangerous for drivers and pedestrians.
	The intersection has become more dangerous because more people live in the neighborhood.
	It is a noisy neighborhood because there are brakes squealing and horns honking.

Part B

Underline the supporting details in paragraph 3 that BEST support the answer to Part A.

Use the Reading Guide to help you understand the passage.

Reading Guide

What is an important detail that supports the main idea of paragraph 1?

What detail supports the main idea of paragraph 3?

How does the last paragraph help you understand the main idea of the passage?

Table Tennis

If you are looking for a sport that is fun and easy to learn, try table tennis. This game, first started in England, was originally called Ping-Pong. Many people still use that name today. It can be played by two or four people.

To play the game, you need a rectangular table, divided in half by a net. Each player needs a small, round paddle, which is flat and made of wood. A thin layer of rubber is on top of each side of the paddle. Players also need a ball, which is lightweight, hollow, and small enough to be propelled over the net with the paddles.

The rules of the game are simple. One player serves first, tossing the ball into the air and striking it with the paddle. The ball must first hit the server's side of the table before bouncing over the net to the second player's side. That player must then strike the ball back over the net after only one bounce. The back-and-forth play, often called a *volley*, continues until one player does not successfully return the ball over the net. The second player then wins a point.

There are other ways to earn a point as well. If a player serves and the opponent does not return the serve over the net after one bounce, the server wins the point. A point can also be won if a player violates a rule, such as touching the table with a free hand during play. Games are played until one player reaches eleven points.

If you follow these simple rules and use the right equipment, then a game of table tennis may just be the sport for you!

Answer the following questions.

8. This passage is MAINLY about how table tennis is

A. an enjoyable sport.

B. a simple game to learn.

C. played all over the world.

D. similar to Ping-Pong.

9. Which detail BEST tells more about the main idea of paragraph 2?

A. The table is divided in half.

B. Paddles are small, round, and made of wood.

C. Each player needs a paddle.

D. The table is rectangular.

10. What is the main idea of paragraph 3?

A. how to serve

B. the basic rules of table tennis

C. how to score a point

D. the best way to volley

11. Which detail from the passage tells a rule violation in table tennis?

A. touching the table with your free hand

B. using a paddle with a layer of rubber

C. bouncing the ball when you serve

D. playing with more than two players

12. Write two sentences that summarize the entire passage.

_____

_____

_____

_____

9 Use Factual Details for Support

Getting the Idea

As you read informational texts, you need to pay attention to the details. You know that a **detail** is a piece of information. Names, dates, and descriptions are all types of details. Pay close attention to the details. This will help you to understand what is happening in the text.

Types of Details	Examples
names of people	George Washington served as commander of the Continental Army.
names of places	They fought in Boston and New York.
dates and times	Martin Luther King Jr. was born in 1929.
facts in an article	Blue whales can reach up to 108 feet in length.

There are many other kinds of details not listed in the chart. As you read, pay attention to all of the details in the text. The better you understand an article or essay, the easier it will be for you to answer questions about it, form ideas, and make statements about it.

Sometimes the author does not tell you exactly what is happening. This means that you have to figure things out on your own and make an inference. You already know that an inference is a decision based on available details. In order to make an inference, you must have some form of support to back up your inference.

When making an inference from informational texts, you use the facts available to you. Because inferences are often based only on the information in a piece, they can be incorrect. Sometimes an inference will be a generalization about what you have read. A **generalization** is a broad statement based on specific details. Read the paragraph below.

> Before World War II, it was not unusual for low-income women to have jobs outside of the home. Women worked in sweatshops and other factories so they could support themselves and others. However, many middle-class women did not have jobs before the war. They were expected to stay at home and raise families. During the war, middle-class women took all sorts of jobs, including physical labor in factories. After the war, many of these women wanted to keep their jobs.

What generalizations and inferences can you make about this text? Well, because many of the middle-class women wanted to keep their jobs, you could say that working in factories was satisfying work for many middle-class women. You might also say that many low-income women worked in sweatshops and factories. But you might be incorrect. The paragraph says, "it was not unusual" for low-income women to work. This doesn't mean that "many" of them worked. Make sure that any inferences and generalizations you make are supported by specific words or facts from the text.

Thinking It Through

Read the following paragraph, and then answer the questions that follow.

By the 1920s, African Americans began to prosper in some parts of the United States for the first time. People whose grandparents had lived through slavery became educated and had good jobs. In the New York neighborhood of Harlem, African American culture blossomed between 1920 and 1940. Music, dance, politics, literature, and art were all parts of the Harlem Renaissance.

Do you think the Harlem Renaissance could have happened before the 1920s? Which details in the paragraph support your inference?

_____

_____

_____

_____

 **HINT** Reread the paragraph. Remember, any inference you make must be based on specific details.

💬 **DISCUSS** Based on details in the text and the illustration, how would you define the Harlem Renaissance? Discuss your answer with the class.

Coached Example

Read the passage and answer the questions.

The Secret Garden by Frances Hodgson Burnett takes place in Misselthwaite Manor in England during the Victorian era. A spoiled orphan named Mary returns to England from India when her parents die. She is sent to live in Yorkshire with her uncle in his mansion. She meets all sorts of people like Martha, Dickon, and Colin. Martha is a maid on the grounds who has taken a fancy to Mary, and Dickon is her brother. Mary becomes interested in a secret garden that the children aren't allowed to enter. She is determined to clear it out and bring it back to life. *The Secret Garden* is a great story with colorful characters and a positive message.

Frances Hodgson Burnett

1. Based on the passage, you can infer that the author

   A. liked the book.

   B. did not like the book.

   C. thought the book was boring.

   D. wants to live in a mansion.

   HINT Remember, an inference is a conclusion based on available details.

2. Which sentence from the passage supports the idea that the author recommends the book?

   A. *"The Secret Garden* by Frances Hodgson Burnett takes place in Misselthwaite Manor in England during the Victorian era."

   B. "A spoiled orphan named Mary returns to England from India when her parents die."

   C. "She meets all sorts of people like Martha, Dickon, and Colin."

   D. *"The Secret Garden* is a great story with colorful characters and a positive message."

   HINT Reread the passage. Look at each answer choice and see which one supports the inference.

Use the Reading Guide to help you understand the passage.

Reading Guide

What generalization can you make about pollutants?

What can you infer about volcanic eruptions?

Which details support the generalization that industries can be harmful?

Air Pollution

When most people talk about pollution, they are talking about the release of smog, soot, dirt, and chemicals into Earth's atmosphere. Anything that pollutes the earth or its atmosphere is called a pollutant. Pollutants are often put directly into the air by factories, machines, and automobiles. They can also be generated when chemicals are released and react with air molecules.

Some common air pollutants are dust, volcanic gases, and smoke from forest fires. These pollutants are often released when volcanoes erupt or when lightning strikes a forest. However, other pollutants are made by humans in factories, power plants, and elsewhere. These include carbon monoxide, dust, smoke, and chemicals, which mix with natural substances in air.

Oil, natural gas, or coal is burned to run factories and cars, also providing electricity for homes and businesses. These fuels occur naturally and are called fossil fuels because they come from decayed fossils. When fossil fuels are burned, harsh chemicals are released. These chemicals react with particles in the air.

One product of these reactions is smog, or gray, stinky vapor. Smog makes it hard to breathe. Smog can also change an area's weather. When air pollutants mix with water in the air, acids are produced. When it rains, acids mix with the water to form acid rain or acid snow. Acid rain or acid snow can harm plants, animals, and even buildings and structures. Over time, the acid in the rain and snow eats away at the materials that make up buildings.

Air pollution can come in many forms. All of these forms are highly dangerous. Hopefully, we will reduce pollution over time.

Answer the following questions.

1. Air pollution PROBABLY

    A. is not that dangerous.

    B. is something that humans need to address.

    C. has always been a problem.

    D. will be removed in the near future.

2. Based on the passage, you can infer that

    A. humans can stop all pollutants from entering the air.

    B. all pollutants are created by humans.

    C. pollutants do not mix with natural substances.

    D. humans can stop some, but not all, pollutants from entering the air.

3. Which detail from the passage backs up the idea that smog is harmful?

    A. Homes and businesses need electricity.

    B. Pollutants occur naturally.

    C. Smog makes it harder to breathe.

    D. Chemical reactions produce acids.

4. Which sentence from the passage does NOT support the idea that smog is caused by humans?

    A. "These pollutants often occur when volcanoes erupt or when lightning strikes a forest."

    B. "Oil, natural gas, or coal is burned to run factories and cars, also providing electricity for homes and businesses."

    C. "When fossil fuels are burned, harsh chemicals are released."

    D. "However, other pollutants are made by humans in factories, power plants, and elsewhere."

5. How does pollution affect living things indirectly? Which details in the passage support your inference?

    _____

    _____

    _____

Use the Reading Guide to help you understand the passage.

Reading Guide

What details about Lake Superior are included in the passage?

What generalizations can you make about Lake Superior?

How does the last sentence of the passage help to reinforce the writer's main points?

Lake Superior

The Great Lakes are a chain of five freshwater lakes that border the United States and Canada. The five lakes—Ontario, Erie, Huron, Michigan, and Superior—connect to the Atlantic Ocean by way of the Saint Lawrence Seaway. The lakes serve as a transportation system for large cargoes of goods.

The largest of these lakes is Lake Superior; it is also the deepest and the coldest. Its average temperature is 40°F, which makes it a very cold place to swim, even in the middle of summer. But surprisingly, Lake Superior rarely freezes completely. In fact, typically, it freezes over only once every twenty years.

By surface area, it is the largest freshwater lake in the world. It covers an area of 31,700 square miles. This is the same size as the entire state of South Carolina!

Lake Superior is the clearest of the Great Lakes. In some places, at a depth of one hundred feet, the underwater visibility is thirty to fifty feet. Scuba divers can search for the 350 sunken ships located there. The cold, fresh water preserves these shipwrecks, making the lake ideal for underwater exploring.

The last major shipwreck was on November 10, 1975. The *Edmund Fitzgerald* sank carrying 26,000 tons of taconite pellets, marble-sized balls of iron ore. The 729-foot ship lies on the floor of Lake Superior in two pieces.

Lake Superior is the most western Great Lake of the chain. Some say this lake is "superior" to all the other great lakes.

Answer the following questions.

6. Choose all the sentences from the passage that support the idea that many ships have sunk in Lake Superior. There is more than one correct choice listed below.

   A. "In fact, typically, it freezes over only once every twenty years."

   B. "The 729-foot ship lies on the floor of Lake Superior in two pieces."

   C. "The largest of these lakes is Lake Superior; it is also the deepest and the coldest."

   D. "Scuba divers can search for the 350 sunken ships located there."

   E. "It covers an area of 31,700 square miles."

   F. "The last major shipwreck was on November 10, 1975."

---

7. Use your answer to Part A to answer Part B.

   Part A

   What details from the passage support the sentence: "Some say this lake is 'superior'"? There is more than one correct choice listed below.

   A. "Lake Superior is the clearest of the Great Lakes."

   B. "But surprisingly, Lake Superior rarely freezes completely."

   C. "Lake Superior is the most western Great Lake of the chain."

   D. "By surface area, it is the largest freshwater lake in the world."

   E. "The lakes serve as a transportation system for large cargoes of goods."

   F. This is the same size as the entire state of South Carolina!

   Part B

   Does the writer's use of factual details effectively support his claim about Lake Superior? Why or why not?

   _____

   _____

   _____

   _____

Use the Reading Guide to help you understand the passage.

Salt Flats of the World

Reading Guide

What generalizations can you make about salt flats?

What can you infer about the importance of salt flats?

Which details tell how salt flats are formed?

People have used salt for thousands of years to prepare and preserve food, and even as money. Salt occurs naturally all over the world in seawater and in lakes. When salt is found on Earth's surface it is usually the dried-up residue of lakes and ancient oceans. These dried-up oceans and lakebeds are called *salt flats*.

Salt flats form in closed places where there isn't enough drainage or rainfall to wash away salt deposits. In dry climates, like deserts, salt flats form because evaporation happens fast. Salt is left behind as a flat, solid layer. Some ancient ocean beds have been pushed underground by Earth's tectonic activity. These beds become salt mines that people excavate for salt.

The surfaces of salt flats are constantly changing. When salt crystals expand, they push the crust of the salt flat. These newly formed crystals make new, strange patterns on the surface of the salt flat. Rainstorms come and wash off the new crystals and leave a fresh layer of salt. Occasionally, floods create temporary lakes. The fresh salts dissolve in the floodwater, and the process starts all over again.

Since salt flats are too harsh for most plants and animals to survive, they are usually barren. The delicate salt crystals become exposed to the elements and are easily crushed. The thin upper crust of the salt can often break through to the mud layer below when stepped on. For this reason, vehicles are often prohibited from salt flats.

There are some exceptions, however. The large, extremely flat surface of the Bonneville Salt Flats in Utah has made it a popular place for racing vehicles. The flats were formed when an ancient lake as large as Lake Michigan dried up. People gather every year to race on a special ten-mile track across the flats.

Answer the following questions.

8. Based on the passage, you can infer that

   A. salt flats are a precious natural resource.

   B. salt flats will stop forming eventually.

   C. people need salt flats to survive.

   D. salt is a mineral.

9. What generalization can you make about salt flats based on the passage?

   A. All salt flats are fragile environments.

   B. Rainfall does not affect salt flats.

   C. Salt flats only occur in deserts.

   D. Most, but not all salt flats are fragile environments.

10. Which detail does NOT support the idea that salt flats occur from evaporation?

   A. "When salt is found at the Earth's surface it is usually the dried-up residue of lakes and ancient oceans."

   B. "The flats were formed when an ancient lake as large as Lake Michigan dried up."

   C. "In dry climates, like deserts, salt flats form because evaporation happens fast."

   D. "Since salt flats are too harsh for most plants and animals to survive, they are usually barren."

11. How are salt flats constantly changing? Which details from the passage support this idea?

   _____

   _____

   _____

Lesson

10 Sequence

Getting the Idea

Sequence is the order in which things happen. One of the most common ways in which authors organize their writing is chronological order. Chronological order is time sequence. Time-order words may be used to show what happens first, second, and last.

Some common time-order words are *now, before, next, first, second,* and *finally*. These words help the reader understand when things happen. Other examples of time-order words are *currently, initially,* and *after*. The chronological method is very effective when the author is writing about people and events. Ordering paragraphs chronologically gives the reader a stronger grasp of the topic.

Biographies and histories are often written in chronological order. In the following example, the events in the development of the Tour de France are presented in the order in which they happened. This helps the reader understand when each event occurred. As you read the example, look for the words that tell what happened first, second, and last.

> The Tour de France is an annual bicycle race that winds around France and neighboring countries. Currently, the race is broken up into stages and lasts for three weeks. At first, however, the race was designed to run around the perimeter of France. The race ran for nineteen days. Cyclists would ride through the night. Then, after a few years, the race became very popular. Finally, the racecourse began to zigzag through France, gaining more and more fans.

There are other text structures that authors use to present things in a particular order. Some texts are written to show a series of steps. The different parts of directions and recipes, for example, need to be presented in a particular order. The correct results depend on following the steps in the right order. If you were writing about how to make a sandwich, for example, you would first talk about getting a piece of bread, then about putting something on it, and finally, about putting another piece of bread on top of that. This structure helps the reader to understand what is going on, and why. For example, read these directions for making a paper snowflake.

1) Find a piece of thin, white paper.

2) Fold the paper two or three times to make a small rectangle.

3) Cut small shapes around the edges of the rectangle.

4) Carefully unfold your snowflake to see its unique design.

5) Loop a piece of string through the snowflake and knot the ends.

6) Hang up the snowflake for everyone to see.

The directions show the order in which a project should be done, from first step to last. Think about the sequence. Could any of the steps happen in a different order? Authors use sequence to present their information in the most logical order.

Thinking It Through

Read the following paragraph, and then complete the activity that follows.

Glenn Gould was born on September 25, 1932. Then, he attended the Royal Conservatory of Music in Toronto. His first piano teacher was his mother. Finally, on April 10, 1964, he gave his last public performance in Los Angeles. After leaving the conservatory, he performed with the Toronto Symphony Orchestra.

Rewrite the sentences so that they are in chronological order.

_____

_____

_____

_____

 Look at the time-order words in the paragraph.

DISCUSS Discuss your answer in a group. Tell how the time-order words in the paragraph helped you figure out the sequence of events.

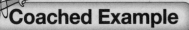

Coached Example

Read the passage and answer the questions.

Exploration of Mars has had a long and interesting history. The Mariner Mission took place between 1964 and 1971. During this mission, spacecraft took photographs of Mars and orbited the planet. The Viking Mission took place between 1976 and 1984. During this mission, U.S. spacecraft actually landed on Mars. During the Mars Pathfinder Mission, which lasted from 1997 to 1998, spacecraft landed and a robot vehicle was released on the planet's surface. This vehicle was called a *rover*. The Mars Global Surveyor Mission began in 1997 and is still going on. In this mission, astronauts are making maps of the planet's surface. In a more recent mission begun in 2003, two rovers have been exploring Mars in search of signs of water. The names of these rovers are *Spirit* and *Opportunity*. This mission began in 2003 and is still in progress.

1. According to the passage, what came BEFORE the Mars Pathfinder Mission?

    A. Viking Mission

    B. Mariner Mission

    C. Mars Global Surveyor Mission

    D. *Spirit* and *Opportunity* rovers

    HINT Reread the passage. Think about the order of the missions.

2. Which exploration occurred FIRST?

    A. Mars Global Surveyor Mission

    B. Mariner Mission

    C. Mars Pathfinder Mission

    D. Viking Mission

    HINT Look at the dates in the passage. Dates and times can help you figure out the sequence.

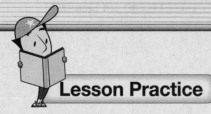

Lesson Practice

Use the Reading Guide to help you understand the passage.

Reading Guide

What words help you figure out the sequence?

What do you do after you spread the clips on your workspace?

What do you do after you write down the number of clips picked up?

Making an Electromagnet

When a magnetic force comes near a metallic object, the object is pulled in the direction of the magnetic force. This experiment will show you how to make and test an electromagnet. You will also see how you can make the magnet more or less powerful.

To do this experiment, you will need the following materials and equipment:

- metric ruler
- 2 wire clips
- 3 pieces of wire, cut at different lengths
- 6-volt battery
- safety goggles
- large steel bolt
- small metal paper clips

1. Put on safety goggles.
2. Attach the end of one wire to a wire clip by wrapping the wire around one side of the clip. Then attach the clip to one of the battery terminals.
3. Neatly wrap the wire around the bolt. Count the number of coils. Write this number down. Leave some of the piece of wire uncoiled. Attach the end to the other wire clip.
4. Spread paper clips on your work space. When you are ready, connect the second wire clip to the battery.
5. Use the electromagnet to pick up paper clips. Count the number of clips the electromagnet picks up at one time. Record this information.
6. After writing down the number of clips, disconnect the electromagnet right away.
7. Attach the other pieces of wire to the battery, repeating steps 2 through 6.

Answer the following questions.

1. According to the passage, what should you do FIRST?

   A. Put on safety goggles.

   B. Use the electromagnet to pick up clips.

   C. Attach the end of one wire to a wire clip.

   D. Count the number of clips you pick up.

2. What step comes BEFORE you spread paper clips on your work space?

   A. Attach the end of the wire to the first wire clip.

   B. Write down the number of clips picked up by the magnet.

   C. Attach the end of the wire to a second wire clip.

   D. Wrap the wire around the bolt.

3. What step comes AFTER you write down the number of clips you have picked up?

   A. Attach the other pieces of wire to the battery.

   B. Disconnect the electromagnet.

   C. Attach one end of the wire to a wire clip.

   D. Spread paper clips on your work space.

4. Which of the following would be the BEST final step after you have repeated steps 2 through 6?

   A. Put your information into a report.

   B. Make another electromagnet.

   C. Make a different kind of magnet.

   D. Ask for more supplies.

5. Could any of the steps in this process be left out? Explain your answer.

   _____

   _____

   _____

   _____

   _____

   _____

Use the Reading Guide to help you understand the passage.

Reading Guide

How did the author organize this biography?

Look for time-order words and dates to help you follow the sequence of events.

What facts does the author include about Sonia Sotomayor's childhood?

What important events happened in Sonia Sotomayor's life after she became a lawyer?

Sonia Sotomayor, Supreme Court Justice

The "American Dream" is the idea that if you work hard, you can achieve your goals in life. Many people believe Sonia Sotomayor achieved the American Dream.

Sotomayor was born on June 25, 1954, to parents who moved to the United States from Puerto Rico. Her family lived in housing for families with low incomes in New York. Sonia's mom knew that education and hard work were the ways her children could achieve their dreams and aspirations.

Sonia loved to read. As a young girl, her favorite books were the Nancy Drew mysteries. Sonia wanted to solve mysteries the way Nancy Drew did. Some people told her she wouldn't be able to do that, especially after she was diagnosed with diabetes at the age of eight. Sonia didn't listen. She held onto her dream and continued to work hard in school.

Sotomayor graduated as valedictorian of her high school class. After high school, she attended Princeton University. Next, she went to Harvard Law School to earn her law degree.

Sotomayor became a lawyer. First, she worked as an assistant district attorney, prosecuting those accused of crimes. Then, she became a private attorney. In 1992, President George H.W. Bush appointed her as a judge to the U.S. District Court. Later, she was appointed to a higher level in the court system by President Bill Clinton.

President Barack Obama nominated her to the U.S. Supreme Court, the highest court in our country. She assumed her new role as Associate Justice of the Supreme Court on August 8, 2009.

Sonia Sotomayor is said to have achieved the American Dream, because through education and hard work she reached her goals.

Answer the following questions.

6. The following are events from the passage. In each box, write the number 2, 3, 4, or 5 so that the events are in the correct order.

| 1 | Sonia Sotomayor is born on June 25, 1954. |

| | She works as an assistant district attorney. |

| | President George H.W. Bush appoints her as a judge to the U.S. District Court. |

| | She graduates as valedictorian of her high school class. |

| | She is diagnosed with diabetes. |

| 6 | Sonia Sotomayor assumes the role of Associate Justice of the Supreme Court. |

7. Read paragraph 5 from the passage. Circle the words and phrases in the paragraph that provide clues to the sequence of events.

> **Sotomayor became a lawyer. First, she worked as an assistant district attorney, prosecuting those accused of crimes. Then, she became a private attorney. In 1992, President George H.W. Bush appointed her as a judge to the U.S. District Court. Later, she was appointed to a higher level in the court system by President Bill Clinton.**

Use the Reading Guide to help you understand the passage.

Reading Guide

How many years of Freed's career are described in this passage?

What time-order words do you notice in the text?

How do the time-order words in the second paragraph help you understand Freed's career better?

"Moondog" Freed: Rock 'N' Roll Pioneer
by Hamilton West

Did you know that the term "rock 'n' roll" was first used by an Ohio deejay named Alan Freed? Freed had a huge influence on the music industry and on music history itself. Freed helped dismantle racial barriers during the 1950s and paved the way for equality among performers.

Freed got his start in radio while working as a deejay for the Armed Forces Radio during World War II. He landed his first professional radio job in Pennsylvania in 1942. After a year, he moved to Youngstown, Ohio, where he worked as a sportscaster. His next move, in 1945, brought him to Akron, Ohio. In Akron, he hosted a jazz and pop show. He soon became a local celebrity. Then, in 1951, a Cleveland record-store owner named Leo Mintz convinced Freed to be a deejay for a rhythm-and-blues show. Freed accepted. He gave himself the nickname "Moondog" and began playing music by African American musicians such as Little Richard and Chuck Berry.

Freed was not the first to play rock music, but he is credited with coining the term "rock 'n' roll" to describe the music. In 1952 he organized the first-ever rock concert, "The Moondog Coronation Ball." The concert, held in the Cleveland Arena, was a huge success. Freed became an influential deejay, and later he appeared in several major films about popular African American musicians.

Following this success, Freed was booked in Europe at Radio Luxembourg. Record companies bought air time on Radio Luxembourg to promote the albums of African American musicians. Freed's prerecorded shows were broadcast all across Europe. The shows were even broadcast in the town of Liverpool, England. There, members of a then-unknown group called The Beatles were writing their first songs. Today, most people remember Freed for breaking down barriers and promoting African American musicians.

Answer the following questions.

8. What happened FIRST?

   A. Freed dismantled racial barriers.

   B. Freed worked in Pennsylvania.

   C. Freed gave himself the nickname "Moondog."

   D. Freed appeared in several popular movies.

9. What did Freed do immediately AFTER he left his first job?

   A. He worked as a sportscaster.

   B. He moved to Akron.

   C. He worked as a deejay in the army.

   D. He organized the first-ever rock concert.

10. What did Freed do immediately BEFORE he organized the first rock concert?

    A. He accepted a job in Youngstown.

    B. He moved to Akron.

    C. He accepted a job in Cleveland.

    D. He appeared in several popular films.

11. What happened AFTER Freed appeared in several films?

    A. He met Leo Mintz.

    B. He coined the term "rock 'n' roll."

    C. He organized the "Moondog Coronation Ball."

    D. He was booked on a European radio station.

12. What does the word *following* in the sentence below suggest about the relationship between Freed's appearance in the movies and his work with Radio Luxembourg?

    Following the success of these movies, Freed was booked on the European station Radio Luxembourg.

    _____

    _____

    _____

    _____

    _____

    _____

11 Cause and Effect

Getting the Idea

Some passages are organized around a cause and its effect. A **cause** is the reason something happens, and the **effect** is what happens as a result. As you read, look for examples of cause and effect. Ask yourself why things happen. Events in a selection happen for a reason. Anytime one event leads to another, this is an instance of cause and effect. For example, if a tornado forms and destroys several homes, the tornado is the cause and the effect is the destruction of homes. There can also be more than one result of a cause, or more than one cause for a single result. Read this graphic organizer.

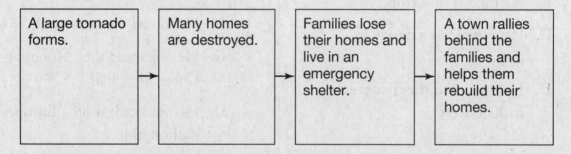

| A large tornado forms. | → | Many homes are destroyed. | → | Families lose their homes and live in an emergency shelter. | → | A town rallies behind the families and helps them rebuild their homes. |

You can figure out the cause by asking yourself why the effect happened. To figure out the effect, ask yourself what happened after the cause occurred. Cause-and-effect words and phrases, such as *so, because, since, thus,* and *if… then,* can help you understand the reason for an event and its result.

As you read informational texts, you will see how different authors use cause and effect to organize texts. Some texts will show the cause and effect in one paragraph. Other times, each paragraph in a longer article or essay will talk about a cause or event. The paragraphs will build toward a conclusion that describes the effects. Look at these two paragraphs from a longer essay.

> In the 1920s, the United States was booming financially, and many people invested money in the stock market. In October of 1929, stocks lost their value in a huge stock market crash. Over two days, the stock market fell 23 percent. It was the beginning of a recession that by 1932 became the Great Depression.
>
> During the Great Depression, people could not pay back money they owed to banks. This meant that the banks lost money. Also, banks had invested in the stock market, just like people had. When the stock market crashed, the banks lost still more money. The banking system collapsed in 1932. By 1933, 15 million people, over one-quarter of the people who wanted jobs, were unemployed. Without money, people could not afford housing. As a result, shantytowns were common. Shantytowns were places where people lived in tents and shacks.

By reading the two paragraphs, you can see that the stock market crash helped begin a recession that turned into the Great Depression. The Great Depression had many effects. People could not pay back loans to banks, banks lost money, companies couldn't afford to pay workers, people lost jobs, people became homeless, and shantytowns were built.

Thinking It Through

Read the following paragraph, and then answer the questions that follow.

Uncle Tom's Cabin by Harriet Beecher Stowe is a book that brought changes to the United States. In 1852, slavery still existed. Stowe wanted to teach readers about the cruelty of slavery. Many people began to see that slavery was wrong after they read the book.

Why did Stowe write *Uncle Tom's Cabin*? What were the effects of the book?

_____

_____

_____

_____

 Reread the paragraph. Remember, a cause is why something happens, and an effect is what happens as a result.

 In a group, talk about something you did recently that had an effect on someone else. Identify the cause and the effect.

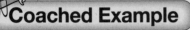

Coached Example

Read the passage and answer the questions.

When two large blocks of earth move past each other quickly and suddenly, the result is an earthquake. The area where they move is called the fault. The location where the earthquake starts is the hypocenter. While the edges of the two blocks stay together, the other parts of the blocks continue moving. Pressure then builds on the point where the blocks touch. When the force of the moving blocks becomes too great, the blocks break and the pressure is released. The energy moves out from the fault in many directions. This movement is often in the form of waves. As these huge waves move through the earth, they shake the ground. They also shake houses, buildings, and other structures, sometimes causing extensive damage.

1. Earthquakes happen because

   A. the ground shakes.

   B. they have an epicenter.

   C. two blocks of earth slip past one another.

   D. two blocks of earth touch one another.

   HINT This question asks for a cause. You must find the reason why.

2. What is the effect of an earthquake?

   A. The ground and anything on it shakes.

   B. Energy is stored.

   C. Two blocks of earth slip past one another.

   D. The epicenter stores energy.

   HINT This question asks for an effect. The effect is what happens because of earthquakes.

Lesson Practice

Use the Reading Guide to help you understand the passage.

Reading Guide

Why didn't the American army think they would win?

Why did Washington decide to go on the attack?

Why didn't the Hessians send soldiers out at first?

The Battle of Trenton

In early December 1776, the American army did not think they would win the Revolutionary War. The Americans had been defeated in New York by the British and their allies. So, the Americans retreated across New Jersey. Ninety percent of the soldiers were gone. Men had deserted because they felt that the cause for independence was lost. The army had fewer than 5,000 men. General George Washington, their commander, was starting to get nervous.

Trenton, New Jersey, was occupied by three regiments of Hessian soldiers. Colonel Johann Rall commanded the 1,400 men. Washington's force had 2,400 men. Washington decided to go on the attack. He crossed the Delaware River on Christmas night. It began to rain. As the air got colder, the rain changed to sleet, and then to snow. Terrible weather conditions delayed the landings in New Jersey. The soldiers began to march toward Trenton before sunrise.

Because of the weather, the Hessians did not send soldiers out. They were surprised by the attack. The Hessians formed ranks and began to advance up the street. But their ranks were quickly broken because of the force of the American army. Since they were soon surrounded, the Hessians surrendered. Washington captured nearly all the Hessians at Trenton on December 26, 1776.

This small but key battle had a large effect. The colonial effort was revived. The Battle of Trenton gave the Americans new confidence. It also caused soldiers to rejoin the Continental Army.

Answer the following questions.

1. Why did men desert the Continental Army?

   A. They felt that the cause for independence was lost.

   B. The weather was making them sick.

   C. They were afraid of the Hessians.

   D. They did not want to go to New Jersey.

2. What was the effect of the severe weather?

   A. Washington crossed the Delaware.

   B. The Hessians did not send patrols out.

   C. The Hessians prepared for battle.

   D. More troops deserted.

3. The Hessians fled because

   A. they were surprised by the attack.

   B. they wanted to surrender.

   C. they were quickly surrounded.

   D. the American army scared them.

4. The Hessians surrendered because

   A. it was Christmas.

   B. their morale was very low.

   C. they were surrounded.

   D. they began to doubt the outcome of the war.

5. What are some of the effects of the Battle of Trenton?

   _____

   _____

   _____

   _____

   _____

   _____

   _____

Use the Reading Guide to help you understand the passage.

Reading Guide

What happens when two plates collide?

Why are the Appalachian Mountains not as tall as they once were?

How are the Himalayas and the Appalachians different?

How the Appalachian Mountains Formed

Earth's crust is not a solid shell. It is made up of eight large slabs of rock called plates. Many of these plates are bigger than the continents, and some are found below the ocean. These plates drift across the globe. Sometimes they collide, or bump into each other.

When two plates collide, the boundary of each plate is compressed and pushed upward, forming mountains. This process can take millions of years. The plates' boundaries are long, creating an extensive mountain range. To help you visualize this, put two flat sheets of paper on your desk. Slowly slide them together so they collide. Notice how the colliding sides are pushed upward creating a peak or bump. Now imagine if these sheets of paper were land masses hundreds of miles long!

The Appalachian Mountains, which extend from Alabama to southeastern Canada, are a result of plate collisions. About 480 million years ago, land masses collided and gave rise to the northern Appalachians. Then, about 130 million years later, another collision along the same plate boundary formed the central and southern Appalachians. Due to the force and location of the collision, this new range connected itself to the northern Appalachians.

When they were first formed, the Appalachians may have been taller than the Himalayas—the highest mountain range in the world today. Because the Appalachians are older than the Himalayas, they are not as tall as they once were. Erosion from rivers, streams, rain, and wind washes away rock and sediment and has caused the Appalachians to diminish.

The plates on Earth's crust are still moving. These slow movements will eventually cause new mountain ranges to form!

Answer the following questions.

6.   Write the phrases from the word box in the correct location on the diagram to show cause and effect.

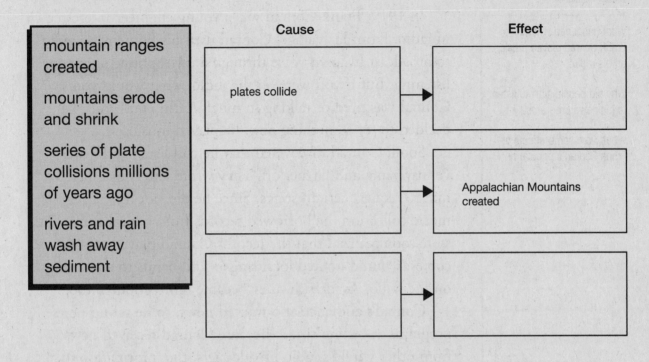

| mountain ranges created |
| mountains erode and shrink |
| series of plate collisions millions of years ago |
| rivers and rain wash away sediment |

Cause

plates collide →

→ Appalachian Mountains created

→

Effect

7.   Choose the causes of the formation of the Appalachian Mountains, based on evidence from the text. There is more than one correct choice listed below.

   A.   Earth's plates divided and split apart.

   B.   Earth's plates collided into one another.

   C.   The northern and southern Appalachian Mountains collided into one another.

   D.   Erosion from rivers built up and deposited sediment.

   E.   Earth's plates moved sideways against one another.

   F.   Landmasses crashed into one another multiple times.

Use the Reading Guide to help you understand the passage.

Reading Guide

What happened when Frank Conrad played music on his radio?

Why did people start to listen to his news programs?

What were some effects of Frank Conrad's popularity?

The Rise of Radio

In 1919, Frank Conrad was a young engineer interested in radio. From his garage, Conrad used his homemade radio to broadcast his own voice through a microphone to anyone listening. But if you were on the radio, what would you say? Conrad was tired of talking so much to thin air. Thus, he decided to try something new: he played music.

Soon, Conrad discovered that he had listeners all over Pennsylvania and farther off. They wrote letters or called him to request certain songs. Since he did not have a big music collection, he borrowed records from a local store. The store soon realized that the records Conrad played sold more copies. Conrad invited local singers and bands to come sing on the radio. As a result, they became more popular, too.

Conrad's audience also wanted news, so he set up news programs at certain times. Because Conrad received news from other wireless radio broadcasters, the information in the morning papers was the same that Conrad had given the night before.

One day, as Conrad was walking past a department store, he saw labels on radios for sale. The labels advertised Conrad's transmissions! Conrad knew he was getting famous. He also realized that he could not run a commercial radio station out of his garage. So Conrad asked his company, Westinghouse, if they wanted to operate his radio station. Westinghouse took over Conrad's music and news programming, becoming the first commercial radio station in the United States, KDKA. The new station proved to be very powerful. When a big presidential election came up, KDKA was able to tell all its listeners who won the election long before any of the newspapers arrived on people's doorsteps. Radio became more popular than ever!

Answer the following questions.

8. Frank Conrad started playing music on the radio because

   A. his radios sold better.

   B. he got tired of talking so much.

   C. he got free records from a store.

   D. people did not want to hear the news.

9. A music store lent records to Conrad because

   A. the records sold better after he played them.

   B. they liked listening to the songs on the radio.

   C. they sold more radios to Conrad's fans.

   D. the records became more popular than live music.

10. What was the effect of KDKA's broadcasting election results?

    A. More radios sold in department stores.

    B. News became more popular than ever.

    C. Frank Conrad gave his station to Westinghouse.

    D. People knew who won before reading the newspapers.

11. Why did Westinghouse take over Frank Conrad's programming?

    A. Conrad was becoming too famous.

    B. Conrad could not run the station out of his garage.

    C. Conrad could not keep up with the daily news.

    D. Conrad sold too many radios in department stores.

12. What are some reasons that radio became more popular?

   _____

   _____

   _____

   _____

   _____

12 Compare and Contrast Informational Texts

Getting the Idea

You know to **compare** things is to tell how they are alike and to **contrast** things is to tell how they are different. When you compare and contrast informational texts, you think about how they are alike and different. There are many things to compare and contrast, including topic, text organization, scope, and main ideas. Comparisons can be made between different articles or essays.

To begin, you can look at how the texts are organized. For example, two books are about the Civil War. But one book tells about the major events in chronological order. The other examines the major causes and effects.

You can also compare and contrast the topics of two texts, or what kind of information they present. For instance, suppose two essays of the same length talk about classical music. One essay might discuss music in the eighteenth century. The other might tell about Italian composers in the eighteenth century. You could say that the first essay is broader, while the second essay is more specific.

Read the following examples.

Passage 1

Thurgood Marshall was the first African American to serve on the U.S. Supreme Court. He was also the lawyer who argued for the Brown family in front of the Supreme Court in the *Brown v. Board of Education* case. President Lyndon Johnson appointed him to the Supreme Court in 1967.

Passage 2

The Supreme Court of the United States is the highest court in the United States. It consists of the chief justice and eight associate justices. Only the president has the power to nominate the justices. The justices are confirmed after voting and discussion by the Senate. Once appointed, justices effectively have life tenure, which terminates only upon death, resignation, or retirement. The Court meets in Washington, D.C., in the U.S. Supreme Court Building.

How are the two paragraphs similar? How are they different? Both paragraphs talk about the Supreme Court. However, the first paragraph talks about a specific Supreme Court justice, and the second paragraph talks generally about the Supreme Court. When comparing and contrasting informational texts, you will find that topic and scope are good initial points of comparison.

Another possible point of comparison is main idea. You may find that two essays or articles that are seemingly unrelated can have similar main ideas. For example, both an essay about a businessman and a magazine article about a writer might have the importance of education as their main ideas.

You will also sometimes compare people, places, or things across texts. For example, two articles might talk about leaders. But one article's leader is cruel, while the other leader is generous. In longer essays or articles, you may compare people, places, or things within the passage. Some texts are organized to show how people, places, or things are alike and different. In these texts, remember to look for these words: *also, as, like, same, similar, not, unlike,* and *yet*.

Finally, you can read two passages in which the writers express a different point of view on a topic. A writer's **point of view** is his or her opinion or perspective on an issue. For example, imagine that a town is planning to build a new mall. One writer may argue in favor of the idea, mainly because the mall will bring more jobs to the community. However, another writer may argue that the mall will be too expensive to build and will take business away from existing shop owners. You can compare each writer's point of view and how effectively he or she develops it in the article.

Thinking It Through

Read the following paragraphs, and then complete the activity that follows.

Passage 1

Typhoons and hurricanes are both tropical cyclones. Tropical cyclones are storms with a mass of thunderstorms centered around a mass of rotating air. They also have an eye, or center, of calm air and winds. They both have wind speeds greater than 74 miles per hour. They can both create widespread damage with their winds and storm surges. Typhoons generally begin in the Western Pacific Ocean. Hurricanes form in the Atlantic Ocean and the Eastern Pacific Ocean.

Passage 2

Typhoon Songda is one of the more famous typhoons in recent times. It began in September 2004, on the coast of Japan's Okinawa islands. After that, it moved along the western coast of Japan, stopping at the island of Hokkaido. At their fastest, the winds of the typhoon were gusting at 115 miles per hour. After the storm, thousands of people had no power. The storm also did several hundred million dollars' worth of damage.

Compare and contrast the topics of the two paragraphs.

_____

_____

_____

_____

 Remember, to compare things means to tell how they are alike, and to contrast things means to tell how they are different.

DISCUSS Discuss your answer in a group, identifying details in each paragraph that support your ideas.

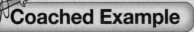

Coached Example

Read the passages and answer the questions.

Andrew Carnegie

Andrew Carnegie and his family emigrated to the United States from Scotland and settled near Pittsburgh, Pennsylvania, in 1848. Carnegie went to work in a cotton mill when he was thirteen. Later, Carnegie became a successful investor, and learned a faster and less expensive method for manufacturing steel from an English company. Carnegie used the technology in his first steel mill. In 1872, he visited the English manufacturer again and realized that U.S. industries had a growing need for steel. On his return to the United States, Carnegie combined smaller companies to make the Carnegie Steel Company. Carnegie sold his steel company in 1901 to J. P. Morgan for about $250 million. With that amount, Carnegie retired as one of the world's wealthiest men. He gave away much of his money. He was famous for building hundreds of public libraries in the United States and other countries.

Henry Ford

Henry Ford was born on July 30, 1863, to Irish immigrant parents. He grew up on the family farm in Greenfield Township, Michigan. He showed an interest in engine mechanics from a very early age. As the founder of the Ford Motor Company, Ford was very original. His goal was to make cars affordable for everyone. He was one of the first people to make cars by using an assembly line. In the process, he changed the way industries produced things. Ford's persistence was his greatest trait. Ford proved that he could change the world with one powerful idea. The foundation he created continues to strive for this goal. The Ford Foundation donates money to people and organizations that reduce poverty and injustice and advance human achievement.

1. How are Andrew Carnegie and Henry Ford similar?

   A. They were both immigrants.

   B. They both made a lot of money and were selfish.

   C. They both made and donated a lot of money.

   D. They both made automobiles.

   HINT Reread the passages. Think about what the two men have in common.

2. How are Andrew Carnegie and Henry Ford different?

   A. Carnegie made his money in steel manufacturing, while Ford manufactured cars.

   B. Carnegie wanted to make steel affordable for every family, while Ford just wanted to make money.

   C. Ford imported a faster and less expensive method for manufacturing steel.

   D. Ford combined smaller car companies to make a large car company.

   HINT Think about each man's actions. How are their actions different?

3. How are the two passages similar?

   _____

   _____

   _____

   _____

   HINT Think about different points of comparison between texts. Structure, scope, and topic are a few different points of comparison.

Lesson Practice

Use the Reading Guides to help you understand the passages.

Reading Guide

How are all fruit bats similar?

What is the difference in wingspan between the largest and smallest fruit bats?

Fruit Bats

There are about 175 species of fruit bats. Bats are the only mammals that can fly. They live in dense forests in Africa, Europe, Australia, and Asia.

Fruit bats have brown furry bodies with long arms, and fingers that are covered by a thin skin. The skin is strong and spreads along the bat's bones, connecting its back, legs, and arms, much as the fabric of an umbrella covers all the parts. Wingspan, the measure of one wingtip to the other when the wings are open, varies greatly among different fruit bats. The largest fruit bat wingspan is six feet, while some fruit bats have a wingspan of less than six inches. Fruit bats are nocturnal, which means you will probably only see them at night. They sleep during the day, hanging upside down in dark places, like caves.

A fruit bat finds its food through its exceptional senses. Fruit bats eat fruit, juice, and nectar. Fruit bats are very important because they help spread fruit seeds from place to place and help pollinate flowers. Spreading seeds and pollen ensures that plants and flowers can grow in new areas.

The Great Horned Owl

Where do Great Horned Owls and fruit bats live?

How do the diets of Great Horned Owls and fruit bats differ?

The Great Horned Owl is common in North America. Because it adapts well to most environments, it can live just about anywhere in the United States.

The Great Horned Owl is a powerful hunter. First, the owl perches. Then, when it sees or hears prey, it launches off into flight. Lastly, it swoops down to get its prey with its talons. It eats large rodents such as rabbits, squirrels, and skunks. The Great Horned Owl hunts at night. It has excellent senses of both sight and hearing.

The owl's very large eyes are a bold yellow color. Its sharp eyesight makes it an effective predator in any available light. The Great Horned Owl also has ears that are very pronounced and very sensitive. The feather tufts around its ears look much like horns, which give the owl its name.

Great Horned Owls do not build their own nests. Instead, they take over abandoned or occupied nests. Sometimes they will take comfort in caves, cliff ledges, or within a group of trees. They often sleep there during the day. These owls spend much of their time alone. However, a female and male pair will return to each other during nesting season for many years. Both parents help to raise young for several months. Young Great Horned Owls can fly, however, when they are only nine or ten weeks old.

Answer the following questions.

1. How are fruit bats and Great Horned Owls alike?

   A. They both hunt prey.

   B. They both sleep during the day.

   C. They both sleep upside down.

   D. They both help disperse seeds and pollinate.

2. How are fruit bats and Great Horned Owls different?

   A. The fruit bat uses all of its senses at night, while the Great Horned Owl uses two.

   B. The fruit bat builds nests, and the Great Horned Owl doesn't.

   C. The fruit bat eats fruit and nectar, and the Great Horned Owl eats rodents.

   D. The fruit bat hunts at night, and the Great Horned Owl hunts during the day.

3. Which of the following is a difference between the two passages?

   A. The first passage discusses a specific animal, and the second passage discusses a group of animals.

   B. The first passage discusses a group of animals, and the second passage discusses a specific animal.

   C. The first passage discusses diet, and the second passage does not.

   D. The first passage discusses environment, and the second passage does not.

4. Which of the following is NOT a difference between Great Horned Owls and fruit bats?

   A. The fruit bat is a mammal, and the Great Horned Owl is a bird.

   B. Only the Great Horned Owl lives in North America.

   C. Only the Great Horned Owl takes over nests.

   D. Only the fruit bat lives in caves.

5. Explain the differences in the way each passage is organized.

   _____

   _____

   _____

Use the Reading Guides to help you understand the passages.

Reading Guide

What is the main idea of this article? How does the last sentence reinforce the main idea?

What details support the main idea?

What are the positive and negative aspects of owning an electric car?

Electric Cars on the Road Today

Nowadays we need batteries for just about everything—television remotes, toys, cell phones, and laptops. Add "car" to the list of some people's battery needs, though replacing the battery of an electric car will cost quite a bit more than a D-size battery for your remote-controlled car.

Electric cars are one alternative that people are using instead of gasoline-powered cars. Electric cars are more energy-efficient and cheaper to run than gasoline-powered cars. On a daily basis, they may be up to four times cheaper to run. However, at this time, they are expensive vehicles to buy. In the future, they may become much more affordable and therefore much more accessible to the general public.

Instead of using gasoline, these cars are run 100 percent by electricity. They use a battery that is similar to those in laptop computers and that needs to be recharged for many hours. Electric car owners could do this at night while they sleep or when they are at work.

Most likely, if you see an electric car, it would be in a city. This is because electric cars are best suited for short- or medium-range driving distances. If you were going on a long road trip, an electric car would not be a good choice.

Electric cars look very different from your typical gasoline-powered car. Electric cars are built for fuel economy. They are designed to reduce wind resistance and to get more mileage.

In the search to find alternatives to gasoline-powered cars, electric cars are one alternative that is available today.

Gasoline-Powered Cars

Use the information in the article to describe how a gasoline-powered car works.

According to the article, why isn't this type of car energy-efficient?

Why do most people own gasoline-powered vehicles?

Think about the differences between the two kinds of cars, as described in the passages.

The typical car you see on the road today has a standard motor. The motor is run with regular or diesel fuel.

When you turn on the ignition, gasoline, which contains chemical potential energy, is transformed into mechanical energy. Mechanical energy is what allows the engine to rotate and the wheels to spin. However, this transformation of energy is not very efficient. A lot of heat is lost as it radiates out of the engine. In fact, according to the United States Department of Energy, only 14–26 percent of the potential energy in gasoline actually moves your car. The remaining energy is lost.

Scientists and engineers are working on other fuel alternatives that are more efficient and produce less pollution. These fuels include ethanol, natural gas, and propane.

Even though gasoline is not very energy-efficient, gasoline-powered cars are usually the most cost-efficient at this time. Gasoline-powered cars are much less expensive than alternative energy cars. Things may change in the future, but currently, our transportation system is convenient for gasoline-powered cars. Gas stations are very common across the United States. A driver pulls into a gas station with a nearly empty tank, fills up the tank, and immediately resumes driving.

In time, we may see less of a reliance on gasoline-powered cars. Many energy-efficient vehicles are being tested and used now. But if you look on the highway today, you will still see that gasoline-powered cars far outnumber any of the alternatives.

Answer the following questions.

6. Write the facts from the word box in the correct locations on the graphic organizer to compare and contrast electric cars to gasoline-powered cars, as described in the articles "Electric Cars on the Road Today" and "Gasoline-Powered Cars."

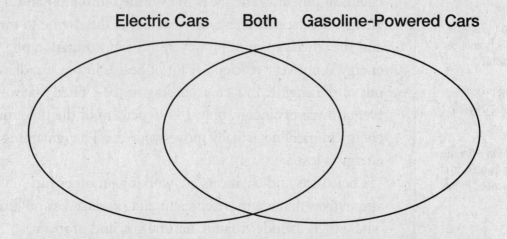

Electric Cars   Both   Gasoline-Powered Cars

A. more convenient to fuel

B. better suited to a long road trip

C. more expensive to buy

D. require planning and time to fuel

E. less expensive to run

F. a current mode of transportation

7. Use your answer to Part A to answer Part B.

Part A

What is one way that electric cars are different from gasoline-powered cars?

A. Electric cars are much more practical and convenient.

B. Overall, electric cars are more cost-efficient.

C. Electric cars are best suited for short or medium driving distances.

D. The change of energy from chemical to mechanical is not very efficient.

Part B

Which detail from the passages BEST supports the answer to Part A?

A. A lot of heat is lost as it radiates out of the engine.

B. The batteries need to be recharged for many hours.

C. Electric cars may be up to four times cheaper to run.

D. A driver fills up the tank and immediately resumes driving.

E. Energy-efficient vehicles are being tested now.

---

8. Choose all the words or phrases that describe an electric car but do NOT describe a gasoline-powered car, based on evidence from the articles. There is more than one correct choice listed below.

A. practical

B. accessible

C. cost-efficient

D. energy-efficient

E. economical to buy

F. runs on alternative energy

Use the Reading Guides to help you understand the passages.

Reading Guide

What sentence in the first paragraph explains what the passage is mainly about?

What do all these animals have in common?

How do the animals get food in the winter?

Where Do They Go in the Snow?

In many northern states in the United States the forest floor is covered with three or more feet of snow in the winter months. Temperatures plunge into the 10s and 20s. Think about the animals. How do they survive these cold, snowy months?

Some use the snow to keep warm. When animals burrow under the snow, air is trapped inside the snow, and they can keep warm. The snowshoe hare is one of these animals. It finds a depression in the snow under an evergreen tree or bush to hide and rest during the day. At night, the hare comes out and looks for small plants and branches to eat. Its fur is white during winter so fox or coyote cannot see it easily.

Small animals like mice have dark fur, and predators can see them in the snow. So they dig tunnels to keep themselves safe. They burrow through the tunnels until they find seeds, plants, or bark from bushes to eat.

Beavers live in lodges in lakes and ponds, and they don't venture out in the snow. These lodges have been made from sticks and mud and are warm inside. The beavers eat bark and wood. Before the water freezes, they gather food and store it in the water. When they get hungry, they swim under the ice, tear away the food they have stored, and bring it back to the lodge.

Deer eat an enormous amount of food during the summer and fall to prepare for the winter months. They live off their fat and supplement it with buds from trees or tiny saplings. Deep snow is dangerous for deer. They move as little as possible to save energy so their fat will last until spring. Thus deer tend to stay the southern side of hills where it's warmer.

How Bears Survive Winter

Reading Guide

What do bears do that is similar to the animals you read about in the first passage?

What things do bears do differently from the animals you read about in the first passage?

How is this passage organized?

To survive the winter, bears start gorging on food in August. They will eat dead animals, berries, pine nuts, and insects, adding a layer of fat five inches thick to their bodies. They will need the fat to live on during the months when there is no food available. Bears won't eat again for another five months! During this time, their body temperature falls a few degrees, which means they use less energy. Using less energy means that they will burn off the fat more slowly.

Grizzly bears choose a spot on a north-facing slope. The weather gets colder there, and the snow won't thaw and wet their fur during warmer days. Then they dig their den in the dirt. Finally, they settle in their dens, where they fall asleep.

Black bears have many different kinds of dens. Some dig a shallow bowl under a fallen tree. Others might locate a cave or hollow tree. When they do make a den, they cover it with bark, twigs, leaves, grasses, and mosses. Inside the den, it still isn't very warm. The bear's fur and body fat must keep it warm all winter.

Other black bears don't use a den at all. They somehow know that it will soon snow. The snow acts likes a blanket, trapping in the warm air from the bear's body. So these bears just curl up on the ground and wait for the snow to cover their bodies!

Female bears have their young during the winter. They wake up to give birth to their cubs, and then they go back to sleep. The cubs don't hibernate. They are busy drinking their mother's milk and growing bigger.

The amazing thing about bears is that even after five months in hibernation, their muscles are still strong. The day a bear wakes up, it can easily walk up a mountain!

Answer the following questions.

9. What main idea do both passages share?

   A. Animals have different ways of surviving the cold winter months.

   B. Animals are able to live off of their own fat during the snowy winter.

   C. To survive the cold winters, animals use their fur, sunny slopes, and movement to keep warm.

   D. To survive snowy winters animals must store food in secret places in order to survive.

10. Which of the following describes a major difference in the two passages?

   A. The first passage describes how small animals survive winters, while the second discusses large animals like bears.

   B. The first passage details what animals in winter eat, but the second does not mention food.

   C. The first passage discusses how many animals survive winter, but the second discusses only one.

   D. The first passage details how animals survive in the northern winters, while the second explains how bears survive in the south.

11. What do some bears and snowshoe hare do similarly to survive the winter?

   A. They both build up fat on their bodies to live on during in the winter.

   B. They both come out at night to search for food.

   C. The both dig tunnels where they can hide under the snow.

   D. They both use snow to help keep them warm.

12. How are the structures of the two passages different?

   A. The first passage is based on main ideas and details, while the second passage is based on cause and effect relationships.

   B. The first passage compares and contrasts animals, while the second passage discusses only one animal.

   C. The first passage is structured around cause and effect, while the second passage is based on main ideas.

   D. The first passage is based on main ideas and details, while the second passage is based on sequence.

13. What do bears and deer both do to survive the winters? What things do they do differently?

_____

_____

_____

_____

_____

_____

_____

_____

_____

_____

13 Using Different Sources

Getting the Idea

Reference materials are published works that contain information. One very familiar reference material is a **textbook**. Textbooks contain extensive information on subjects studied in schools. Common subjects for textbooks include math, science, and social studies. Dictionaries, encyclopedias, periodicals, atlases, and Web sites are all examples of reference materials. The key to selecting a reference is knowing which reference will give you the information you want.

A **dictionary** is a book that lists words alphabetically, tells how to pronounce them, and gives their definitions. If you are looking for the meaning of a word, you can use a dictionary. A dictionary entry has four main parts: the word, the pronunciation, the part of speech (such as a noun or a verb), and the definitions. Sometimes it also gives you the language of origin for the word. Look at this dictionary entry:

> **clock** (klok): *n.* (1) a device that displays the time;
> (2) a measuring instrument with a dial or digital display;
> (3) the seed head of a dandelion; (4) an electronic circuit
> that synchronizes computer processes; (5) a design
> on a stocking or sock. *v.* (1) to record somebody's or
> something's time.

Use a dictionary when you want to find the meaning of a word and can't figure it out from the context of the sentence.

An **encyclopedia** is a book or set of books that gives information, through short articles, about subjects listed alphabetically. An encyclopedia may give facts about many topics. Some encyclopedias focus on one subject, like science or history. Use an encyclopedia when you want to read a brief passage about a person, place, or thing.

A **periodical** is a publication, such as a newspaper, magazine, or brochure, which is released daily, weekly, monthly, or yearly. Some periodicals cover many different subjects at once, such as culture, news, and sports. Other periodicals cover very specific subjects or topics, such as engineering or dance. Because periodicals are released daily, weekly, monthly, or yearly, they are great resources for reading new articles. Use periodicals when you want current information.

An **atlas** is a book of maps. Atlases typically have a map of Earth as well as specific regions. Many atlases will feature information about specific countries or regions, such as population and economic data.

Online directories are very much like search engines. However, rather than give you a list of all Web sites containing information related to your topic, they provide you with a list of sub-topics and directories of sites that might be related to your topic. This allows you to locate more specific information about part of your topic easier and faster. Search engines and online directories both point you to Web sites that contain information related to your search terms. You must always be very careful when using Web sites for research. Just as with articles, you need to consider the source of your information before relying on it as fact. Sites that generally contain reliable information include:

- government Web sites (any Web address ending with .*gov*)

- college and university Web sites (any Web address ending with .*edu*)

- official Web sites of reputable news organizations

- official Web sites of reputable professional organizations and not-for-profits (sometimes ending with .*org*)

Many traditional reference books, such as encyclopedias and dictionaries, are also available as CD-ROMs or on Web sites.

Thinking It Through

Read the following paragraph, and then answer the question that follows.

In Congress and in state government, a bill is legislation that lawmakers are trying to make official. A bill later becomes law if it is approved. Ideas for bills can come from individual lawmakers, the president, the governor, citizens, or special groups.

What reference material would be useful in finding out more about how a bill becomes a law?

_____

_____

_____

_____

 Think about which reference source gives basic information about a broad topic.

DISCUSS Use the reference source you identified to learn more about the process of how a bill becomes a law. Then share your findings with the class.

Coached Example

Read the passage and answer the questions.

Imagine riding a train that doesn't touch the ground. For years, scientists have been researching Maglev, or magnetic <u>levitation</u>, technology. If you've ever played with magnets, you know that if you put the magnet ends together, they push away from each other. This is the basic principle behind the Maglev train. This train floats above the track, while a conventional train rolls along it. The other difference between these two trains is that a conventional train has an engine, while a Maglev train does not. Instead, the magnetic field created by the electrified coils in the track moves the Maglev train forward. In China, the Shanghai Transrapid line currently runs to and from the city's center and the airport. It travels at an average speed of 267 mph.

1. Which reference material would be MOST useful in finding the definition of <u>levitation</u>?

   A. atlas

   B. dictionary

   C. encyclopedia

   D. periodical

   HINT Think about the different reference materials listed. Which one lists words and definitions?

2. Which reference material would NOT be useful in finding out more about electromagnetic fields?

   A. atlas

   B. encyclopedia

   C. periodical

   D. Web site

   HINT Think about the different reference materials listed. What information does each reference material give you?

Lesson Practice

Use the Reading Guide to help you understand the passage.

Reading Guide

Which reference material would be most useful in finding out about countries that surround Germany?

Which reference material would be most useful in finding out more on John Augustus Roebling's fatal accident?

If you wanted to find out the meaning of the word *catenary*, where would you look?

The Making of the Brooklyn Bridge

Today the city of Brooklyn is considered part of New York City because of a bridge that connects Brooklyn to the island of Manhattan. The man who designed that bridge was one of America's greatest engineers.

John Augustus Roebling emigrated from Germany as an industrial engineer. The Brooklyn Bridge was the first steel-wire suspension bridge in the world. Roebling had a fatal accident at the proposed site of the bridge before construction began. After he died in 1869, his son, Washington A. Roebling, took over as chief engineer.

Roebling used many workers, nicknamed "sandhogs." Sandhogs dug until they found bedrock at the bottom of the river. This bedrock was a strong foundation for the bridge. They could put layers of granite rock on the bedrock to build the pillars. The pillars then reached the surface of the water and beyond.

Roebling and the sandhogs suffered from a painful condition called "caisson disease" or "the bends," which is caused from going deep into water. Roebling became paralyzed for the rest of his life. Several sandhogs died from the bends. Roebling turned over the bridge's construction to his wife Emily. To prepare for the job, Emily studied higher mathematics and <u>catenary</u> curves, with her husband's guidance.

On May 24, 1883, the bridge opened, and Emily was the first to ride across it. Within 24 hours, over 250,000 people walked across the Brooklyn Bridge. It took 14 years to build and involved over 600 workers. Over two dozen people died during its construction. The Brooklyn Bridge is over 125 years old, and over 150,000 people cross it every day.

Answer the following questions.

1. If you wanted to learn more about what industrial engineers do, what reference material would you use?

   A. an atlas

   B. an online directory

   C. a dictionary

   D. an encyclopedia

2. Which reference material would be MOST useful in finding out more about John Augustus Roebling's fatal accident?

   A. a periodical

   B. an atlas

   C. an encyclopedia

   D. a dictionary

3. Which reference material would be MOST useful in finding the definition of catenary?

   A. an encyclopedia

   B. an atlas

   C. a dictionary

   D. a periodical

4. If you wanted to learn more about the different events happening in Brooklyn or Manhattan at the time, you would use

   A. an atlas.

   B. an encyclopedia.

   C. a dictionary.

   D. a history book.

5. In your own words, explain how an atlas could be useful to learn more about the Brooklyn Bridge.

   _____

   _____

   _____

   _____

   _____

   _____

   _____

Use the Reading Guide to help you understand the passage.

Reading Guide

Based on the article, how can ordinary citizens help in scientific studies?

What are examples of citizen science projects?

What types of resources do you think the author used to write this article?

Citizen Science

Ordinary citizens are contributing to the field of science every day by making observations, recording data, and taking photographs. They are volunteering their time to help scientists. These volunteers are taking part in a program called citizen science.

The New York State Department of Environmental Conservation recently requested that citizens with swimming pools take part in a survey. They wanted people to monitor their pools in order to look for the Asian long-horned beetle. If people found this beetle, they were asked to contact the department. A project like this involves many community members actively looking for an invasive beetle. If they can find the beetles early enough, they can prevent harmful damage to trees.

Another project, the Worm Watch Lab, asks people in the community to record data for scientific research. A group of scientists have discovered that if a certain type of worm lays fewer or more eggs than normal, it may have a specific gene defect. The understanding of this defect can help scientists understand and help humans. The problem is that it takes too long for scientists to identify which worms have the defect. The time involved in finding the right worms takes away from the time needed to study them. So, scientists ask people to watch worms being recorded on webcams. The people watch worms and record when they lay eggs. The scientists use the data to identify worms that they should study.

Scientists have an important job to do, but they often don't have enough people to help with their studies. However, with the help of other people in the community, scientists can gather more information than they ever could on their own.

Answer the following questions.

6. Read the question in each choice. Then match the question to the reference source on the right.

A. Which reference material would you use to find the definition of the word <u>invasive</u>?

1. almanac

2. atlas

B. Which reference material would you use to find out more information about the Asian long-horned beetle?

3. dictionary

4. encyclopedia

C. Which reference material would you use to find a map of New York?

5. periodical

D. Which reference material would you use to find an article about the results from the Worm Watch Lab?

6. thesaurus

7. Why is it important to choose Web sites carefully when using them as a source for research?

A. No information on Web sites is trustworthy.

B. Not all information on Web sites is reliable.

C. There is not much information available on Web sites.

D. Government Web sites are not intended for student use.

Use the Reading Guide to help you understand the passage.

Reading Guide

What reference material would be most useful for researching ancient Mesopotamia?

Which reference material would be most useful in finding out about *cristallo*?

Which reference material would be most useful in finding out where Venice is?

The Early History of Glass

Ever wonder how glass is formed? Natural glass occurs when certain types of rocks melt as a result of intense, high-temperature natural events like volcanic eruptions and lightning strikes. When the rocks are hit suddenly with intense heat during these events, they melt and cool very quickly, solidifying into glass.

People have been making tools with natural glass for thousands of years. Phoenician merchants discovered glass in the region of Syria around 5000 BCE and began experimenting with melting it. They would heat blocks of nitrate on the shore when they would land and combine it with the sand over fire to form a liquid. The liquid "glass" then could be used to make shapes.

The first glass beads date back to around 3500 BCE in Mesopotamia and Egypt. People also began to make pots and vases with glass. Historians believe it was the Phoenician merchants who spread this new art as they traveled along the coasts of the Mediterranean.

By the first century CE, glassmaking had become a craft. Romans discovered they could inflate a mass of glass through the end of a hollow tube. This method allowed them to produce objects made from glass quickly. Ordinary objects for household use became popular.

Several hundred years later, people began experimenting with new glassmaking techniques. Islamic glassmakers used a combination of Roman techniques and new forms of glassmaking to make ornamental glass. Their glass objects had bright colors and intricate patterns.

Some of the most sophisticated glassmaking techniques were developed in Venice, Italy. In the mid-fifteenth century, highly skilled Venetian glassmakers on the island of Murano made *cristallo*, a thin, colorless glass that looked like crystal. Knowledge of their technique spread throughout Europe, where it remains celebrated and popular today.

Answer the following questions.

8. What reference material would be MOST useful in finding where ancient glasswork is displayed?

    A. a periodical

    B. a museum Web site

    C. an encyclopedia

    D. a dictionary

9. Which reference material would be MOST useful in locating the trade routes of Phoenician merchants?

    A. a history book

    B. a periodical

    C. a historical atlas

    D. a dictionary

10. Which reference material would be the BEST source for finding the meaning of the word <u>nitrate</u>?

    A. a periodical

    B. an atlas

    C. an encyclopedia

    D. a dictionary

11. If you wanted to learn about current experiments in glassmaking, you would use

    A. a history book.

    B. a periodical.

    C. an atlas.

    D. an encyclopedia.

12. In your own words, explain how the source you chose for the last question above might help you learn more about current events in glassmaking.

    _____

    _____

    _____

    _____

    _____

    _____

    _____

    _____

14 Reasons and Evidence

Getting the Idea

Point of view is the way an author feels about someone or something. Many passages that you read make claims, or arguments. A claim expresses a writer's point of view. A claim is also normally an opinion. An **opinion** is a statement that cannot be proven. Although you can't prove a claim, necessarily, you can defend it. Writers defend their arguments with reasons that justify their opinion. If a writer supplies a reason, he or she will also supply evidence that supports that reason. This is where facts come in handy. A **fact** is something that can be proven true and can be used to prove something else true.

The purpose of a piece of persuasive writing is to convince people to take action or to think a certain way. Car advertisements, political speeches, and newspaper editorials on the environment are examples of persuasive writing. The writer clearly states his or her position, or argument, in support of something or against it. Then, he or she goes on to explain the reasons behind the claim. For the argument to be successful, those reasons have to be backed up by relevant evidence. As a reader, you should be able to identify relevant evidence when you see it.

Relevant evidence is any information that is related to the issue and supports a position. This isn't as simple as it sounds. Let's use an easy example. In an editorial about recycling in your community, the author states that we should recycle because it saves the environment. As evidence, the author supplies a chart of the chemicals factories release as they turn out new products. Another reason might be that recycling would clean up the community. In this case, relevant evidence would be quotes from residents who have noticed a difference in the area. If the author included a quote from a resident that simply stated how nice recycling was, that would not be relevant. Why? Because, while it supports the main argument, it simply repeats the author's point of view. It would not help to convince someone to start recycling.

The following chart outlines a claim, its reasons, and some evidence to support those reasons.

Claim: The citizens of Yakville should talk less on their cell phones.		
Reason: Talking on your cell phone can be distracting and dangerous.	Reason: Your conversations might cause a public nuisance.	Reason: Cell phones are hazardous to your health.
Evidence: A teenage girl was talking on her cell phone, riding a bicycle, and eating ice cream last Wednesday, and she ran into a tree.	Evidence: Last Thursday, an older woman on a bus had a loud argument with a girl who was talking too much on her cell phone. The girl and the woman had to be asked to leave the bus.	Evidence: Studies have shown that some cell phones emit powerful amounts of radiation.

Writers may try various tricks to convince their readers. One of the most common tricks of argument is appealing to the emotions. Writers appeal to your emotions when they express their own sadness, anger, or excitement through their word choice. For example, if a writer says, "Try to imagine the sadness parents will feel if their children can no longer use the library on Saturdays," he's appealing to your emotions. With the phrase *try to imagine* or the word *sadness*, the writer is clearly asking readers to feel something, or to imagine it. Also, appeals to the emotions often use exaggerated language. Appeals to the emotions are less solid supports than factual evidence, and they are often less convincing for readers.

Thinking It Through

Read the following paragraph, and then complete the activity that follows.

Clearcutting is a terrible logging practice in which most or all of the trees in an area are cut down. Logging companies support clearcutting. Their owners argue that it is safe and economical. However, they are wrong. They do not talk about the negative impacts. Clearcutting destroys natural habitats. It also contributes to global warming. This harmful process must be stopped.

List two facts and two opinions from the paragraph.

_____

_____

_____

_____

 Remember, an opinion states someone's belief or judgment. It is not something that can be proved.

 Which specific words in the paragraph helped you determine if a sentence is a fact or an opinion? Discuss your ideas with a partner.

Coached Example

Read the passage and answer the questions.

excerpted and adapted from

Common Sense
by Thomas Paine

Some say that because America prospered under Great Britain in the past, America needs Great Britain to do well in the future. Nothing can be more wrong. We may as well say that because a child lived on milk, it should never have meat. Or, that the next twenty years of our lives will be just like the last twenty years. I think that America would have done just as well, and probably better, without Great Britain.

---

1. What is the author's argument?

    A. America needs Great Britain to do well.

    B. America does not need Great Britain to do well.

    C. America is a young country.

    D. Some things never change.

    HINT Reread the passage. What is the author trying to say? How do the author's reasons support the argument?

2. Read this sentence.

    We may as well say that because a child lived on milk, it should never have meat.

    The sentence above is

    A. relevant evidence.

    B. irrelevant evidence.

    C. a statement of opinion.

    D. a fact based on science.

    HINT Reread the sentence. Think about how the sentence works in the author's argument.

Lesson Practice

Use the Reading Guide to help you understand the passage.

Reading Guide

Which statement in paragraph 1 is an opinion?

Can all of the statements in paragraph 2 be proved?

What are the facts in paragraph 3?

Living in a Greenhouse

Imagine standing in a house made of glass, or a "greenhouse." The glass windows let the sun in, but the glass doesn't let the heat escape. Some gardeners build greenhouses so they can grow plants during the cold months. Scientists call some harmful gases "greenhouse gases." These gases can't leave Earth's atmosphere. When there are enough of them, they create a thick layer that won't let heat escape our planet. The atmosphere around Earth then becomes much like a greenhouse. We call that increase in temperature "global warming."

During the last fifty years, Earth's temperature has risen faster than ever before. We must be doing something to make Earth so warm. Earth is billions of years old, and the temperature has never changed like this in the past. Earth's average temperature would be about 60 degrees Fahrenheit colder without greenhouse gases.

Cars produce 1.5 billion tons of carbon dioxide gas each year. Carbon dioxide is one of the gases that causes global warming. Electricity and gas used every day create 2.5 billion tons of carbon dioxide. And the planet gets warmer and warmer.

Also, cutting down forests in recent years has helped to cause global warming. Trees reduce carbon dioxide in the air. Because humans have cut down a lot of forests to use the wood for lumber, the Earth's temperature has risen rapidly.

Our actions are changing the world for the worse. We need to start treating our planet better, or our children's futures will be in danger.

Answer the following questions.

1. Which sentence from the passage expresses an opinion?

    A. "We must be doing something to make Earth so warm."

    B. "During the last fifty years, Earth's temperature has risen faster than ever before."

    C. "Cars produce 1.5 billion tons of carbon dioxide gas each year."

    D. "Electricity and gas used every day create 2.5 billion tons of carbon dioxide."

2. Read the following sentence from the passage.

    Earth's average temperature would be about 60 degrees Fahrenheit colder without greenhouse gases.

    The sentence above is

    A. relevant evidence.

    B. irrelevant evidence.

    C. an appeal to emotions.

    D. an opinion.

3. Why does the author write "Cars produce 1.5 billion tons of carbon dioxide gas each year"?

    A. to state an opinion about cars

    B. to provide an opinion about greenhouse gases

    C. to appeal to the reader's emotions

    D. to provide relevant evidence

4. Read this sentence.

    We need to start treating our planet better, or our children's futures will be in danger.

    The sentence above is

    A. relevant evidence.

    B. irrelevant evidence.

    C. an appeal to emotions.

    D. a fact based on science.

5. List two facts and two opinions from the passage.

    _____

    _____

    _____

Use the Reading Guide to help you understand the passage.

Reading Guide

What is the author's point of view about sports participation?

What claims does the author make about sports participation?

What relevant evidence does the author provide to support the claims made in the passage?

Benefits of Sports Participation

Research has shown that participation in sports can be extremely valuable for children. Not only can it be fun and enjoyable, it is good for them physically, mentally, and socially.

The Centers for Disease Control and Prevention reports that one-third of children and adolescents are overweight. They have too much weight on their body for their height. The Centers recommend that children get sixty minutes or more of physical activity each day. Using a scale of 0 to 10, where 0 represents sitting on the couch and 10 is the highest level of activity, the Centers recommend that children should be active at a level of at least a 5 or a 6. Sports get children active at a moderate level while doing something they enjoy.

Researchers have found that if children are active, their self-esteem increases. When people have good self-esteem, they think well of themselves. When your self-esteem increases, you may be more likely to make healthy choices. The President's Council on Physical Fitness and Sports reports that girls who are active have a healthier body image than girls who aren't active.

Playing sports also provides opportunities for social growth. Children in sports learn about teamwork. They learn the importance of working with others toward a shared goal.

Participation in sports helps children in several ways. Being active allows the body to become physically fit. Many active children have more confidence and have a better attitude about themselves. In addition, participating in sports teaches how to work well with others.

Answer the following questions.

6. Below are three claims that one could make, based on the passage "Benefits of Sports Participation."

Claim	Playing sports is fun and enjoyable.
	Active children have higher self-esteem.
	Involvement in sports teaches about teamwork.

Part A

Circle the claim that is supported by the MOST relevant and sufficient evidence in the passage "Benefits of Sports Participation."

Part B

Circle two facts in the passage that BEST provide evidence to support the claim selected in Part A. Write the facts below.

_____

_____

_____

_____

7. Choose all the reasons the author gives to support his or her opinion. There is more than one correct choice listed below.

   A. Children in sports have an increased sense of self-esteem.

   B. Sports get children active at a recommended moderate level.

   C. Being on sports teams teaches children leadership skills they need in life.

   D. Participation on sports teams is great for learning time management skills.

   E. Participating in sports provides opportunities to learn to work and play with others.

   F. Physical activity as a child increases the likelihood of physical activity into adulthood.

Use the Reading Guide to help you understand the passage.

Reading Guide

What is the author's point of view about eating breakfast?

What relevant evidence does the author provide to support the claim that breakfast is the most important meal of the day?

What relevant evidence does the author provide to support the claim that eating breakfast isn't that important?

Eating Breakfast

Breakfast is the most important meal of the day. Or is it? The topic has been the subject of debate for many years. For years, parents have scolded their children, "Eat your breakfast!" So where did the idea come from, and how did it become such a hotly debated topic?

Nearly one hundred years ago a health magazine published an article stating that breakfast is more important than any other meal. The editor of that magazine was Dr. John Harvey Kellogg. You might recognize the name Kellogg as the company that makes breakfast cereal. Dr. Kellogg was both a doctor and a businessman. He had a product to sell. Getting more people to eat breakfast meant more cereal sales! This is one way the idea became popular.

Eating breakfast was not a new idea. Breakfast has been a regular meal for centuries. However, the health benefit of that meal is still up for debate. One group of scientists did a six-week study of people who did and did not eat breakfast regularly. They did not find many health differences, but they did find that people who ate breakfast tended to be more active in the morning.

Another scientific study, done over a period of sixteen years, showed that skipping breakfast did have a negative effect on people's health. In that study, people who regularly skipped breakfast were more likely to have heart problems.

So is breakfast really the most important meal of the day? No one really knows. The best advice is to do what feels right. If you're usually hungry in the morning, eat. If you're not hungry, maybe it's okay to skip breakfast now and then. Your body is your best guide.

Answer the following questions.

8. Which sentence from the passage expresses the author's opinion?

   A. "Breakfast is the most important meal of the day."

   B. "They did not find many health differences."

   C. "The best advice is to do what feels right."

   D. "Skipping breakfast did have a negative effect on people's health."

9. For what reason does the author write that Dr. Kellogg "had a product to sell"?

   A. to state an opinion about Dr. Kellogg's purpose

   B. to provide evidence about Dr. Kellogg's reasoning

   C. to appeal to the reader's emotions about the product

   D. to provide irrelevant evidence about the cereal

10. Read this sentence.

    People who regularly skipped breakfast were more likely to have heart problems.

    The sentence above is

    A. relevant evidence.

    B. irrelevant evidence.

    C. an appeal to emotions.

    D. an opinion.

11. Read this sentence.

    Your body is your best guide.

    The sentence above is

    A. irrelevant evidence.

    B. relevant evidence.

    C. a fact based on science.

    D. an opinion.

12. Use facts from the passage and your own opinion to tell whether or not you think that breakfast is the most important meal of the day.

    _____

    _____

    _____

    _____

15 Compare and Contrast Texts Across Genres

Getting the Idea

When you compare and contrast informational texts that address the same topic, you think about how they are alike and how they are different. There are many things to compare and contrast in informational texts— how the texts are organized, the details each author uses to support the main ideas, and the author's purpose for writing each text, to name a few.

Informational texts come in different genres, or forms. All informational text contains facts, but the way the facts are presented in different texts can vary considerably. For instance, in a biography, an author writes about someone else's life. In an autobiography, an author writes about his or her own life. Both are informational texts, but the information is presented differently. One is presented from an outside observer, and one is presented in the first person. A biographical account can present a broader historical picture of the time and events affecting the subject. On the other hand, an autobiographical account will include emotions and thoughts that a biography could not.

Biography and autobiography are just two examples of different genres of informational text. Others include informational articles, news articles, memoirs, historical accounts, and public speeches. When you read different types of text that are about the same subject, you get a much fuller and richer understanding of the topic. For instance, a reader who has already read an objective history of a famous battle might enjoy reading a soldier's eyewitness account of the same battle much more.

Read the two paragraphs below about iguanas. Think about how the texts are similar and how they are different.

Passage 1

The marine iguanas of the Galapagos Islands are unique. They are herbivores that feed both on land and in the ocean. Their faces are small, with wide-set eyes, and their skin is knotty and rough. They have blunt snouts and sharp teeth that help them scrape tough, hardened algae off ocean rocks for food. Marine iguanas search for food not only on land but also underwater. Their dark gray color allows them to absorb sunlight after they emerge from feeding in the cold Galapagos waters. Often when they emerge from the water, they sneeze to expel the salt from the ocean water they have inhaled. Sometimes the salt lands on their heads, giving them a distinctive white "wig."

Passage 2

The marine iguana is the world's only marine lizard. Scientists believe that land-dwelling iguanas from South America drifted to the Galapagos Islands on logs and other debris and adapted to the island environment. Although marine iguanas have evolved to successfully protect themselves against predators, they still face many threats. Dogs, cats, and rats that have been introduced to the Galapagos by humans eat iguanas and their eggs, causing a decline in the iguana population. Rising ocean temperatures also threaten their survival. As temperatures rise, the algae the lizards feed on dies off, and other algae species grow in its place. Disasters such as oil spills are another threat. One oil spill off the coast of the Galapagos caused the deaths of over 60 percent of the marine iguana population.

These texts are from informational articles about the marine iguana of the Galapagos Islands. Both texts give information that helps build the reader's understanding of the marine iguana, but the details the authors provide are different. The first passage addresses the iguana's appearance, its habitat, and what and how it eats. The second passage offers broader details about the animal's environment and threats to its survival. By comparing and contrasting the information in both texts, the reader gets a better understanding of marine iguanas than either text alone could offer.

Thinking It Through

Read the following paragraphs, and then answer the question that follows.

Passage 1

In some countries, people don't have access to clean water through plumbing. They must carry their water for long distances. Traditionally, women and children carried twenty-liter buckets on their heads. Now, an invention called the Hippo Roller has enabled women, children, and the elderly to collect five times that amount of water. The Hippo Roller is a large, barrel-shaped container with a handle that can be rolled on the ground. It is made of inexpensive plastic and metal. The Hippo Roller is a simple, effective solution with enormous benefits. It saves people the time, energy, and hardship involved with toting water long distances.

Passage 2

The Hippo Roller is a great way for anyone to transform the lives of others. In some parts of the world, people must carry water for long distances on their heads. As a result, they suffer neck problems, bone issues, and muscle damage. It can take many hours just to carry a day's worth of water for cooking, cleaning, and drinking—hours that could be spent doing more productive things. Investing in the Hippo Roller is a way to positively impact the lives of others. For a few dollars, anyone can purchase a Hippo Roller for people living without ready access to water and radically improve their lives.

Compare and contrast the two paragraphs. Think about the main idea in each and the way supporting details are presented. Why were the two paragraphs written?

_____

_____

_____

 Think about who the intended audience is for the two texts.

 **DISCUSS** What is the author's purpose for writing each passage?

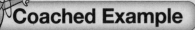

Coached Example

Read the passages and answer the questions.

The Cacao Tree

Cacao is a tropical evergreen tree that grows in the lowland rain forests of the Amazon and surrounding river basins. The cacao tree is the source of cocoa beans that have been used to produce chocolate for generations.

Cacao trees usually grow between twenty and forty feet tall. The flowers of the cacao can be a variety of colors as they grow and develop. Depending on the plant, the flowers can be pink, yellow, or bright red. The flowers are pollinated by tiny flies called *midges*.

After four years, the mature cacao tree produces fruit. These fruits, or pods, are called *cherelles* and resemble squash. They range in color from bright yellow to deep purple. A cacao tree may yield up to seventy pods per year.

The cherelles ripen after six months, when they have reached a length of about fourteen inches. The pods are hard and have ridges running along their sides. Nestled in the center of the pods are cocoa beans. The beans are about one inch long and are covered with a sweet, sticky white pulp.

The cacao tree is also known as *Theobroma cacao*, which means "food of the gods" in Greek. Aztecs and Mayans of Central America had a long tradition of cultivating the plant. Today it is processed in a variety of ways around the world and still considered a divine gift.

Threats to the Cacao Plant

One of the biggest threats to the cacao plant is fungus. A fungus has killed off nearly all the cacao plants in Central America, where cacao was first cultivated by Mayans 1,500 years ago. As a result, nearly 70 percent of the world's cacao crop is now grown in West Africa.

The cacao trees in West Africa have no resistance to the fungus found in Central America. Fungus varieties such as the "frosty pod" easily form spores that are scattered in the wind. If farmers are careless, the fungus can easily spread and infect the pods.

To combat this threat, biologists are identifying and breeding plants that are naturally resistant to the fungus. All of their efforts are a race against the clock. Scientists believe that if just a few cacao pods are infected by the fungus, it could lead to the loss of one third of the world's production of the cacao plant.

1. How are the passages alike?

    A. Both passages are meant to inform readers.

    B. Both passages have fungus as the main idea.

    C. Both passages are types of biographies.

    D. Both passages are meant to persuade readers.

    HINT Think about the topic of each text.

2. Which of the following is true?

    A. One passage tells about the cacao plant, and the other does not.

    B. Both passages are about cacao, but they have different main ideas.

    C. Both passages address threats to the cacao plant.

    D. Both passages discuss the African cacao crop.

    HINT Is one passage more specific than the other? How?

3. How are the passages different? Use details to support your answer.

    _____

    _____

    _____

    _____

    HINT Consider the details that are used to support the main idea of each passage. How does each passage help you to better understand the cacao plant?

Lesson Practice

Use the Reading Guides to help you understand the passages.

Duplicating any part of this book is prohibited by law.

Reading Guide

How does structure help convey the main idea of the passage?

What is the author's purpose for writing the passage?

A Solar-Powered Lantern

In some areas of Africa, families live without electricity. Though it is possible to adapt to a life without electricity, living without it is difficult. People without access to electricity must rely on kerosene and firewood for light, warmth, and cooking. Using kerosene and firewood can cause problems. First, the two resources can be expensive. Many people will spend a majority of their income on just these items. Using kerosene and firewood may also cause health problems due to constant exposure to smoke. And when someone's only source of light is fire, it can result in eyestrain because firelight is not very bright. Activities like studying and reading stop as soon as the sun sets.

In 2004, a man from Kenya named Evans Wadongo created a solar-powered lantern to help his fellow Africans have access to safe, affordable light. Wadongo's lantern works by using a solar panel to produce electricity for a light-emitting diode (LED). A solar panel is a device that turns the sun's light into electricity. The electricity produced by the solar panel is captured and used to power the LED. The lanterns can be adapted to match the conditions of the villages where they're used.

Wadongo found a way to make and distribute ten thousand free lanterns. With Wadongo's invention, many families have access to free, safe, and efficient light. With what they can save on kerosene and firewood, families have more money for other necessities like food. Wadongo's solar-powered lantern has truly changed lives for many people in Africa.

How is the information presented in the passage?

How does the previous passage help you appreciate and understand this one?

What is the author's purpose in writing this text?

Evans Wadongo: Africa's Hero

When citizens of Nairobi, Kenya, meet Evans Wadongo, their faces light up, just like the solar-powered lantern he invented. Men, women, and children gather around him to sing the praises of the inventor who truly touched their lives.

When Evans Wadongo was growing up in Africa, education was a top priority. Wadongo grew up in a home of four children, and his father, a high school teacher, firmly believed in the value of education. Like many in surrounding areas, the family had no electricity. Wadongo had to study by a kerosene lamp or share one lantern with his siblings and other family members when he wanted to study after dark.

Wadongo remembers the frustration he felt when he could not finish his homework because he did not have enough light. He would have to pack up his books and go to bed before he was able to finish studying for his exams the next day, and as a result, he performed poorly. "I couldn't compete effectively with other kids who had access to lighting," Wadongo said. "In every home in the village it was the same . . . many children drop out of school for these reasons . . . so they remain poor for the rest of their life."

Wadongo wondered what he could do about this situation. In 2004, while attending university, Wadongo found his answer. He experimented with LED lights used for Christmas lighting and realized that the lights could be used to light homes. Around the same time, he came across a discarded solar panel. It struck Wadongo that he could combine the LED and solar panel to create an affordable solution to his country's light problems. He went on to create just such a solar-powered lantern.

Wadongo's lantern is a huge success. Through his organization, Use Solar, Save Lives, he was able to create and offer lanterns to villagers for free. Wadongo worked with a local artist to design the solar lantern. Together, they named it *MwangaBora*, which is Swahili for "good light." His community considers Wadongo a hero.

Answer the following questions.

1. "A Solar-Powered Lantern" is written mainly to

    A. provide general information about the solar-powered lantern.

    B. provide information about Evans Wadongo's life and work.

    C. persuade readers to address problems in Africa.

    D. inform about the health risks of kerosene and firewood.

2. "Evans Wadongo: Africa's Hero" is written mainly to

    A. inform readers about Evans Wadongo's family.

    B. inform readers about Evans Wadongo's life and accomplishments.

    C. instruct readers how to build a solar-powered lantern.

    D. educate readers about life in Nairobi, Kenya.

3. Which genre BEST describes "Evans Wadongo: Africa's Hero"?

    A. memoir

    B. autobiography

    C. technical account

    D. news article

4. What type of details are in "Evans Wadongo: Africa's Hero" but not in "A Solar-Powered Lantern"?

    A. facts about Evans Wadongo's solar-powered lantern

    B. direct quotations from Evans Wadongo

    C. information about African villagers' problems

    D. facts about how a solar panel works

5. Explain how "Evans Wadongo: Africa's Hero" helps you to understand the details in "A Solar-Powered Lantern."

    _____

    _____

    _____

    _____

Use the Reading Guide to help you understand the passage.

Reading Guide

Journals and memoirs are nonfiction. How does this form of writing help readers understand the information?

What questions does this passage raise?

Think about why Amare cannot attend school, although her brother can.

Amare's Journal

The three journal entries below were written by Amare, an eleven-year-old girl from Kenya.

July 16, 2014

Akon woke me up again getting ready for school. Then at the breakfast table he was boasting about his math studies, saying he needs an extra serving of *mandazi* to fuel his long day at school. If he needs an extra serving of *mandazi*, then I do too! I will be at home with the cows all day, working hard. Akon doesn't understand. It's so hard watching him go to school while I have to stay home and work on our farm. I really wish I could go to school, but my family needs my help. Those math problems he describes don't sound so hard.

August 20, 2014

I almost can't believe it! My aunt came to tell us that she and her family are moving nearby. They will help with the farm, and I can go to school! My mother looked so relieved and excited. Now both of her children can go to school! All of the chores will get done, and soon I will be as good at math as Akon. Next week we are going to the school to register. I'll start in September when the third term begins!

January 4, 2016

I'm about to start my second full year of school. School can be very difficult, but I love it, and I feel like I understand so much more. Reading in the school library is my favorite thing. I have learned much about the history of Kenya and other countries in Africa. It is hard for many people in my country to get an education, so I feel extremely lucky. At first Akon resented my going to school because he could no longer brag about his math studies, but his attitude quickly changed. Someday I hope to open a school for girls. I want all the girls of Africa to have an education!

Reading Guide

Think about Amare's firsthand account as you read the passage.

How does this passage help you understand and appreciate "Amare's Journal"?

Which details in the two passages are similar? Which are different?

Education for Everyone in Africa

The Kibera School for Girls in Kenya, Africa, is one of many schools that are being created for female students there. At times, girls were left behind in Africa and given little to no chance for an education, but times are changing.

If families could not afford to send all of their children to school, they would often send the boys first. Girls stayed home to herd livestock and perform household chores to support the family.

Today, people are realizing that it is just as important to send girls to school as it is to send boys. Many girls who are being given the opportunity to have an education are extremely excited about it. They will brave walking at night just for an opportunity to attend special night classes and other free community classes.

Often when people are given the opportunity to learn, they help others who also yearn to learn because they know how valuable their own education is. One woman who was given a scholarship to go to school was motivated to share her experiences and help others. She helps girls with their homework on a volunteer basis. She is overjoyed to see their grades improve, knowing she helped them become more confident in themselves.

Everyone in Africa should be given access to education. Everyone has a role to contribute to the community. As more schools for girls are opened and more chances are given for girls to attend them, the communities will prosper from their education.

Answer the following questions.

6. Read the first paragraph of "Amare's Journal."

> **Akon woke me up again getting ready for school. Then at the breakfast table he was boasting about his math studies, saying he needs an extra serving of *mandazi* to fuel his long day at school. If he needs an extra serving of *mandazi*, then I do too! I will be at home with the cows all day, working hard. Akon doesn't understand. It's so hard watching him go to school while I have to stay home and work on our farm. I really wish I could go to school, but my family needs my help. Those math problems he describes don't sound so hard.**

Underline the sentence that BEST supports a similar idea found in "Education for Everyone in Africa."

---

7. Use your answer to Part A to answer Part B.

Part A

Which sentence BEST describes how "Amare's Journal" is organized?

A. It is organized around the idea that girls in Kenya get to go to school.

B. It is organized chronologically around events in Amare's life.

C. It is organized around the cause and effects of Amare's attending school.

D. It compares and contrasts the experiences of boys and girls in Kenyan schools.

Part B

Which detail from the passage best supports the answer to Part A?

A. "I'm about to start my second full year of school. I'm so excited."

B. "If he needs an extra serving of *mandazi*, then I do too!"

C. "I really wish I could go to school too."

D. "Someday I hope to open a school for girls."

8. Use your answer to Part A to answer Part B.

Part A

Based on the information in the passages, what is the main difference between education for boys and girls in Kenya?

A. Girls have more access to school than boys do.

B. Girls and boys have equal access to school.

C. Boys have more access to school than girls do.

D. Boys have less access to school than girls do.

Part B

Based on the passages, how are Kenyan girls' lives changing?

_____

_____

_____

9. Use Part A to answer Part B.

Part A

Read each choice in the chart below. Circle the choice that supports the main idea of BOTH passages.

Main Idea	I really wish I could go to school, but my family needs my help.
	If families cannot afford to send all of their children to school, they will often send the boys first.
	She is overjoyed to see their grades improve, knowing she helped them become more confident in themselves.

Part B

Use the detail you circled to, write a three-sentence summary of both of the passages.

_____

_____

Use the Reading Guides to help you understand the passages.

Reading Guide

How did Twain's family play a role in his life?

How many jobs did Twain have? How did these experiences shape him as a writer?

What kind of informational text is this?

Mark Twain's Adventures

The writer Mark Twain created the famous character of Tom Sawyer, and his *Adventures of Huckleberry Finn* is considered one of the great American novels. The various jobs and travels of Twain's early life helped to make him the writer he became.

Mark Twain began working early in his life. At twelve years of age, Mark Twain went to work full-time as an apprentice printer for a newspaper in Hannibal, Missouri. When his older brother Orion bought a newspaper company, Twain went to work with him. Twain became a typesetter, and he even began to write articles for the newspaper. Eventually, he left Missouri and traveled around the country, working as a printer in different cities.

A few years later, Twain tried his hand at piloting riverboats. He became an apprentice on the steamboat *Pennsylvania*, which traveled up and down the Mississippi River. Twain got his brother Henry a job on board the *Pennsylvania* as well. Some time later, there was an accidental explosion on the boat, and Henry was killed. Twain was heartbroken but continued on to get his pilot's license.

In 1861, shortly after the Civil War began, he joined the Confederate militia to show loyalty to his Southern roots. Twain didn't believe in the war and, luckily, the militia he joined quickly disbanded once it heard that Union troops were approaching. It was then that Twain left to travel west with his brother Orion.

Twain had many adventures in the West. Like so many others who traveled there in search of fortune, he made an attempt at silver mining. When he failed at that, he returned to his former profession, reporting for a Nevada newspaper. It was during this time that he established his pen name "Mark Twain." Thus it was on the wild American frontier that Mark Twain the writer was born.

Reading **Guide**

How does the genre of the memoir help you learn more about Mark Twain?

How does this passage compare and contrast to the previous passage?

What information in the first passage helped you appreciate this memoir excerpt?

excerpted from Mark Twain's travel writing

Roughing It

Roughing It *tells about Mark Twain's adventures in the western United States before they were part of the union. This excerpt tells about a typical day Twain had riding a stagecoach across the plains.*

By eight o'clock everything was ready, and we were on the other side of the river. We jumped into the stage, the driver cracked his whip, and we bowled away and left "the States" behind us. It was a superb summer morning, and all the landscape was brilliant with sunshine. There was a freshness and breeziness, too, and an exhilarating sense of emancipation from all sorts of cares and responsibilities, that almost made us feel that the years we had spent in the close, hot city, toiling and slaving, had been wasted and thrown away. We were spinning along through Kansas, and in the course of an hour and a half we were fairly abroad on the Great Plains. Just here the land was rolling—a grand sweep of regular elevations and depressions as far as the eye could reach—like the stately heave and swell of the ocean's bosom after a storm. And everywhere were cornfields, accenting with squares of deeper green, this limitless expanse of grassy land. But presently this sea upon dry ground was to lose its "rolling" character and stretch away for seven hundred miles as level as a floor!

Our coach was a great swinging and swaying stage, of the most sumptuous description—an imposing cradle on wheels. It was drawn by six handsome horses, and by the side of the driver sat the "conductor," the legitimate captain of the craft; for it was his business to take charge and care of the mails, baggage, express matter, and passengers. We three were the only passengers, this trip. We sat on the back seat, inside. About all the rest of the coach was full of mail bags—for we had three days' delayed mails with us. Almost touching our knees, a perpendicular wall of mail matter rose up to the roof. There was a great pile of it strapped on top of the stage, and both the fore and hind boots were full.

Answer the following questions.

10. How are the passages alike?

    A. They are both biographies about Mark Twain.

    B. They both address Mark Twain's relationship with his brothers.

    C. They both address Mark Twain's adventures out West.

    D. They both share the same author's purpose.

11. Which statement about the passages is correct?

    A. One passage mentions Twain's travels, and the other does not.

    B. One is from a biography, and the other is from a memoir.

    C. Both passages have the same tone and viewpoint.

    D. Both passages inform readers about Twain's early life.

12. Which sentence from "Mark Twain's Adventures" expresses the main idea of the passage?

    A. "A few years later, Twain tried his hand at piloting riverboats."

    B. "Twain became a typesetter, and he even began to write articles for the newspaper."

    C. "In 1861, shortly after the Civil War began, Twain joined the Confederate militia to show loyalty to his Southern roots."

    D. "The various jobs and travels of Twain's early life helped to make him the writer he became."

13. How does the excerpt from *Roughing It* give readers a fuller understanding of the final paragraph of "Mark Twain's Adventures"?

    A. Twain's description of the geography helps readers understand the factual information.

    B. The information presented in the memoir explains how Twain became a writer.

    C. The tone of the memoir helps readers appreciate how exciting this period of Twain's life was.

    D. The information presented in the memoir explains why Twain decided to use a pen name.

14. Read this sentence from *Roughing It*.

> There was a freshness and breeziness, too, and an exhilarating sense of emancipation from all sorts of cares and responsibilities, that almost made us feel that the years we had spent in the close, hot city, toiling and slaving, had been wasted and thrown away.

What information from "Mark Twain's Adventures" helps readers appreciate this line from his memoir?

_____

_____

_____

_____

15. Tell how *Roughing It* helps you to understand "Mark Twain's Adventures" better.

_____

_____

_____

_____

Cumulative Assessment

Read the passage and answer the questions that follow.

The Battle of Fort Sumter

A Short Battle Leads to a Big War

In 1861, there was a disagreement among the states. Newly elected President Abraham Lincoln had spoken out against slavery. He also believed that the federal government should make laws for the states. Some states agreed with him, and some did not. People called states that agreed with Lincoln the "Union states." They were also called "free states." These were mainly northern states. People called states that did not agree with Lincoln the "Confederate states." These were mainly southern states.

Leading Up to the Battle

Early on in 1861, several Southern states seceded, or separated, from the United States. As tensions grew, there were more and more disagreements. The North and South were close to declaring war.

Fort Sumter was an army fort located near Charleston, South Carolina. Because of its location, it was important to both the Union and the Confederate armies. So both sides were interested in the fort. At the time, the Union army controlled the fort. But the Confederate army planned to take it over.

On April 10, 1861, General Beauregard led Confederate soldiers to the fort. As soon as they arrived, he demanded that the Union soldiers surrender. The leader of the Union forces, Major Anderson, refused.

Shots Are Fired

In response, another group of Confederate soldiers traveled to the fort. They joined Beauregard's forces. The Union soldiers were in a difficult situation. Defending a fort is not an easy task. A fort can contain only a few supplies: weapons, cannons, food, and water. It's sometimes impossible for soldiers in a fort to get more supplies. To do so, soldiers have to leave the fort. Then they have to get past the enemy. Soldiers in a fort can starve if a battle goes on for too long.

With the extra forces, Beauregard knew he could take over the fort. On the morning of Friday, April 12, he sent a message to Major Anderson. He told Anderson to surrender the fort. But Anderson did not return a message to Beauregard. As a result, fighting began.

The heavy firing continued on Saturday, April 13. Smoke billowed out of the fort, but the Union flag still flapped above the fort. Soon, the Union soldiers had to take down the Union flag. They lifted a white flag into the air instead. This white flag was a sign of surrender. They could not continue. At this point, both armies agreed to end the fight. On Sunday, April 14, the Union soldiers left the fort, tired, hungry, and thirsty.

The Aftermath of the Battle

Luckily, no one died as a result of the battle. While the fighting only lasted for one weekend, it was very important. Most historians think that the Battle of Fort Sumter was the start of the American Civil War.

1. This passage is MAINLY about

   A. Abraham Lincoln.

   B. the Battle of Fort Sumter.

   C. Major Anderson.

   D. Union soldiers refusing to surrender.

2. What happened BEFORE General Beauregard led Confederate soldiers to Fort Sumter?

   A. Major Anderson refused to surrender.

   B. Union and Confederate soldiers began to fight.

   C. Union soldiers left the fort.

   D. Several Southern states seceded.

Read the passage and answer the questions that follow.

The Battles of Lexington and Concord

At Lexington, Massachusetts, the first shots of the American Revolutionary War were fired. On April 18, 1775, British General Thomas Gage gave 700 soldiers a very specific mission. First, they were to find guns and supplies stored by American colonists in Concord, Massachusetts, near Boston. After destroying these items, they were also ordered to arrest Samuel Adams and John Hancock. These two men were important leaders of the patriot movement. The colonists knew about this mission several weeks before the soldiers arrived. Spies warned them that the British were coming to search their homes. To be safe, they moved much of their supplies to safety. On the night before the British came, the colonists received extensive details about British plans, which they passed on to the militia.

When Dr. Joseph Warren learned about these plans, he told Paul Revere, who lived in Boston, to inform Hancock and Adams about the developments. Revere promised that he would warn them when the British soldiers were about to enter the city. However, he wasn't entirely sure that he would be able to deliver the message on time. Therefore, he planned to alert people by putting lanterns in the city's Old North Church steeple. He would light one lantern if the British were coming by land, and he would light two lanterns if the British were coming by sea.

The British troops boarded ferries on the night of April 18. They were sailing into Boston Harbor, where they would begin the march to Lexington. Revere lit two lanterns in the steeple of the Old North Church, sending a signal that the British were coming by sea. Then Revere left with Dr. Samuel Prescott and William Dawes, on their way to tell the colonists that the British were coming. Revere went to Lexington, where he told Hancock and Adams. These two men managed to escape before the British could reach Lexington.

The colonists were prepared to battle the British soldiers. They had formed a group of brave soldiers called the minutemen. They got their name because they could begin to fight with only a minute's notice. A group of seventy-five armed minutemen, led by Captain Jonas Parker, met the British soldiers when they got to Lexington. Unfortunately, there were far more British soldiers than minutemen. The British were the first to fire. Eight minutemen were dead, and ten were injured, after the battle.

Revere tried to reach Concord, but he was captured before he could get there. The men working with him managed to avoid capture, and they warned the people about the coming invasion. As the British kept moving toward Concord, the town's citizens hid their guns and supplies in towns nearby. Only a small part of the supplies were left when the British arrived. The soldiers burned those supplies immediately.

The messengers rapidly spread the word about the British; the smoke from burning supplies was a strong signal, as well. The minutemen, along with other local citizens, got their weapons and gathered together. They were ready to fight.

The British soldiers began their return to Boston. The colonists attacked them as they passed through Lexington and Concord. The British army lost seventy-three soldiers before they reached Boston; 174 more were wounded. The patriot army lost forty-nine soldiers, and thirty-nine were wounded.

The fighting did not stop there. The militia army attacked Boston the following morning. The colonists had formed an army of 200,000 soldiers, and it kept growing as more and more colonists joined up. This group of loyal patriots would eventually form the Continental army.

---

3. Why did the British march to Lexington and Concord?

   A. to start the war between Great Britain and the colonies

   B. to arrest Paul Revere

   C. to arrest Samuel Adams and John Hancock

   D. to arrest the minutemen

4. How were the Battle of Fort Sumter and the Battles of Lexington and Concord alike?

   A. They were both small battles that started large wars.

   B. They were both battles against the British.

   C. They were both battles against the Confederate soldiers.

   D. They were both long battles that cost many lives.

---

5. How are both passages organized?

   _____

   _____

Read the passage and answer the questions that follow.

excerpted and adapted from

Gray's Anatomy
by Henry Gray

The muscles are connected to bones, cartilages, ligaments, and skin. Some are directly connected. Others are connected through tendons. Tendons are thin and wiry, like fibers.

The muscles have different forms. In the limbs, they are very long, especially the ones closer to the skin. They surround the bones, and they provide protection for the joints. In the trunk, they are broad, flattened, and expanded. They help to form the walls of the trunk cavities. This is why we call muscles *long, broad,* or *short.*

The fibers of certain muscles are arranged with the tendons in many different ways. In some muscles the fibers are parallel. They run directly from their starting point to the place where they join with the muscle. These are quadrilateral muscles. In other muscles the fibers are convergent. This means that several of them join together, or converge, at one point. In some muscles the fibers are slanted. They all converge on one side of a tendon. Finally, in some muscles, the fibers are arranged in curved bundles. The arrangement of the fibers is important. It affects the strength of the muscle. It also affects the way the muscle moves. The muscles where the fibers are long and few in number can move in many different directions. But they are not as strong. On the other hand, if the fibers are short and there are a lot of them, they have great power. But, they have a smaller range of movement.

The names given to the various muscles have been given for many reasons:
(1) their location
(2) their direction
(3) their uses
(4) their shape
(5) the number of divisions they have
(6) the places where they attach to tendons and bones.

In the description of a muscle, the *origin* is its more fixed or central attachment; the *insertion* is the movable point where the force of the muscle goes.

We should pay attention to the exact *origin, insertion,* and *actions* of each muscle. More importantly, though, we should pay attention to the muscle's *relations* with other parts. Knowing where the muscles are attached is important in finding out about their actions. But neither of these pieces of information is the most important. A muscle's action should not be studied by itself. It is impossible for anyone to use only one muscle at a time. In other words, the brain gives commands for movements, not for individual muscle actions. To carry out a movement, a combination of muscles must be used. People have no power to leave out a muscle or to add one to it. One (or more) muscle of the combination is the chief moving force. When this muscle passes over more than one joint, other muscles join in the movement. In the case of the limb movements, a third set of muscles is used. These muscles keep the limb steady and also prevent the balance of the body from being disturbed. A further point to consider is that in certain positions, a movement can be affected by gravity. And in such a case, the muscles in action oppose those that might normally be in action.

Thinking about the actions of the muscles can help surgeons explain the causes of dislocation in various types of fractures, or broken bones. In doing so, he or she can choose proper treatment in each case.

6. What is the passage MAINLY about?

    A. movement

    B. muscles

    C. origins

    D. tendons

7. Which sentence from the passage supports the idea that the parts of the body must work together?

    A. "To carry out a movement, a combination of muscles must be used."

    B. "They all converge on one side of a tendon."

    C. "They surround the bones, and they provide protection for the joints."

    D. "In doing so, he or she can choose proper treatment in each case."

8. Which of the following sentences from the passage expresses an opinion?

    A. "The muscles have different forms."

    B. "In some muscles the fibers are parallel."

    C. "Finally, in some muscles, the fibers are arranged in curved bundles."

    D. "But neither of these pieces of information is the most important."

9. Which reference material would be MOST useful in finding out about bones and tendons?

    A. atlas

    B. dictionary

    C. encyclopedia

    D. periodical

10. What is paragraph 6 MOSTLY about?

_____

_____

_____

_____

_____

_____

_____

CHAPTER

3 Writing

Chapter 3: Diagnostic Assessment

Chapter 3: Cumulative Assessment

Diagnostic Assessment

The following passage contains mistakes. Read the passage and answer the questions that follow.

Summer in the City

(1) My family vacations a lot; we have been on vacation trips to Kalamazoo, Chicago, and even Mexico. (2) Each trip was terrific in its own way, but the most fantastic trip I ever had was our vacation in New York.

(3) There were so many activities to do! (4) Next, we went to Battery Park and ate hot dogs and falafels. (5) First, we went to Ellis Island and the Statue of Liberty. (6) Dad described our great-grandmother's voyage by steamship from Italy. (7) It must have been pretty exciting for her to see the Statue of Liberty after traveling on a boat for such an extended period. (8) Then, we rode in a taxi to Central Park. (9) We'd never seen such an enormous park; there were so many people lying on the grass, playing Frisbee, and picnicking. (10) It made me think of the parks back home and how empty they seem. (11) Back home, most people never walk, they always drive everywhere.

(12) New York is not only an extraordinary place to have fun, but it is also an incredible place to learn. (13) There were so many museums in New York. (14) We didn't have time to see all of them. (15) My mom chose one museum. (16) My dad chose another museum. (17) I chose a third museum. (18) First, we went to the American Museum of Natural History, which was amazing. (19) My favorite part was the giant blue whale that seemed to float in the sky. (20) Next, we went to the Metropolitan Museum of Art. (21) The Metropolitan Museum was so gigantic that we got disoriented and couldn't find our way out. (22) Finally, we went to the Museum of Modern Art, where we saw a lot of paintings.

(23) The food in New York is like nowhere else in America. (24) There are so many great restaurants. (25) Anyone who wants to travel to an exciting place where you can learn, have fun, and eat great food should definitely go to New York.

1. Which sentence is in the wrong order in paragraph 2?

   A. sentence 3

   B. sentence 4

   C. sentence 6

   D. sentence 9

2. Which sentence does NOT belong in paragraph 2?

   A. sentence 4

   B. sentence 5

   C. sentence 8

   D. sentence 11

3. What is paragraph 3 MAINLY about?

   A. the Statue of Liberty

   B. Central Park

   C. New York museums

   D. food

4. Which would be the BEST detail to add to paragraph 4?

   A. the history of Central Park

   B. stories about the narrator's great-grandmother

   C. different artists' names in the museums

   D. examples of food in New York

5. Which heading would NOT be in an outline used for this passage?

   A. Food in New York

   B. Fun Things to Do

   C. Parks Across America

   D. Museums

6. Which resource would NOT be helpful when researching what to do in New York?

   A. a book

   B. a thesaurus

   C. a Web site

   D. a newspaper

Narrative Prompt

Think about the early settlers to this country. Think about the hard times that they encountered and how they survived. They had to live with few resources. Imagine that you are a settler in a strange country. What would you be most concerned about? Write a story about your first day as a settler. Be sure to include details describing your setting.

Use the checklist below to help you do your best writing.

Does your story

❏ have a situation and characters?

❏ use dialogue or description to develop the story?

❏ have a clear plot?

❏ use good word choice?

❏ have a satisfying ending?

❏ have good spelling, capitalization, and punctuation?

❏ follow the rules for good grammar?

Write your response in the space provided. You may use your own paper if you need more space.

16 Write Opinions

Getting the Idea

In **persuasive writing**, you offer the reader a certain point of view. You also try to get the reader to agree with that point of view. In doing that, you present facts and give your opinion on a topic. A **fact** is information that is true and can be proven. An **opinion** is a statement that cannot be proven.

When writing a persuasive letter or essay, the first thing you should do is identify the issue you will write about at the beginning of your paper. Then, state your position clearly. It is always important, when writing the introduction to a persuasive piece, to start off with your position. Otherwise, the reader will not understand your point. After you have written your opening statement, review it to make sure it is clear. Readers should not be confused about where you stand.

After you have stated your position, you need to support it. To do that, you must first decide how to organize your writing. The best method is to order your points from strongest to weakest. This means that your strongest and most relevant points should come first. Then, your less important points should follow. If you begin with your weaker points, your reader might think your position is weak. To see which points are strongest and which are weakest, think about how much you have to say about each point. If you can easily write an entire paragraph about one of your points, it is likely a strong point. If another one of your points is very simple, then it is probably a weaker point.

It is also a good idea to allow for opposing arguments in your piece. To do this, first think of what someone who disagreed with your position might say. Then, respond to that argument, pointing out why your position is more reasonable. When you present opposing arguments, it shows that you have thought through your position thoroughly.

A key to good writing is to make sure that your paragraphs flow smoothly from one to the next. The best way to do this is to use proper details and transitions when writing. **Transitions** are words writers use as they move between one idea and another. Examples of transitional words include: *at first, earlier, while, next, for example*, and *therefore*. Transition words are also used to compare and contrast; these include *but, by the same token, conversely, however, instead, nevertheless, on one hand, still, yet, in contrast, likewise*, and *similarly*.

The final paragraph is the summary, or **conclusion**. The conclusion restates the argument. It also summarizes the most important points, ideas, and details. It brings the paper to an end. Unlike the introduction, the conclusion does not lay out the groundwork for the presentation of the topic. It reminds readers of the most important point of the paper.

Prewriting is sometimes tricky but very important. As you think about your subject, you should organize your ideas before you start to write. One way to do this is by using a graphic organizer. A **graphic organizer** visually illustrates your ideas and helps you keep them clear as you write.

For example, a person writing about a new city plan might use the graphic organizer below. In this example, the main claim is: "The city should not build a new toll road." It goes on the top row of the chart. The reasons that support the claim are in the three rows following that row. The conclusion is on the last row of the chart.

Claim	The city should not build a new toll road.
Reason	The toll road will cost the city millions of dollars.
Reason	The proposed toll road will destroy thousands of acres of nature.
Reason	It will displace endangered wildlife.
Conclusion	Building a new toll road will bring more problems than benefits.

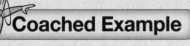

Coached Example

Read the following opinions. Then rewrite each one so that the opinion is clearer.

1. Some people argue that every child in every school should have access to computers. Others believe that computers in the classroom may not be that valuable. They believe that computers may actually interfere with the learning process. I think computers might be good for students. They might be able to help students learn.

_____

_____

_____

_____

HINT Think about the effect that phrases such as "I think" and "they might" have on a piece of writing. Are there other ways the sentences might be phrased?

2. Millions of people visit zoos around the world every year. However, some people believe that zoos are inhumane and that animals should not be kept in captivity. A lot of people learn about animals by visiting them at the zoo. But I guess some animals might be better in the wild and should not be held in captivity.

_____

_____

_____

_____

HINT Remember that when you write an opinion piece, you need to be certain of your opinion. Look for spots here where the writer doesn't seem certain.

Lesson Practice

Use the Writing Guide to help you understand the passage.

Writing Guide

What is the author's position?

How does the author support the position?

Food for Everyone

School cafeterias should be required to provide low-fat and vegetarian lunch choices for all students. Currently, the cafeteria has a very limited menu, without meals that are right for everyone.

Not all students have the same eating habits. My friends who are vegetarians always have to bring their lunches. According to the Vegetarian Resource Group, there are millions of vegetarians in the United States. The school should not leave out an entire group of people because of their eating habits.

The school should also offer low-fat meals. A certain amount of fat is good for you. But too much can be harmful to your health. By offering low-fat menu items, the school can help students' general health. It would be nice if the school stopped serving deep-fried foods that are high in fat. It would be a step in the right direction. But I think that would be too great a change. Instead, the school can continue serving the regular menu while also offering other choices.

Along with the regular menu, the school can start serving salads and other vegetable dishes. In time, I think students will find that the healthier dishes taste just as good, if not better, than the food that is not as healthy. The school should give everyone the option to choose.

What would make a strong conclusion? Write the final paragraph of the essay.

_____

_____

_____

_____

Plan Your Writing

Read the writing prompt, and then plan your response below.

In some schools across the nation, students do not earn grades. Instead, they receive written and oral evaluations. Some people believe this is more helpful than the grading system. They believe grading systems reward students unevenly. They also believe grading systems push students to compete instead of learn. Write an essay either in favor of grades or against them. Use specific reasons and examples to support your answer.

Claim	
Reason	
Reason	
Reason	
Conclusion	

Write Your Response

Write your response on the pages provided.

Checklist for Persuasive Writing

Use the checklist below to help you do your best writing.

Does your essay

- ❏ have a clear topic?
- ❏ show a point of view about the topic?
- ❏ have a logical structure?
- ❏ support reasons with details?
- ❏ present and respond to opposing arguments?
- ❏ use transition phrases properly?
- ❏ connect reasons and details with the right words or phrases?
- ❏ use a style and vocabulary that is correct for the audience and purpose?
- ❏ have a solid concluding paragraph?
- ❏ have good spelling, capitalization, and punctuation?
- ❏ follow the rules for good grammar?

Use the Writing Guide to help you understand the passage.

Writing Guide

Find the author's opinion about libraries in the first paragraph. What opposing opinion does the author include in this paragraph?

Notice how each paragraph develops the author's argument. What reasons and examples does the author use to support his opinion?

Is the author's argument convincing? Why or why not?

Libraries Are for Everyone

Some people say that we no longer need public libraries. They claim that because of the Internet, money no longer needs to be spent on keeping libraries open, staffing them with librarians, or buying print books. However, I do not agree. I believe that we need to continue spending money on public libraries so that everyone has access to information.

Libraries are the foundation of our communities. The public library system provides a physical building for people of all backgrounds to check out books, use computers, or otherwise find information. For example, if you go into a library, you might see a volunteer reading to a group of children, a person using a computer to look for a job, or a group of students researching information. Libraries are used and needed by all.

When libraries are taken away, librarians are also taken away. Librarians are the human connection to information. They teach skills on a one-on-one basis when they show how to use keywords in an online search for print or digital materials, how information is organized, or how to choose appropriate materials. Have you ever gone to a public library and asked a librarian for help? Information is not always easy to find, and a librarian can guide you to the best resources.

Although many people read books and do research online, there is still a need for library books. Many people cannot afford the technology to access information at home. Those people may only use computers in the library, at school, or at work. When they get home, they still need books to read.

We need public library buildings in our communities. They provide the space to access information, people to help, and materials to read.

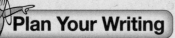

Plan Your Writing

Read the writing prompt, and then plan your response below.

In 2009–2010, nineteen percent of public schools in the United States had a policy that required students to wear uniforms to school. Those in favor of uniforms believe that they allow students to concentrate on their studies, reduce differences among students, increase their sense of belonging, and help identify trespassers. Those against school uniforms believe that they do not allow students to express themselves freely, are an additional cost for parents, and will not actually prevent fighting or bullying. Write an essay either in favor of or in opposition to school uniforms in public schools. Use specific reasons and examples to support your opinion.

Claim	
Reason	
Reason	
Reason	
Conclusion	

Write Your Response

Write your response on the pages provided.

_____

_____

_____

_____

_____

_____

_____

_____

_____

_____

_____

_____

_____

_____

_____

_____

_____

_____

_____

_____

_____

_____

_____

_____

_____

_____

_____

_____

17 Write Informative or Explanatory Pieces

Getting the Idea

Informational writing is writing that tells the reader about something or explains something. It must have a clearly defined topic, supported by well-chosen facts.

All informational writing includes an introduction. The **introduction** is the opening, or first part. It can be several sentences or several paragraphs. It provides the basic framework for the paper's topic or subject and shows the goal of the paper.

Once you have chosen your topic, you must think about your main idea, your topic sentence, and the details you want to include. A **topic sentence** is a sentence that tells the central idea of a paragraph or passage. It usually lies near the beginning of the paragraph. You will have one topic sentence in the first paragraph of the composition, and each paragraph that follows it should have a topic sentence as well. You should develop the essay with facts, examples, or quotations. Details that are off-topic should be removed. Remember to use precise language and terms that relate to your topic. For example, in a report about earthquakes, you might use terms such as *fault*, *stress*, and *Richter scale*.

Finally, write a strong **conclusion**. The conclusion is similar to the introduction, but they contain slightly different types of information. The conclusion is more specific, while the introduction is more general. The conclusion also serves to restate the points made in the introduction. It should also neatly tie up the paper with a closing statement.

When doing your research, use more than one source whenever you can. Different sources provide a wider range of information. Ask yourself these questions as you choose sources: Do I need up-to-date information? Or can I use an older source? If you need up-to-date information, a newspaper or magazine is probably your best bet. If you don't need particularly recent information, you can try a book or a Web site.

Sometimes, you may want to use an exact quotation from a source in your paper. Quotations, or quotes, are someone's exact words. They are also the words that you have found in a book or other source. Place this type of text in quotation marks. Use quotes when the exact words are necessary for the passage.

Other times, you may choose to paraphrase the information. This means putting information in your own words. You can make information easier to understand this way. When you paraphrase, it's important to mention the source, or the writer you are paraphrasing, so that readers will know who wrote or said the words. Additionally, you will need to list your sources in a bibliography.

As you present information to the reader, you will need to arrange your facts, examples, and quotes in a way that makes sense. You already know about different ways texts are organized. Some passages will compare and contrast things or ideas. Some passages include information in the order in which events happen. Make sure to include transition words, such as *however, therefore, also, in addition, next, first,* and *finally*. Good writing flows smoothly from one paragraph to the next.

A graphic organizer is a good way to sort out your thoughts. Think about your topic sentence first. Then, think about details that will support the main idea. In the example below, the center of the web has the main idea. The surrounding ovals contain supporting details. Remember that the information in your graphic organizer can later change. The important thing is to organize your thoughts and notes before you begin writing.

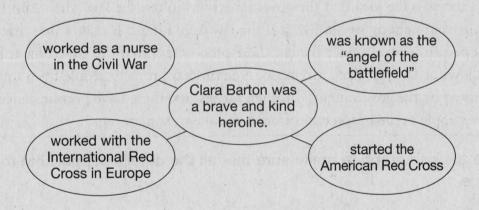

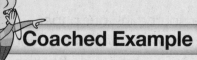

Coached Example

Read the following paragraphs. Then rewrite each one so that the topic sentence is clearer.

1. Skinks are a group of lizards that are like other animals, but not quite. Skinks are the largest of the lizard families with about 1,200 species. Skinks look like lizards, but most species have very short necks. They often have relatively small legs. Some skinks have no limbs at all. Skinks move more like snakes than lizards.

How can you rewrite the first sentence to make the main idea of the paragraph clearer?

_____

_____

_____

HINT   Remember, a topic sentence tells the central idea of a paragraph or passage. Look at the supporting details. What main idea do they support?

2. Due process is the idea that the government has to use the law fairly. And I am sure that nobody would like it if the law were unfair. It makes sure that every person is equal under the law. Due process says that the government has to follow the law just like citizens do. Due process protects people from unfair treatment by the government. Throughout history, there have been instances where people needed protection from someone or something.

Rewrite the paragraph to make sure that all the details support the topic sentence.

_____

_____

_____

_____

HINT   Reread the paragraph. What is the main idea of the paragraph? Which sentences do not belong in the paragraph?

Lesson Practice

Use the Writing Guide to help you understand the passage.

Writing Guide

What is the main idea of the passage?

Do the supporting details back up the main idea?

What is the main idea of paragraph 3?

Together and Equal

Imagine not being allowed to go to school. In the early 1950s, African American students were not allowed to go to certain schools in many states and cities. Two events helped change the education system and the United States: *Brown v. Board of Education* and the Little Rock Crisis.

Linda Brown, a third grader, had to walk six blocks to her school bus stop to ride to her segregated black school one mile away. Meanwhile, a white school was only seven blocks from her house. The Brown family went to court. They wanted to force the Board of Education of Topeka, Kansas, to allow Linda to attend a closer, all-white school.

On May 17, 1954, the Supreme Court decided the case of *Brown v. Board of Education*. The case challenged the "separate but equal" law. Under that law, African Americans were separated from whites in public places. African American students went to different schools from white students. The U.S. Supreme Court sided with the Brown family.

In September 1957, nine African American students wanted to attend Central High School in Little Rock, Arkansas. But there were many people there to stop them from going into the building. President Dwight D. Eisenhower sent troops to make sure the Little Rock Nine were allowed to go to school at Central High. Even so, many schools did not want to integrate, or allow black and white students to go to the same school.

How could paragraph 3 be made more informative?

_____

_____

_____

Plan Your Writing

Read the writing prompt, and then plan your response below.

There are inventions today that did not exist when your parents or grandparents were young. Some of those inventions are essential, and others are less important. But they have all changed modern life in some way. Think about something that was invented in the last hundred years. Write an essay on how that invention changed people's lives. Explain how life was then, how it is different today, and whether the result is positive or negative.

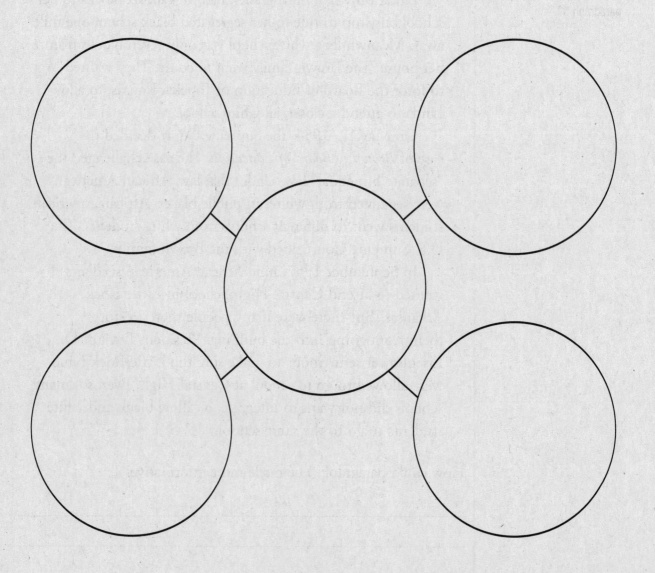

Write Your Response

Write your response on the pages provided.

_____

_____

_____

_____

_____

_____

_____

_____

_____

_____

_____

_____

_____

_____

_____

_____

_____

_____

_____

_____

Checklist for Informative/Explanatory Writing

Use the checklist below to help you do your best writing.

Does your essay

❏ have a clear and focused topic?

❏ have a topic sentence?

❏ have a logical structure?

❏ use precise language and terms that relate to the topic?

❏ use linking words and phrases to connect ideas?

❏ have a solid conclusion?

❏ have good spelling, capitalization, and punctuation?

❏ follow the rules for good grammar?

Use the Writing Guide to help you understand the passage.

Writing **Guide**

How do topic sentences help readers understand the information in an informative article?

How are all the details in the passage relevant to the topic?

What are the similarities and differences between the introduction and the conclusion?

The White House Vegetable Garden

Michelle Obama, First Lady of the United States, planted a vegetable garden on the south lawn of the White House. This is not the first garden ever planted on White House grounds; however, it is one of the most noteworthy.

Before Michelle Obama's Kitchen Garden, the most notable vegetable garden planted at the White House was the Victory Garden. That garden was planted by First Lady Eleanor Roosevelt during World War II. Roosevelt encouraged others in the United States to plant their own Victory Gardens. Home gardens allowed people to grow and produce their own fruit and vegetables during wartime, a time of food shortages.

One of the reasons that Michelle Obama planted a garden was to promote healthy eating for families and children. Her own family always had a very busy schedule. Before her family lived in the White House, she started noticing that they were eating out a lot and making poor food choices. Therefore, she decided that they needed to make changes in their diet. She said, "And the changes that we made were very simple. We added more fruits and vegetables to our plates."

The Kitchen Garden provides healthy food to many people. Fifty-five varieties of vegetables have been planted in the garden. In addition to being prepared for the Obama family meals, food from the garden is served to White House guests. It is also donated to local food kitchens that feed those needing a meal.

The vegetable garden at the White House serves a practical purpose, to feed the Obama family and their guests, but it also serves as a reminder to eat healthy. Simple choices, such as adding more fruits and vegetables to one's diet, can improve one's health.

Plan Your Writing

Read the writing prompt, and then plan your response below.

Use the information provided in the article "The White House Vegetable Garden," and what you already know, to write an informational essay about the importance of local or home vegetable gardens. Choose three or four details about the topic that can be developed into paragraphs. Be sure to include a strong topic sentence and concluding statement. Use headings if they help you to organize your ideas.

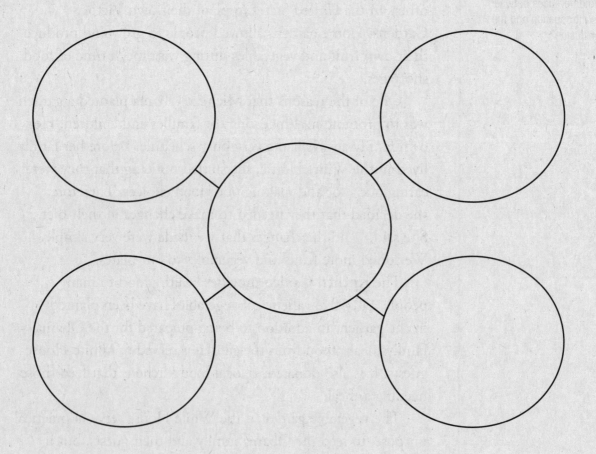

Write Your Response

Write your response on the pages provided.

_____

_____

_____

_____

_____

_____

_____

_____

_____

_____

_____

_____

_____

_____

_____

_____

_____

_____

_____

_____

_____

_____

_____

_____

_____

_____

_____

_____

18 Write Narratives

Getting the Idea

Narrative writing tells a story. All stories have some parts in common: characters, setting, and plot.

Each story includes at least one **character**. Authors can develop a character in several ways. You could begin by asking yourself what you want the reader to know about the character. What does the character look like? What would other characters think of this character?

The **setting** is the place and time in which a story takes place. The setting can depend on the story you're telling. For a ghost story, you might choose an old house at night. If it's an adventure story, you might choose an ancient mythical village.

A narrative must also have a plot. A **plot** is a series of events that depends on a conflict, or a problem the characters have. Every problem must be solved with a **resolution**. The resolution you choose for the conflict will affect the story's **theme**, or message.

After you have an idea about your plot, choose a point of view and narrator. **Point of view** is the position from which a story is told, and the **narrator** is the character who tells it. In a first-person story, the story is told by an *I*, while a third-person story is told about a *he*, a *she*, or even an *it*. If you want to surprise the reader in some way, a first-person narrator might be better. The *I* of the story is experiencing events for the first time, and so is the reader. If you want the reader to know something that the characters do not, the third-person point of view is a better choice.

Once you have started writing your story, you have to try to make it as interesting as possible. Begin by showing rather than telling. This means that you should try to show how it feels for someone to do an action, instead of just saying he or she did it.

Using the same words over and over can also make your writing dull. Use a variety of words when possible. Try thinking in more specific terms when you write. Instead of saying that someone sat down, think about how the character would sit. If it is a large, tired old man, for example, perhaps he *settled* into his chair. A small, energetic child might *leap* into her chair. Someone who is exhausted might *collapse* onto the sofa.

A good ending is hard to write, but a bad ending is hard to forgive. Often, writers get so involved in their plot and characters that they forget to work out an ending that would affect the reader. Try thinking about your story's end before you start writing. You do not have to have all the details, but you should have a basic idea. Is it a happy ending? A sad ending? You decide.

Figure out the plot, as well, before you get too involved in writing. The plot is your blueprint, or plan, for the story. You can use a graphic organizer to do this. Look at the flowchart below. The first box introduces a problem. The middle boxes show the plot events. The last box is the resolution: the problem has been solved. The story described below follows a logical sequence, or order, from beginning to end.

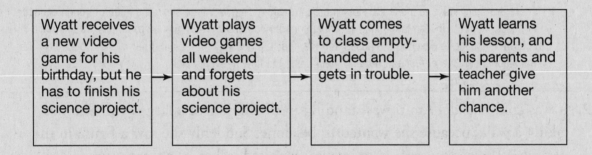

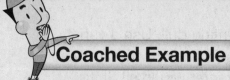

Coached Example

Read the following stories. Then rewrite each one so that they are more entertaining.

1. Summer had arrived. It was time, once again, for Christie to go on vacation with her parents. This year, they decided to rent a house on the coast instead of going camping. At first, Christie was bored because the only things her parents wanted to do were read books and sleep. But then she met a friend. They went swimming. Then they made sandcastles.

_____

_____

_____

_____

HINT There are many ways to make the story more interesting. One way is to show the action through dialogue or description rather than just telling what happened. Another way is to give more details. You can use colorful language to describe the house and the beach, as well as Christie and her friend. Notice how the transitional phrases *at first* and *but then* help make the flow of events clear.

2. It was cold outside. Amiri was standing in the middle of a large field. She was taking a walk, because she wanted to be alone. Suddenly she saw a figure in the distance. The person seemed to be wearing a red jacket. She wasn't sure who it was. Then the figure came closer. She saw it was her cousin Ahmad. She was relieved. She had thought it was going to be her little brother. She and Ahmad kept walking.

_____

_____

_____

_____

HINT In this story, you could tell about the field. How did it smell? What was growing there? Additionally, you could say where the field was. Was it near her house? Was she visiting someone? Then you might tell more about the figure approaching, giving more clothing details. You might also explain why Amiri was relieved it was not her little brother.

Lesson Practice

Use the Writing Guide to help you understand the passage.

Writing Guide

Is the conflict clear?

Does the author tell or show the action?

How could the author make the story more interesting?

All Even

Lionel and Wayne were best friends. Still, they always tried to outdo each other, even as children. As they grew older, they learned to appreciate each other's talents. During the school year, the boys were often too busy trying to get the highest test grades to play games. But when summer arrived, they competed constantly.

On the first day of summer, Lionel challenged Wayne to a game of checkers. Lionel easily beat Wayne in the first game, but Wayne wanted a rematch. Six hours later, the boys were tied. If Lionel's mother hadn't stopped the competition, the boys would have played through the night.

The next day, Wayne challenged Lionel to a game of basketball. Lionel gladly accepted, boasting about how he would make Wayne look like he had two left feet. Lionel took the lead early. However, Wayne had a few new tricks up his sleeve. Wayne spent extra time during the year watching his favorite basketball players and trying to imitate them. The boys had to call the game a draw when the sun set. Wayne talked all the way home about how he would have won if they had ten more minutes of daylight.

A few days later, Lionel decided that they should have a bike race. Wayne agreed and guaranteed that Lionel would be too busy eating his dust to finish. The boys started at the top of Blind Man's Cliff and stared down to the bottom of the hill.

Write a good ending for the story above.

_____

_____

_____

_____

Plan Your Writing

Read the writing prompt, and then plan your response below.

Suppose that Celia wakes up one Saturday morning to find she has been turned into an animal. Think about what animal she might become. Describe what happens to Celia on the day she discovers that she has been turned into an animal. Be sure to include descriptions of the setting.

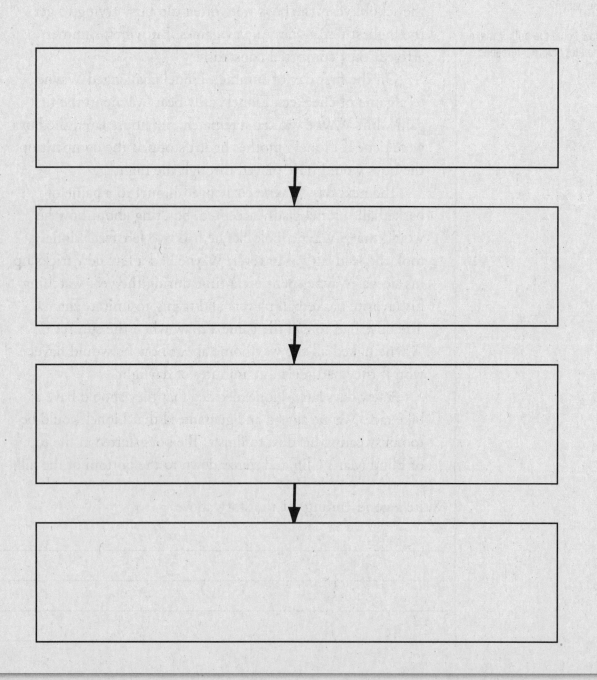

Write Your Response

Write your response on the pages provided.

_____

_____

_____

_____

_____

_____

_____

_____

_____

_____

_____

_____

_____

_____

_____

_____

_____

_____

_____

_____

_____

_____

_____

Checklist for Narrative Writing

Use the checklist below to help you do your best writing.

Does your story

❏ have a situation and characters?

❏ use dialogue and/or description to develop the story?

❏ have a clear plot with a logical series of events?

❏ use precise word choice?

❏ have a satisfying ending?

❏ have good spelling, capitalization, and punctuation?

❏ follow the rules for good grammar?

Use the Writing Guide to help you understand the passage.

Writing Guide

From what point of view does the author write the story? Is the point of view effective?

What are the plot events of the story? How does the author organize them?

Is the ending of the story satisfying? How might the story continue?

Campout at the Farm

The cousins prepared for their annual backyard campout at their grandparents' farm. The only difference this year was that no adults were allowed. In the past, aunts, uncles, cousins, and grandparents all joined in the fun. Everyone, young and old, helped to make the event a success by pitching tents, collecting firewood, preparing food, and cleaning up. Then they all played games, sang songs, and told stories.

This year, the cousins declared that they wanted the campout to include only themselves and no adults. The adults all grumbled, but they agreed. So, all six cousins started to set up the campsite behind the barn. Max and Mackenzie wrestled with the tents. Gabe and Audrey tripped through the woods. Kate and Blake struggled with the food.

By the time that camp was halfheartedly set up, the cousins were hot, sweaty, and crabby. Usually by this time, they were playing games and snacking on treats. This year, they sat together by the tents, but no one said a word.

When their stomachs started rumbling, Blake tried to make a campfire but had no luck. The cousins ate cold hot dogs for dinner. Max attempted to get a game of tag started, but no one was enthusiastic enough to play. Mackenzie and Kate climbed into the tent, only to have it fall on top of them.

Audrey and Gabe declared that the campout just wasn't the same this year. The cousins ran to the house, ready to plead with their parents and grandparents to join them. When they got back, all of the adults were sitting on the porch, patiently waiting for an invitation to the campout.

Plan Your Writing

Read the writing prompt, and then plan your response below.

In the passage, the author developed a plot around a group of cousins. Think about the details that the author used to create an interesting sequence of events. What else do you want to know about these characters? Write an original story that continues where the passage ended. In your story, be sure to use what you have learned about setting and characters as you tell what happens next. Use the graphic organizer to determine the order of the plot events that will introduce a new conflict and lead to the resolution of the conflict.

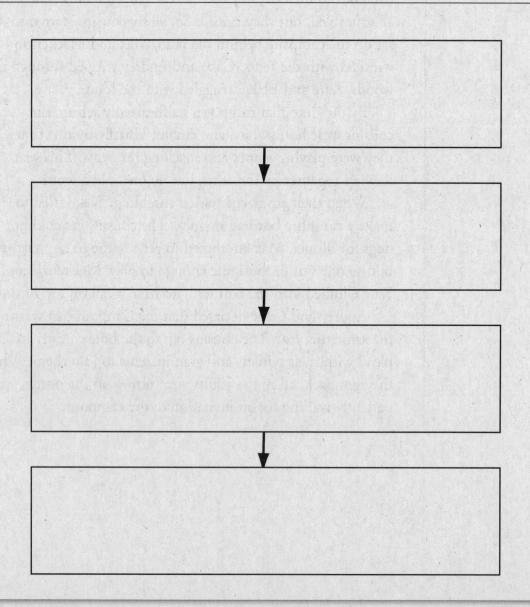

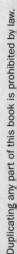

Write Your Response

Write your response on the pages provided.

_____

_____

_____

_____

_____

_____

_____

_____

_____

_____

_____

_____

_____

_____

_____

_____

_____

_____

_____

_____

_____

_____

_____

_____

_____

_____

_____

_____

_____

_____

_____

_____

_____

19 Respond to Literature

Getting the Idea

Literature includes written works such as novels, short stories, poems, and plays. For an assignment or during a test, you may be asked to respond to a work of literature by answering a short-answer question or writing a longer essay. This is your chance to express your ideas about and reactions to the text. For example, you may be asked to tell how the writer develops the plot of a story or to interpret the actions of one or more characters. When you **interpret** a character's thoughts, words or actions, you decide what they show about a character's personality. You may also be asked to compare elements in two stories or plays.

Be sure to read the prompt carefully. Underline the words in the prompt that tell you what is expected. Read the example below.

> Provide <u>two examples</u> that show where the story takes place. Use <u>details from the text</u> to support your answer.

This prompt is asking you to focus on the setting and **analyze**, or think more deeply about, the ways in which the author establishes it. Sometimes, a writer does not describe the setting directly. Instead, he or she will provide clues that help the reader figure it out. Read this response to the example prompt.

> The story takes place in a remote, wooded setting. The author uses examples to show this. For example, "As the students walked, they realized they hadn't seen another person in two hours." This detail shows that the students are very isolated. If the friends haven't seen anyone in two hours, most likely they are in a remote area. The author writes, "Surrounded by so many trees, it was dark." Trees suggest a forest.

The topic sentence of this response answers the prompt: Where does the story take place? The statement is supported with examples shown in quotation marks, which indicate that these are words taken directly from the story.

Whether you are writing a short answer or a long essay, it is important to organize your response. You need a clearly defined topic, supported by well-chosen details from the story. By using a graphic organizer and taking notes, you can develop stronger answers. Read the following prompt.

> Compare and contrast the two main characters, Sam and Alex. What do they have in common? In what ways are they different? Use evidence from the story to support your answer.

First, think about composing your topic sentence. For example, you may write: *The two main characters in the story, Sam and Alex, are brothers and share a few of the same character traits. But in many more ways, they are very different from each another.* Then identify the details from the story that you will use to support this idea. Details can include examples, anecdotes, descriptions, or quotations from the story. For example, the author may portray Sam as introverted or shy and Alex as extroverted or outgoing. The characters reveal their traits through specific actions and behaviors. A graphic organizer like the one below will help you organize your thoughts.

In this example, you may plan to write two supporting paragraphs about the boys' differences and one paragraph about what they have in common. Remember to include a strong conclusion. It should sum up the main points in your essay and let the reader know that you have addressed all parts of the prompt.

Character	Character Traits	Supporting Details
Sam	• introverted • intelligent • punctual	• stands to the side at a party • enrolled in honors classes • is always on time for everything
Alex	• extroverted • intelligent • clumsy	• tells jokes to a crowd • enrolled in honors classes • bumps into things often

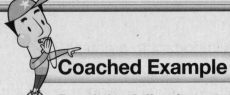

Coached Example

Read the following passage, and then answer the questions that follow.

> Matthew and Jason were inseparable; they never left each other's side until they had to go home from school. People always wondered why the two boys were friends. Matthew didn't talk much. Jason, on the other hand, loved to talk. He could talk from morning until night, and his mom said he even talked in his sleep. Matthew loved anything technical. Anytime something broke down in the neighborhood, it was sure to find its way to Matthew's garage. Jason wasn't into anything technical. He'd rather be doing something outside instead of spending time on a computer. But what people didn't know is that both boys loved taking things apart and trying to put them back together. When they were given something that didn't work, they would tinker with it until it was working again. They both loved a good challenge.

1. In what ways are Matthew and Jason similar? In what ways are the boys different? Provide examples from the passage.

    _____

    _____

    _____

    HINT Look for words and phrases that signal similarities and differences, such as *both*, *but*, and *on the other hand*.

2. What might the theme of this passage be?

    _____

    _____

    _____

    HINT Theme is the message that the writer wants to convey. The theme is often a lesson about life. Here, two boys share a friendship that may seem unlikely to other people. What theme does that suggest?

Lesson Practice

Use the Writing Guide to help you understand the passage.

Writing Guide

What words does the author use to describe Sydney as she wakes up?

How is Grandma described in paragraph 2? How does the author develop Grandma's personality in the passage?

What happens at the end of the passage? What new information about the characters do the last two paragraphs reveal?

Grandma and Sydney

"Rise and shine!" Grandma said as she opened the curtains.

Bright sunlight streamed onto Sydney's face. She groaned and burrowed deep under her covers.

"Time to get up! The garden is not going to plant itself."

Sydney grunted. Grandma was always too perky in the morning. Sydney knew Grandma had already gone for a walk, washed a load of laundry, and eaten a hearty breakfast of eggs, bacon, and hash browns.

Slowly, Sydney stumbled out of bed. It was no use to hide, because Grandma would continue to pester her until she got up.

At the table, Sydney ate her preferred breakfast of cereal and juice. She didn't say a word while Grandma babbled on and on about what she had seen on her walk and the most interesting news of the day. Once in a while, Sydney mumbled a response, but mostly she just listened and nodded.

The instant that Sydney finished the last mouthful of cereal, Grandma whisked her outside to start the planting. Grandma was meticulous about her gardens. The rows of flowers and vegetables needed to be planted in straight lines, like little toy soldiers. Sydney liked it that way, too.

The combination of the warm sun and the damp earth filled Sydney with energy. She became more animated and energetic as the morning progressed. She chattered away, asking Grandma about the news and whom she had seen on her morning walk.

Grandma and Sydney worked hard until noon, when they stopped for lunch. After eating, they retired to the living room. Sydney played games on the computer while Grandma snored, taking her afternoon nap.

Plan Your Writing

Read the writing prompt, and then plan your response below.

Grandma and Sydney are different and alike in many ways. Use the graphic organizer below to show their similarities and differences. Write the characters' names in the first column. Write the character traits you identify for each character in the second column. In the last column, list a detail from the passage that supports why you chose that particular character trait. Then, using your graphic organizer and evidence from the story, write an essay comparing and contrasting the two characters.

Character	Character Traits	Supporting Details

Write Your Response

Write your response on the pages provided.

_____
_____
_____
_____
_____
_____
_____
_____
_____
_____
_____
_____
_____
_____
_____
_____
_____
_____
_____
_____
_____
_____
_____
_____
_____

Checklist for Responding to Literature

Use the checklist below to help you do your best writing.

Does your response

❏ include a topic sentence that states your thesis, or main idea?

❏ have a logical organization, with linking words to connect paragraphs?

❏ answer the prompt completely by comparing *and* contrasting?

❏ include text evidence that supports your response?

❏ include details about characters, setting, or plot related to your response?

❏ have a concluding statement that sums up your response?

❏ express your ideas and reactions in your own words?

❏ use a formal and respectful tone?

❏ have good spelling, capitalization, and punctuation?

❏ follow the rules for good grammar?

Use the Writing Guides to help you understand the passages.

Real Letters

Writing Guide

How does Colin feel about receiving letters from his grandma?

What do the letters represent to Colin?

Why doesn't he share the letters with his dad?

Colin waited patiently by the mailbox. The mail carrier came every day at the same time to deliver the mail to his apartment building. She was due to arrive any minute.

At exactly four o'clock, she opened the door to his building, walked into the mailroom, and began to stuff mail into each person's mailbox. Colin never asked for his mail while she was there; he always waited until she was gone to check his mailbox.

As soon as she left, he hurried to open his mailbox. Inside was a letter from his grandma. Hastily, he ripped the envelope open and read the news from home. Her letters felt like a direct connection to her and Ireland.

Just two months earlier, Colin and his father had moved to the United States because his father had received a promotion. Colin didn't want to move, but he didn't have a choice. He wrote to his grandma every day—real letters that had stamps on them and got mailed in the mailbox. His grandmother said she had no time for computers. Besides, it was nice getting something special in the mail that he could hold and tuck away to take out when he was having a bad day.

He didn't share his grandma's letters with his dad. They were something special that he shared with his grandma. He could tell his grandma everything. Dad didn't like to hear about how the kids at school made fun of Colin's accent or how he was having a little trouble making friends. Dad only wanted to hear the positive things, and Colin was having a hard time coming up with anything positive lately.

But his grandma always seemed to understand. He told her everything. Her replies gave him the courage to look for the positives.

What is so important about the letter?

What does the letter represent to Joe?

How does Joe's family respond to the news in the letter?

What detail in the letter shows that the passage was written a long time ago?

excerpted and adapted from

Baseball Joe on the Giants

by Lester Chadwick

Joe was returning from the post office, where he had stopped for the mail. He carried in his hand a big, official-looking letter that bore the name of the New York Baseball Club.

He felt sure that it contained the contract. But eager as he was to know what it contained, he restrained himself until he reached home, so that all could read it together.

"Here it is at last!" he shouted, as he burst into the living room, waving the envelope.

"Oh, I'm so glad!" said his mom.

"Open it up, open it up!" pleaded his sister Clara.

Into the laughing group came Mr. Matson.

"What's all the noise about?" he asked.

"Oh, Dad!" cried Clara. "It's the letter from the New York Club."

"Perhaps it's just a note telling me that, after thinking it over, they don't want me after all," teased Joe.

"Well, now that we're all here, suppose you settle the question by reading it," suggested Mrs. Matson.

There was a moment of breathless suspense. Joe's hand was not quite steady as he tore open the envelope. There was a big formal letter inside.

Joe cleared his throat and began to read. The New York Club agreed to contract Joseph Matson for three years to play baseball for their team and to pay the sum of four thousand five hundred dollars a year!

Joe looked up at this point to see three shining pairs of eyes fixed upon him. The precious document was read and reread and discussed at length. It is safe to say that in all of Riverside that night, there was no happier family!

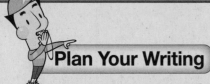

Plan Your Writing

Read the writing prompt, and then plan your response below.

In the two passages that you read, the main characters both receive important letters in the mail. Use the graphic organizer below to compare and contrast Joe's and Colin's reactions to the letters and what the letters mean to them. Write the characters' names in the first column. Write the characters' reactions in the second column. In the last column, list a detail from the passage that supports why you chose that particular reaction. Then, using your graphic organizer and evidence from the stories, write an essay comparing and contrasting the two characters' reactions. Use specific examples from the text to support your essay.

Character	Reaction	Supporting Details

Write Your Response

Write your response on the pages provided.

_____

_____

_____

_____

_____

_____

_____

_____

_____

_____

_____

_____

_____

_____

_____

_____

_____

_____

_____

_____

_____

_____

_____

_____

_____

_____

Checklist for Responding to Literature

Use the checklist below to help you do your best writing.

Does your response

❏ include a topic sentence that states your thesis, or main idea?

❏ have a logical organization, with linking words to connect paragraphs?

❏ answer the prompt completely by comparing *and* contrasting?

❏ include text evidence that supports your response?

❏ include details about characters, setting, or plot related to your response?

❏ have a concluding statement that sums up your response?

❏ express your ideas and reactions, in your own words?

❏ use a formal and respectful tone?

❏ have good spelling, capitalization, and punctuation?

❏ follow the rules for good grammar?

20 Respond to Informational Text

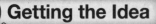

Getting the Idea

Informational text is writing that explains something and communicates facts about it. Being able to write an intelligent response to an informational text is an important skill to have. Whether the response is in the form of a short answer or a longer essay, we all need to be able to think about information and form an opinion about it. What is the author trying to say? Are the author's ideas convincing?

Before responding, analyze the text. Is it an opinion piece in which the author expresses a personal **point of view**, or is it an objective informational article? Knowing the difference will help you evaluate the writing. Can you identify the reasons and evidence that the author provides? If so, do those reasons and evidence clearly support the author's point of view?

Read and reread the prompt. Highlight or underline what it is asking. Decide exactly what is being asked and is expected from you in your response. You don't want to write a long essay only to realize that you didn't address all parts of the question. Read the prompt below.

> How does the writer build an argument in favor of wearing seatbelts while riding in any vehicle? Provide facts included in the article to support your response.

Notice that the prompt asks for *facts* from the article, not opinions. So, if the passage includes opinions, then you have to distinguish the facts from the opinions. Also, the prompt asked for facts *from the text*. You may know additional facts about seatbelts or you may have your own opinions about their use; neither of these is needed, or wanted, according to this prompt.

Responses to informational texts may require you to do a lot of thinking and reasoning before you actually start to write. Your essay should look like the informational texts that you often read. Include an introduction and a conclusion, as well as supporting paragraphs with topic sentences and supporting details. Cite details, examples, and quotations from the article to strengthen your response. These provide **evidence**, or proof, that shows how and why you formed your conclusion.

If you are asked to compare more than one text, make sure to distinguish between the texts that you quote. Read the following short response.

Many teachers have differing opinions about the assigning of homework. According to Mr. Parker, "Homework teaches responsibility. Students should have at least thirty minutes of homework every night." However, the second opinion piece that we read by Mrs. Evans was dramatically different. According to her, "Students work hard in school all day. Their evening hours should be devoted to family and recreation."

Each quote is credited to its specific author. This makes it easy for the reader to know where you obtained your evidence.

Suppose you read an article about ice hockey. Here is a prompt relating to it.

Identify the details that the author uses to support the main idea that hockey is a physically intense, fast-paced sport.

Though this prompt is short, it requires a number of things for you to do. First, confirm the main idea. Next, identify the details that the author uses to support the main idea. By highlighting, underlining, or taking notes before you start writing, you can identify the important information for your response. Then you can organize your ideas and evidence by using a graphic organizer. Look at the graphic organizer below.

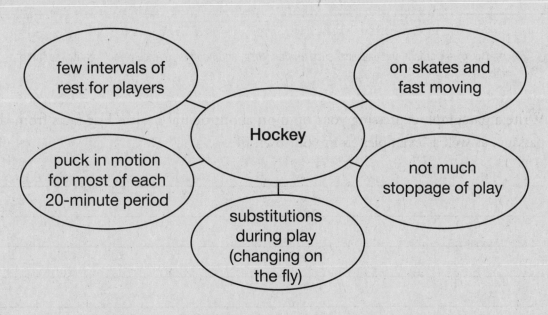

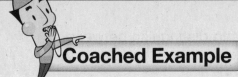

Coached Example

Read the following passage, and then answer the questions that follow.

Cavities can be prevented by practicing good dental health. Some of the most important things you can do to prevent cavities can be done right in your own home. First, brush your teeth at least twice a day. Brush after breakfast and before bed. Then, floss at least once a day. Flossing removes all the food particles that get caught between teeth or in the gums. Leftover food causes cavities and bad breath! Another preventative measure is to schedule dental visits every six months. The staff will clean your teeth and remove any plaque buildup that you may have.

1. What are three things you can do to prevent cavities? Use specific examples from the passage in your answer.

   _____
   _____
   _____

   HINT Look for clue words in the passage, such as *first*, *then*, and *another*, that help you identify the three activities.

2. Write a paragraph expressing your opinion about dental health. Use facts from the passage, as well as examples from your own life.

   _____
   _____
   _____
   _____
   _____

   HINT Think about your personal experience. For example, maybe you brushed your teeth regularly twice a day, every day, and still got six cavities. You may have a different opinion than someone who never gets cavities without brushing regularly.

Lesson Practice

Use the Writing Guide to help you understand the passage.

Writing Guide

Why do people grow extra food in their garden?

What two types of processes for preserving food are described?

What are the pros and cons of each process?

What is the author's purpose in writing this informational text?

Fresh Fruits and Vegetables All Year Long

Many gardeners grow an abundance of fruits and vegetables each season. They grow more than they can possibly eat, so they have extra produce to freeze or to can. This allows them to eat food from their garden even during the most frigid months of winter. So is it better to freeze or to can? Experts say it all depends on your preferences for taste, as well as availability of time and space.

Canning food is typically a more time-consuming process. It requires more specific equipment than freezing. Although this process is called canning, people usually use glass jars, not cans, to store their food this way. For safety, you need to follow specific directions to make sure that the food is cooked properly. This ensures that bacteria don't grow in the food and make it unsafe to eat. After canning, store the jars in a cool, dark space. Many foods can be canned. Pickles, jams, jellies, salsa, spaghetti sauces, peaches, and applesauce are all commonly canned items.

Freezing is typically a faster process than canning. However, frozen food can take up valuable space in a freezer. Usually you just boil the food for a short time, give it a "bath" in ice water, put it in a freezer bag, and place the bag in the freezer. Blueberries, strawberries, onions, green beans, peas, and corn are examples of foods that can be frozen whole. They don't need to be mashed or cut up before storage. Some foods, such as squash and eggplant, are preserved better when frozen rather than canned.

Canning or freezing the food you grow in your garden is an excellent way to have delicious fruits and vegetables all year long.

Read the writing prompt, and then plan your response below.

> The author explains two ways that people preserve fruits and vegetables. Use information from the passage to write an essay about preserving food. Before writing, use the web below to organize your thoughts and ideas. This will help you to write a well-organized essay.

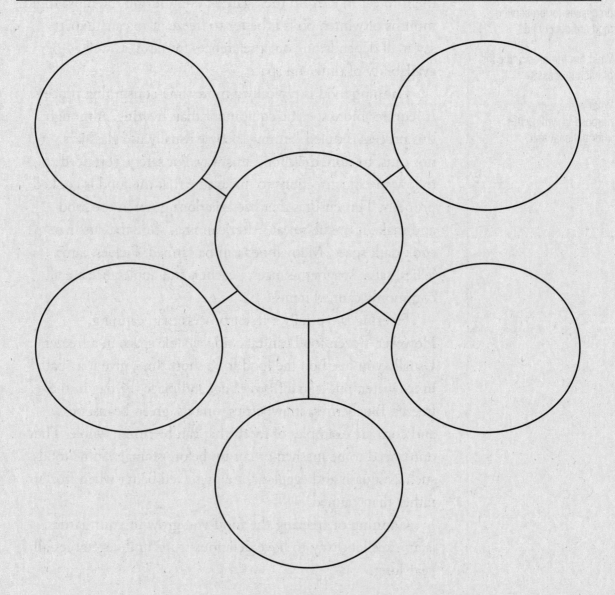

Write Your Response

Write your response on the pages provided.

_____

_____

_____

_____

_____

_____

_____

_____

_____

_____

_____

_____

_____

_____

_____

_____

_____

_____

_____

_____

_____

_____

_____

_____

Checklist for Responding to Informational Texts

Use the checklist below to help you do your best writing.

Does your response

❏ answer the prompt completely?

❏ state the writer's ideas or opinions?

❏ include text details that support the writer's ideas or opinions?

❏ include text evidence that supports your response?

❏ have a concluding statement that sums up your response?

❏ use a formal and respectful tone?

❏ have good spelling, capitalization, and punctuation?

❏ follow the rules for good grammar?

Use the Writing Guides to help you understand the passages.

Writing Guide

What is the difference between good bacteria and bad bacteria?

What is the purpose of an antibiotic?

What are probiotics, and how are they helpful to your body's health?

Good Bacteria and Bad Bacteria

How can introducing bacteria or microorganisms into your body be good for you? Not all bacteria are harmful; some are actually good for you and may help you stay healthy. Probiotics, types of good bacteria, are live cultures that can be included in your diet to help aid in digestion and keep your body's health in balance.

If you've ever taken a prescription antibiotic for an illness, you may have experienced such unpleasant symptoms as gas, diarrhea, and cramping. These symptoms may not be caused by your illness; instead, they may be a side effect of taking the antibiotic.

The antibiotic that your doctor prescribed killed the bad bacteria that caused your illness. This was good. Unfortunately, the antibiotic doesn't know the difference between good bacteria and bad bacteria. So, it may destroy some of the good bacteria, too.

The good bacteria, bacteria you always have in your body, help keep systems in your body working properly. So, when when good bacteria are killed, it may prevent systems from working correctly, leading to some unpleasant effects.

One way that people try to balance the effects of antibiotics is to introduce probiotics into their diet. Yogurt is probably the most well-known food that contains probiotics.

Some people eat yogurt all the time, not just when they are taking an antibiotic. They know that in addition to yogurt's nutritional benefits, it also introduces live cultures into their body. This may help them digest food properly.

Why does the author believe that walking is a better exercise than running?

What type of writing is this passage: narrative, opinion, or informative?

Why does knowing the type of passage help in analyzing the text?

Walking Is the Better Exercise

The great debate in our household is whether running or walking is the better exercise to keep you healthy and active. I wholeheartedly believe that walking is the better alternative.

Walking is an exercise you can do anywhere and anytime. If you are at a mall, you will often see people speed-walking around the perimeter of the stores. They do this during the coldest winter months or the hottest summer months. They can do this on a Saturday when the mall is packed with people. However, you don't see people running laps in a mall on a Saturday. They can't; it is too dangerous. You'd see people crashing into each other. Runners would be bumping into people, and no one would want to go shopping anymore. So, during the coldest months when sidewalks are covered in ice and during heat waves when being outdoors is unhealthy, a person can walk in a mall and get exercise.

Walking is better for your joints than running. Many runners experience pain in their knees, hips, spine, and ankles. The force of your body weight on your joints as you run on hard pavement causes your joints to wear out faster than if you walk. Walkers, on the other hand, don't have the same pressure and wear on their joints. That's because the force of your body weight does not bear down on your joints very much with every step. It's just a little easier on your joints when you walk.

I prefer walking over running. I can exercise virtually anywhere and at any time, and I'm not doing great damage to my joints with every step.

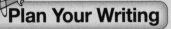

Plan Your Writing

Read the writing prompt, and then plan your response below.

Each passage, "Good Bacteria and Bad Bacteria" and "Walking Is the Better Exercise," addresses an aspect of health and staying healthy. Use information from both passages to write an essay about taking personal responsibility for your health and the ways you can stay healthy.

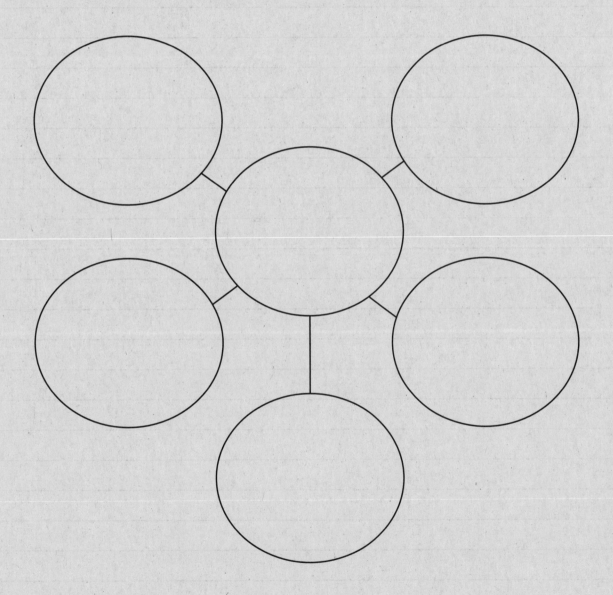

Write Your Response

Write your response on the pages provided.

_____

_____

_____

_____

_____

_____

_____

_____

_____

_____

_____

_____

_____

_____

_____

_____

_____

_____

_____

_____

_____

_____

_____

_____

_____

Checklist for Responding to Informational Texts

Use the checklist below to help you do your best writing.

Does your response

❏ answer the prompt completely?

❏ have a logical organization?

❏ state the writer's ideas or opinions accurately?

❏ include text details that support the writer's ideas or opinions?

❏ include text evidence that supports your response?

❏ have a concluding statement that sums up your response?

❏ use a formal and respectful tone?

❏ have good spelling, capitalization, and punctuation?

❏ follow the rules for good grammar?

21 Revising, Editing, and Publishing

Getting the Idea

A writer does not usually hand in his or her first attempt at writing. A **draft** is one of the first versions of a writer's work. A writer may make more than one draft before he or she is ready to hand in the work. In the first attempt you make to write a paper, your goal is to list the information you want to provide. Because you are focusing on getting the information down on paper, you are likely to make errors in spelling, grammar, and punctuation. It is also common for a first draft to include errors in clarity, meaning that what you have written is not exactly what you meant to say. After you have finished your first draft, you need to review, evaluate, and revise it.

A writer can revise a draft to make it better. When you **revise**, you read your draft carefully and make improvements. If you're writing an argument, you might switch paragraphs so that your strongest supporting point comes first. If you're writing a story, you might change the order of events to increase suspense. You might also come across a point about which you have more to say. Maybe there is an additional detail you want to add, or maybe you want to further justify or describe something. When you have more to say, you will want to add a sentence or several sentences. When you do this, be sure to read the paragraph completely first. Then insert the new sentence, or sentences, where you feel they make the most sense. In some cases, you might take out a sentence, if you feel it gives unnecessary information.

You might also want to choose a better word to express your idea. Remember, you are familiar with your topic, but your readers may not be. So clarity is very important. If you're writing about geology, for instance, you might want to say *quartz* instead of *rock*, or *trilobite* instead of *fossil*. Ask another classmate or your teacher to read your draft. Their feedback can help you decide what needs to be revised.

Editing is the process of preparing your paper for its final draft. This means that when you edit, you change the way in which you present information, to help ensure clarity.

Proofreading is a basic part of editing. **Proofreading** is the process of reading your writing and looking for errors in spelling, capitalization, and punctuation. Here are some pointers that will help you as you proofread:

Be careful not to confuse *it's* and *its*. *It's* is the contraction for *it is*. *Its* is the possessive form of *it*.

> Incorrect: Its awfully hot outside, for September.

> Correct: It's awfully hot outside, for September.

> Incorrect: The dog chased it's tail for a while and then bit my leg.

> Correct: The dog chased its tail for a while and then bit my leg.

Don't confuse *their, they're,* and *there*. *Their* is the possessive of *they*. *They're* is the contraction for *they are*. *There* is a pronoun used to indicate a specific place.

> Incorrect: There leaving they're backpacks their, but they'll be back for them later.

> Correct: They're leaving their backpacks there, but they'll be back for them later.

Be sure that sentences end with the proper punctuation mark.

> Incorrect: Do you know the way to Fernando's Hideaway!

> Correct: Do you know the way to Fernando's Hideaway?

Editing also involves checking for mistakes in grammar or sentence structure. You might, for instance, check for subject-verb agreement. A singular subject must be followed by a singular form of a verb.

> Incorrect: He go to the same restaurant for breakfast every morning.

> Correct: He goes to the same restaurant for breakfast every morning.

You should also avoid run-on sentences. These should be broken up into smaller sentences, or they should be shortened with conjunctions.

> Incorrect: We went to the mall and we went to the movies and we went to the zoo.

> Correct: We went to the mall, the movies, and the zoo.

Thinking It Through

Read the following paragraph, and then answer the questions that follow.

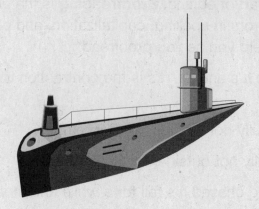

    A submarine is a vessel, or ship, that can go underwater. Submarines are called "subs" for short. The words *submarine, sandwiches,* and *substitute* are also sometimes shortened to *sub*. Militaries and scientists use submarines to travel deep under the ocean. The *Turtle* was the first submarine used in combat. David Bushnell designed it to sink British ships during the American Revolutionary War. David Bushnell also designed other weapons.

Which details do NOT belong in the paragraph? Why?

_____

_____

_____

_____

 Reread the paragraph. Look for details that have nothing to do with the rest of the paragraph. Remember, all details should support the main idea.

 Discuss your answers with a partner. Do you both agree on what the main idea of the paragraph is?

Coached Example

Read the passage and answer the questions.

(1) Elizabeth Coleman, later known as Bessie Coleman, was a famous African American aviation pioneer born on January 26, 1893, in Texas. (2) As a child, she was very good in math. (3) When she grew older, she became fascinated by aviation. (4) However, it was hard for her to get into aviation school because many of these schools did not accept African Americans. (5) There were a lot of aviation schools at that time. (6) When she was twenty-seven, she started aviation training in France. (7) She got her pilot's license in 1921. (8) She was the first woman to get this license. (9) She became an expert stunt flier and parachutist. (10) In 1921, she became the first African American woman to make a public flight. (11) She became a very popular stunt flier in America, where they're weren't many female fliers. (12) Sadly, Coleman died in a plane crash in 1926.

---

1. Which is the correct way to write sentence 11?

    A. She became a very popular stunt flier in America, where their weren't many female fliers.

    B. She became a very popular stunt flier in America, where there weren't many female fliers.

    C. She became a very popular stunt flier in America, where there aren't many female fliers.

    D. She became a very popular stunt flier in America, where they're werent many female fliers.

    HINT Watch out for words that sound alike but are spelled differently.

2. Which sentence in the passage is unnecessary?

    A. sentence 5

    B. sentence 6

    C. sentence 7

    D. sentence 9

    HINT Look for sentences that do not have a clear connection to the main idea of the passage.

Lesson Practice

Use the Reading Guide to help you understand the passage.

Reading Guide

Do all of the details support the main idea?

Are all the sentences in the correct order?

As you read the passage, try to find sentences that do not help support the main idea.

Poison Frogs

Poison frogs are tiny frogs found in warm Central and South American rain forests. Rain forests are forests that receive over eighty inches of rainfall per year. Poison frogs are brightly colored in shades of red, orange, yellow, blue, green, and black. The bright coloring helps to protect the frog by warning other animals.

We also call these frogs "poison dart" frogs. In South America, the Choco Indians coat the tips of hunting darts with their poison. They get the poison from the frogs' skin. Next, the hunters dip their blow darts in the skin secretions. Blowguns are used by different cultures in South America and Asia. First, the Indians pick the frogs up with waxy leaves because the skin is toxic. One small drop is enough to kill a mammal or a bird. A single golden poison frog can supply enough poison for thirty to fifty darts.

The poisons in these tiny frogs come from the ants, termites, centipedes, and tiny beetles they eat. Then the toxins are collected in glands in the frog's skin. Frogs born at zoos eat different food from the frogs in the wild, so they aren't poisonous. When the frog eats the bugs, it gets their poison. Frogs taken from the wild lose much of their poison when fed regular food.

Most types of frog species are most active at night, but poison frogs are more active in daylight. Animals see their colors and avoid them.

Answer the following questions.

1. Which sentence does NOT belong in paragraph 1?

    A. "Poison frogs are tiny frogs found in warm Central and South American rain forests."

    B. "Rain forests are forests that receive over eighty inches of rainfall per year."

    C. "Poison frogs are brightly colored in shades of red, orange, yellow, blue, green, and black."

    D. "The bright coloring helps to protect the frog by warning other animals."

2. Which would be the BEST detail to add to paragraph 1?

    A. the size and weight of poison frogs

    B. the names of rain forests

    C. the other kinds of animals in the rain forest

    D. what poison frogs eat

3. Which sentence does NOT belong in paragraph 2?

    A. "We also call these frogs 'poison dart' frogs."

    B. "Next, the hunters dip their blow darts in the skin secretions."

    C. "Blowguns are used by different cultures in South America and Asia."

    D. "One small drop is enough to kill a mammal or a bird."

4. Which would be the BEST detail to add to paragraph 3?

    A. where the poison frog gets its poison

    B. what other animals live in the zoo

    C. why the poison frogs hatched at the zoo aren't poisonous

    D. the diet of poison frogs in zoos

5. Which sentences are in the wrong order in paragraphs 2 and 3?

    _____

    _____

    _____

    _____

The following questions do not relate to a passage.

6. Look for errors in spelling, capitalization, and punctuation. Choose all of the sentences that are correctly written. There is more than one correct choice listed below.

    A. This spring in Minnesota their was snow.

    B. Its really hot walking on the sand at the beach.

    C. The Brother and Sister slid down the slide at the park.

    D. We ate dinner at Pablo's Pizza Palace to celebrate my mom's birthday.

    E. Her name was Mackenzie, and she went to Round Lake Elementary School.

    F. Do you understand the directions for how to complete the test.

---

7. The following paragraph is from the first draft that a student wrote about Sally Ride. Read the paragraph. Then rewrite it, revising it to correct errors in spelling, grammar, and punctuation.

    Sally attended stanford university and studied physics and English. In 1978 she answered a advertisement in a school newspaper? NASA were recruiting women to become part of there astronaut program. She was one of six women chosen among thousands of applicants.

    _____

    _____

    _____

    _____

    _____

    _____

    _____

    _____

    _____

    _____

8. Read the following paragraph from a student's article about Indian festivals.

> **In India, Holi is a festival that honors spring and the color it brings. People gather to eat special foods. Diwali is another festival in India. Holi means "the festival of color." People celebrate by throwing powdered colors, "coloring" friends and family!**

Underline the sentence that is unnecessary in this paragraph and should be deleted or moved to another paragraph.

---

9. Read the following paragraph from a student's article about Native Americans. Then rewrite the paragraph, arranging the sentences in the correct order.

> **Native Americans traveled by canoe, carving each canoe by hand from large trees. They started a fire and allowed the inside of the log to burn to soften the wood. Then they used the steam to soften the wood. Then they used a tool to make the log hollow. Fire was a valuable tool back then. To further shape the canoe, they heated water over a fire. But how did they carve logs without the tools of today?**

_____

_____

_____

_____

_____

_____

_____

_____

_____

_____

_____

22 Research and Resources

Getting the Idea

Finding facts and other information in books, encyclopedias, and newspapers is called **research**. The materials where you find information are called **resources**. You can also use digital resources, such as Web sites and online encyclopedias. Writing often requires research. If you are writing a narrative set in colonial times, you might research how people talked and dressed in that period to make your story more realistic. If you are writing an opinion piece about a landmark that is being torn down, you might find out about the history of the landmark. If you were writing an informational paper about the life of a famous artist, you'd find biographical information to put in the paper.

When you are researching your topic, you should never rely on one source for all of your information. That source may not have the most current information. It may also be unreliable. Use at least two reference sources. Make sure the references are trustworthy. You don't want to put opinions or incomplete facts in a research paper.

As you know, when you read books and passages, you find lots of important and useful information. To help yourself remember key ideas and facts, you can take notes. When you take notes, don't try to write down everything from the passage. Notes should include important concepts, or ideas. Ask yourself, "What is this passage mainly about?" or "What is this paragraph mainly about?" If the passage explains how to do or make something, take notes on the steps in the process. Remember to **paraphrase** the information, or express it in your own words.

Before you write, organize your notes. As you learned, webs can be used to sort notes and ideas by importance. Start with the topic in the center. Then branch out to the topic's main ideas. Draw more branches to add supporting details. For informational writing, ask *who, what, where, when, how*, and *why* questions to fill the web. For persuasive writing, each part of the web will be a reason that supports your opinion.

An outline is another way to help you get organized. An **outline** lists your ideas in the order you plan to write about them. An outline will help to keep track of main ideas and facts that have been gathered. Each main idea will be a heading. Put supporting details under each main idea and place smaller details under each supporting detail. An outline can look something like this:

I. Photography

   A. History

      1. The first black-and-white photograph was taken in 1826.

      2. Color photography was made available to the public in 1907.

        a. Instant color film was invented in 1963.

        b. Digital cameras are popular today.

   B. Uses of Photography

      1. People keep pictures of family members in photo albums.

      2. Museums often have artistic photographs in their exhibitions.

When you are doing research, you need to keep track of all the resources you use in your writing. A **bibliography** is a listing of the resources used for a written project. Here are some sample bibliographic entries:

A Book by a Single Author
Morris, Pat. *Giraffe Habitats*. Denver, Colorado: Long Neck, 2009.
   (Author)   (Title of work)   (City)   (Publisher)   (Year)

A Book by More Than One Author
Bock, Jan, and Kim Chen. *Your Health*. Athens, Georgia: Blue Books, 2003.
     (Authors)   (Title of Work)   (City)   (Publisher)   (Year)

A Magazine Article
Lederer, Kim. "Our World." <u>Geology Today</u> 23 July 2008: 138–56.
   (Author)   (Title of article)   (Name of publication) (Date of issue) (Page numbers)

Thinking It Through

Read the following bibliography, and then answer the question that follows.

Little, Clyde, and Omar Smith. *Frank Lloyd Wright's Influence*. Baltimore: Big Little Press, 2007.

McGuire, Shawn. *Frank Lloyd Wright*. San Francisco: Organic California Publishing, 2004.

Wolff, Katherine. "The Houses of Frank Lloyd Wright." <u>Houses Monthly</u> February 2008: 135–148.

Based on the bibliography, what is the topic of the research report?

_____

_____

_____

_____

HINT   Reread the entries. What do they have in common?

 DISCUSS   Do some research in the library about a topic you are interested in. Choose two sources, and write bibliography entries for them like the ones you learned about in this lesson. Share your bibliography in a group.

Coached Example

Read the passage and answer the questions.

A volcano is a kind of mountain. An opening inside it stretches far beneath Earth's surface. At the bottom of that opening is a pool of liquid, which is actually melted rock. Pressure sometimes builds up at that depth. When the pressure is strong enough, it may push gas and rock through the opening in an eruption. Eruptions can have various results. They can cause mudslides, floods, avalanches, earthquakes, and other natural disasters.

The most active volcanoes in the United States are found in Hawaii and Alaska. However, they may also be found in California, Oregon, Montana, or Washington. Mount St. Helens, in Washington, erupted on May 18, 1980, killing fifty-eight people and causing over a billion dollars in property damage. The area within twenty miles of a volcano is considered highly dangerous.

1. Take notes on paragraph 1.

_____

_____

_____

_____

HINT What is the paragraph mainly about?

2. Take notes on paragraph 2.

_____

_____

_____

_____

HINT Are there any important dates, events, or facts that you should take notes on?

Lesson Practice

Use the Reading Guide to help you understand the passage.

Reading Guide

What is paragraph 2 mainly about?

What resources would you use to research John Wilkes Booth?

What headings would you use to make an outline for this passage?

Abraham Lincoln

Abraham Lincoln was the 16th president of the United States. He was elected president twice, in 1860 and 1864. Although he was born in Kentucky, he spent most of his life in Illinois. He was a lawyer, a state legislator in Illinois, and a representative in Congress for the state of Illinois.

Lincoln did not want slavery to spread to new states and territories. Some states wanted slavery to be more common, though. Before the 1860 election, South Carolina's governor said that if Abraham Lincoln won the election, the state would leave the Union. When Lincoln won, South Carolina seceded, or withdrew from the Union.

Before Lincoln began serving as president, six other states seceded. Over the next year, four other Southern states followed. Together these Southern states formed the Confederate States of America. Lincoln stated in his first inaugural speech, given in March 1861, that no state could lawfully withdraw from the Union. Shortly after the secession, the Civil War began.

On the night of April 14, 1865, actor John Wilkes Booth, who agreed with the Confederates, shot Lincoln. Having led his country through one of its worst wars, Lincoln died early the next morning. The Confederates had surrendered in Appomattox Court House just five days before.

Bibliography

The Life of Abraham Lincoln, Geoffrey O'Byrne. Famous Lives Publishing in Atlanta, GA. 2004.

Answer the following questions.

1. Which resource would NOT be helpful when researching the life of Abraham Lincoln?

   A. a textbook

   B. an encyclopedia

   C. a Web site

   D. a current newspaper

2. What is paragraph 1 MAINLY about?

   A. the Civil War

   B. Abraham Lincoln

   C. Illinois

   D. John Wilkes Booth

3. What is paragraph 3 MAINLY about?

   A. the Civil War

   B. Abraham Lincoln

   C. South Carolina

   D. states seceding

4. Which heading would NOT be in an outline used for this passage?

   A. Appomattox Court House

   B. States Seceding

   C. Last Days of Lincoln

   D. Early Life of Lincoln

5. Rewrite the bibliography entry, correcting any errors.

   _____

   _____

   _____

   _____

   _____

The following questions do not relate to a passage.

6. You are writing an informational text about NASA's mission to study the planet Saturn. Choose all of the resources that would be appropriate for your research. There is more than one correct choice listed below.

   A. letter in the opinion section of the newspaper

   B. newspaper article about the mission to space

   C. encyclopedia article about the history of NASA

   D. science textbook about NASA's first trip to space

   E. dictionary to find the pronunciation of the names of the planets

   F. NASA Web site that explains the mission to Saturn

---

7. Below is the bibliography from a student's report about the planet Saturn. He listed three books that he used to research the topic.

Bibliography	Simon, Seymour. *Saturn*. New York, New York: HarperCollins, 1988.
	Nicole Mortillaro. *Saturn*: *Exploring the Mystery of the Ringed Planet*. 2010.
	Saturn: A New View by Laura Lovett, published in 2006.

Part A

Circle the entry from the bibliography that is written correctly.

Part B

Explain why the entry you chose in Part A is correct. In your response, explain the different pieces of information that are included.

_____

_____

_____

8. Ellen has taken notes about the U.S. government for a social studies report. Read Ellen's notes and the directions that follow.

Notes about the U.S. Government

- The government has three branches: legislative, executive, and judicial.

- The legislative branch makes the laws. The executive branch enforces and enacts the laws. The judicial branch decides if the laws are fair and agree with the Constitution.

- Congress is the legislative branch. It is made up of the Senate and the House of Representatives. Congress is elected by the people.

- The president is head of the executive branch. He is in charge of the military. The president is elected by the people.

- The Supreme Court is the main body of the judicial branch. There are nine justices on the Supreme Court. The justices are appointed by the president and confirmed by the Senate.

Use the notes to create an outline for Ellen's paper. Complete the outline below.

I. Topic: _____

    A. Main Idea: _____

        1. Supporting Detail: _____

        2. Supporting Detail: _____

    B. Main Idea: _____

        1. Supporting Detail: _____

        2. Supporting Detail: _____

    C. Main Idea: _____

        1. Supporting Detail: _____

        2. Supporting Detail: _____

3 Cumulative Assessment

The following passage contains mistakes. Read the passage and answer the questions that follow.

Machu Picchu

Machu Picchu stands in the Andes Mountains in Peru. Built and occupied by the Inca people in the mid-1400s, it is now a deserted city. The name Machu Picchu means "old peak" in Quechua, the language of the Inca. Machu Picchu is one of the few American Indian sites from the 1400s to be found nearly intact.

For hundreds of years, few people knew Machu Picchu existed. Then, in 1911, it was rediscovered. When he stumbled upon Machu Picchu, he thought he had found Vilcabamba. At first, Hiram Bingham, a Yale professor, was searching for Vilcabamba, a great undiscovered Incan city. The Inca Empire stretched from modern-day Ecuador to Chile. Machu Picchu was never completely forgotten, as a few people still lived in the area.

There are many theories about what Machu Picchu was used for. Some people believe that the city was built for the gods to live in, or for royal events. Another theory is that it was an agricultural testing station. Most likely, Machu Picchu was a royal estate and religious retreat. About 1,200 people lived in and around Machu Picchu. Among the crops the Inca planted were maize and potatoes. To get the most crops, they used advanced farming methods. These methods lessened the amount of erosion that occurred. Also, they made it possible to cultivate more land.

Machu Picchu was built in the classical Inca style, with polished dry-stone walls. It contained around 200 buildings. Most of the buildings were residences, although there were temples and other public buildings. Most of the structures were built of granite blocks. The blocks fit together perfectly. Another unique thing about Machu Picchu was the use of the landscape. Existing rock formations became part of structures as they were built. Many sculptures were carved into the rock as well.

1. What is this passage MAINLY about?

   A. Machu Picchu

   B. the Inca Empire

   C. Hiram Bingham

   D. South American architecture

2. Which sentence is in the wrong order in paragraph 2?

   A. "For hundreds of years, few people knew Machu Picchu existed."

   B. "Then, in 1911, it was rediscovered."

   C. "When he stumbled upon Machu Picchu, he thought he had found Vilcabamba."

   D. "The Inca Empire stretched from modern-day Ecuador to Chile."

3. Which sentence does NOT belong in paragraph 2?

   A. "At first, Hiram Bingham, a Yale professor, was searching for Vilcabamba…"

   B. "The Inca Empire stretched from modern-day Ecuador to Chile."

   C. "Then, in 1911, it was rediscovered."

   D. "Machu Picchu was never completely forgotten, as a few people still lived in the area."

4. Which would be the BEST detail to add to paragraph 3?

   A. stories about Hiram Bingham

   B. history of the Inca Empire

   C. what the different buildings were used for

   D. why people think Machu Picchu was a royal estate

5. Which heading would NOT be in an outline used for this passage?

   A. Rediscovery of Machu Picchu

   B. Inca Art and Sculptures

   C. The Inca and Machu Picchu

   D. Architecture of Machu Picchu

6. Which resource would NOT be helpful when researching Machu Picchu?

   A. a book

   B. an encyclopedia

   C. a Web site

   D. a current newspaper

Persuasive Prompt

Your class has a field trip coming up. Where would you most like for the class to go? Write a letter to your teacher, explaining your choice and the reasons behind it.

Use the checklist below to help you do your best writing.

Does your letter

❏ have a clear topic?

❏ show a point of view about that topic?

❏ have a logical structure?

❏ support reasons with details?

❏ connect reasons and details with the right words or phrases?

❏ use a style and vocabulary that is correct for the audience and purpose?

❏ have a solid conclusion?

❏ have good spelling, capitalization, and punctuation?

❏ follow the rules for good grammar?

Write your response in the space provided. You may use your own paper if you need more space.

CHAPTER

4 Language

Chapter 4: Diagnostic Assessment

Chapter 4: Cumulative Assessment

Diagnostic Assessment

The following passage contains mistakes. Read the passage and answer the questions that follow.

A Great Ocean Explorer

(1) Experts beleive Jacques Cousteau traveled more of the world's oceans than anyone else in history. (2) He made many <u>contributions</u> to the science of oceanography. (3) In, 1943 he helped to invent oxygen tanks for divers so they could move about freely underwater without wearing, heavy, awkward, diving, suits.

(4) Cousteau spent the second half of his life traveling the oceans on his boat, *Calypso*. (5) He studied rare ocean life. (6) He also explored shipwrecks.

(7) Cousteau was terrified about pollution and other troubles in the oceans. (8) He wanted to make people more aware, so he wrote books and made movies. (9) His books have been translated into many different languages. (10) Three of his movies won <u>Academy Awards</u>. (11) This is the highest honor a movie can win.

(12) Although Jacques Cousteau died in 1997, his work lives on.

1. Which sentence has a spelling error?

   A. sentence 1

   B. sentence 2

   C. sentence 3

   D. sentence 4

2. What is the root of <u>contributions</u>?

   A. contrib

   B. tributions

   C. contri

   D. trib

3. Which is the correct way to write sentence 3?

   A. In, 1943 he helped to invent oxygen tanks for divers so they could move about freely underwater without wearing heavy, awkward diving suits.

   B. In, 1943 he helped to invent oxygen tanks for divers so they could move about freely underwater without wearing heavy awkward diving suits.

   C. In 1943, he helped to invent oxygen tanks for divers so they could move about freely underwater without wearing heavy, awkward diving suits.

   D. In 1943, he helped to invent oxygen tanks for divers so they could move about freely underwater without wearing heavy, awkward, diving, suits.

4. Which of the following sentences contains a conjunction?

    A. sentence 4

    B. sentence 5

    C. sentence 8

    D. sentence 9

5. Which phrase from the passage helps you figure out the meaning of <u>Academy Awards</u>?

    A. "highest honor a movie can win"

    B. "he wrote books"

    C. "have been translated"

    D. "three of his movies"

6. Read the following sentence.

    Cousteau was terrified about pollution and other troubles in the oceans.

Rewrite the sentence using synonyms to better match the rest of the passage.

_____

_____

_____

_____

_____

_____

The following passage contains mistakes. Read the passage and answer the questions that follow.

Video Games at School

(1) Some students think our school should have a video game room. (2) I will have think this is a very good idea. (3) I don't want to make a mountain out of a molehill. (4) But we are under a lot of pressure at school each day. (5) A video game room could help us relax. (6) Allowing us to play video games could be a reward for students when we perform well in our studies. (7) My favorite video game is "Super martian brothers" so, that's the one I would play. (8) Although my <u>antagonists</u>, the people opposing my idea, might say that the video game room could be distracting, that is not true. (9) Our teachers and principals would control who could use the game room but when they could use it.

7. Which sentence from the passage contains an idiom?

   A. sentence 1

   B. sentence 2

   C. sentence 3

   D. sentence 4

8. Read this sentence from the passage.

   I will have think this is a very good idea.

   Which is the correct way to write this sentence?

   A. I will have thought this is a very good idea.

   B. I have thought this is a very good idea.

   C. I have think this is a very good idea.

   D. I think this is a very good idea.

9. Which is the BEST way to combine sentences 4 and 5?

   But we are under a lot of pressure at school each day. A video game room could help us relax.

   A. But we are under a lot of pressure at school each day, and a video game room could help us relax.

   B. But we are under a lot of pressure at school each day, yet a video game room could help us relax.

   C. But we are under a lot of pressure at school each day, for a video game room could help us relax.

   D. But we are under a lot of pressure at school each day, but a video game room could help us relax.

10. Which phrase from the passage helps you figure out the meaning of <u>antagonists</u>?

   A. "that is not true"

   B. "that's the one I would play"

   C. "people opposing"

   D. "the video game room could be distracting"

11. Which is the correct way to write sentence 7?

   A. My favorite video game is "Super martian brothers," so that's the one I would play.

   B. My favorite video game is "Super Martian Brothers" so, that's the one I would play.

   C. My favorite video game is super martian brothers so, that's the one I would play.

   D. My favorite video game is "Super Martian Brothers," so that's the one I would play.

12. Rewrite the following sentence, using the correct conjunction.

Our teachers and principals would control who could use the game room but when they could use it.

_____

_____

_____

_____

_____

23 Capitalization and Spelling

Getting the Idea

Capitalization is the use of capital letters at the beginning of sentences and certain kinds of words. Capital letters, or uppercase letters, are used only in certain situations. For example, all proper nouns are capitalized. A **proper noun** is a word that names a particular person, place, or thing. Capital letters are mostly used at the beginnings of the following words:

- words that begin a sentence
- proper names (Robert, Donna, Uncle Willie, Smith, Johnson)
- geographical places (Mississippi, Chicago, Gulf of Mexico, Rocky Mountains)
- historical periods (Middle Ages, the Jurassic Period)
- days and months (Thursday, October)
- holidays (Veteran's Day, Columbus Day)
- personal titles before a person's name (Dr., Mr., Mrs.)
- organizations (Girl Scouts, Red Sox)
- abbreviations and acronyms (in this case, all letters are usually capitalized—for example, FBI, YMCA, or NAACP)
- first and last word in a title, and other important words (*The Wind in the Willows, Little House on the Prairie*)
- the greeting of a letter (Dear Patricia)
- the closing of a letter (Yours truly)
- proper adjectives (Florida oranges, American flag)
- the pronoun *I* (referring to oneself)

Thinking It Through 1

Read the following sentences. Write them correctly on the lines provided. If the sentence is correct, write "correct as is."

1. Mr. and mrs. sabrowski visited the grand canyon last summer.

_____

HINT Words that name a particular person, place, or thing should be capitalized.

2. in class, Ty presented a report. it was on the Revolutionary War.

_____

HINT Words that begin a sentence should be capitalized.

3. Dr. Adams told My Mother to eat healthier.

_____

4. Alix grew up in miami, florida.

_____

5. Aunt Sharon flew into town on President's Day.

_____

6. Ms. Romero told Me to submit my book report after i revise the errors.

_____

7. The New England Patriots play football in October.

_____

8. Mrs. Andrews studied the stone age in College.

_____

Spelling is the correct arrangement of letters in a word. Different letters can make the same sound—as in *here* and *hear*. The same letters can make different sounds—as with *ou* in *bought, bounce*, and *tour*. Here are some general rules and hints you can follow to spell correctly.

- When adding a suffix beginning with a vowel to a word ending with a silent *e*, drop the *e*.

  Example: The noun form of *behave* is *behavior*.

- When adding a suffix beginning with a consonant to a word ending with a silent *e*, keep the *e*.

  Example: The adverb form of *rare* is *rarely*.

- When pluralizing nouns that end in *s, z, x, sh*, or *ch*, add *-es*.

  Example: The plural of *dish* is *dishes*.

- When pluralizing nouns ending in *y*, drop the *y* and add *-ies*.

  Example: The plural of *body* is *bodies*.

- When pluralizing nouns ending with *f*, change the *f* to *v* and add *-es*.

  Example: The plural of *shelf* is *shelves*.

- When a one-syllable word ends in a consonant after one vowel, double the final consonant before adding a suffix that begins with a vowel.

  Example: *bat* becomes *batting, batted, batter*.

- If the word has more than one syllable, but the emphasis is on the final syllable, the same rule applies: double the final consonant.

  Example: occur becomes *occurred, occurring*.

A word can be broken into syllables. A **syllable** is the smallest unit of sound in a word that contains at least a vowel or a vowel and a consonant. Look at these two words:

> in • for • ma • tion

> mol • e • cule

Breaking a word into parts can help you spell it correctly.

Thinking It Through 2

Read the following sentences. Write them correctly on the lines provided. If the sentence is correct, write "correct as is."

1.   Their nieghbor bakes cookies every Saturday.

_____

   HINT   To determine whether to use *ie* or *ei*, think about how the word sounds. Words with a long *e* are spelled *ie*.

2.   Instead of putting a whole slice of cheddar on the bread, Alice decided to shread the cheese.

_____

   HINT   The same letters can make different sounds, and different letters can make the same sound.

3.   Allison was ecstatic when she received an award at school.

_____

4.   Because Ron barly made the team, he worked harder than his other teammates.

_____

5.   The pack of wolfs ran in the snow.

_____

6.   Corrine spilled a bucket of water when she mopped the floor.

_____

7.   After he finished moving, Timothy had to flaten the moving boxxes.

_____

8.   Rosy was full of greif after a theif broke into her house and stole her computer.

_____

Lesson Practice

This passage contains mistakes. Use the Reading Guide to help you find the mistakes.

Reading Guide

Proper nouns name a particular person, place, or thing and should be capitalized. Are there any proper nouns in paragraph 1?

Which spelling rules are being used improperly in paragraph 2?

Hoover Dam

(1) Hoover dam is nameed after president herbert hoover, the 31st president of the united states of america.

(2) The Colorado river flooded regularly as the snow melted from the Rocky mountains. (3) The floods caused terrible damage. (4) Hoover saw that a dam would control the river. (5) He also knew that a dam would capture fresh water. (6) Before he was president, Hoover sat with state leaders to plan for the dam. (7) The following states formed the Colorado River Compact: Arizona, California, Colorado, Nevada, New Mexico, Utah, and Wyoming. (8) They signed an agreement on November 24, 1922. (9) This agreement was made effective on june 25, 1929, after Hoover became president. (10) During the great depression, over 21,000 men worked on the dam. (11) Although the workers had seven years to build the dam, they completeed the project in five years. (12) hoover said, "This great river, instead of being wasted in the sea, will now be brought into use by man."

(13) Lake Mead was made when the Colorado River was damed up. (14) Lake Mead is the largest reservoir in the United States and has enough water to fill the entire state of New York with one foot of water!

Answer the following questions.

1. Which sentence from the passage has a spelling error?

   A. He also knew that a dam would capture fresh water.

   B. The floods caused terrible damage.

   C. They signed an agreement on November 24, 1922.

   D. Lake Mead was made when the Colorado River was damed up.

2. Which sentence contains a capitalization error?

   A. They signed an agreement on November 24, 1922.

   B. The Colorado river flooded regularly as the snow melted from the Rocky mountains.

   C. Hoover saw that a dam would control the river.

   D. Before he was president, Hoover sat with state leaders to plan for the dam.

3. Which sentence has correct capitalization?

   A. This agreement was made effective on june 25, 1929, after Hoover became president.

   B. During the great depression, over 21,000 men worked on the dam.

   C. The floods caused terrible damage.

   D. hoover said, "This great river, instead of being wasted in the sea, will now be brought into use by man."

4. Which sentence has a spelling error?

   A. Although the workers had seven years to build the dam, they completeed the project in five years.

   B. He also knew that a dam would capture fresh water.

   C. The following states formed the Colorado River Compact: Arizona, California, Colorado, Nevada, New Mexico, Utah, and Wyoming.

   D. Before he was president, Hoover sat with state leaders to plan for the dam.

5. Rewrite the following sentence, correcting any errors in capitalization and spelling.

   Hoover dam is nameed after president herbert hoover, the 31st president of the united states of america.

The following questions do not relate to a passage.

6. Read the sentence in each answer choice. The underlined word or phrase in the sentence is incorrectly capitalized. Match the sentence to the reason the underlined word or phrase should be capitalized.

<table>
<tr><td>A.</td><td>My Uncle Dave took us to the amusement park on <u>valentine's day</u>.</td><td>1.</td><td>abbreviation</td></tr>
<tr><td></td><td></td><td>2.</td><td>geographic place</td></tr>
<tr><td>B.</td><td>He took us to the Mall of America in <u>bloomington, minnesota.</u></td><td>3.</td><td>historical period</td></tr>
<tr><td>C.</td><td>At the mall, Dave saw his professor, <u>dr.</u> Johnson, shopping for a watch.</td><td>4.</td><td>holiday</td></tr>
<tr><td></td><td></td><td>5.</td><td>organization</td></tr>
<tr><td></td><td></td><td>6.</td><td>personal title</td></tr>
</table>

7. Use your answer to Part A to answer Part B.

Part A

Read the following sentence and tell why it is incorrect.

> **Mrs. Kelley brought the class to the science museum of Virginia.**

Circle the words that have errors in capitalization.

Part B

Which sentence has correct capitalization?

A. Mrs. Kelley brought the class to the science museum of virginia.

B. Mrs. Kelley brought the class to the science Museum of Virginia.

C. Mrs. Kelley brought the class to the Science Museum of Virginia.

D. Mrs. Kelley brought the CLASS to the science museum of Virginia.

---

8. The following paragraph is from a student's book report. Read the paragraph. Then rewrite it, revising it to correct errors.

> **The book "hatchet" was written by gary paulsen. it is about a Boy named brian who gets on a plain to fly to canada to spend time with his dad all summer. The plain crashs and brian must learn to survive in the wilderness buy himself. At one point in the book, he heres some rustling in the bushs. it turns out to be a bare looking for berrys.**

_____

_____

_____

_____

_____

_____

_____

_____

24 Punctuation

Getting the Idea

Punctuation marks make sentences easier to understand. **Exclamation points (!)** end sentences that show excitement or strong emotion. **Periods (.)** end sentences that are more declarative or informational. Two common punctuation marks with complex uses are commas and quotation marks.

A **comma (,)** indicates a pause in a sentence. Commas are used after introductory words. For example: *Later, we all went out for ice cream*. They set off the words *yes* and *no* (as in *Yes, I'll have more mashed sweet potatoes. No, I've never liked Brussels sprouts*.). They are used to set off a tag question from the rest of the sentence (as in *It's pretty outside, don't you think?*) They are also used to set off a direct address from the rest of the sentence. We use direct address when we name the person we are speaking to in a sentence. For example: *Karen, you are my favorite cousin*.

Commas are used when linking ideas or phrases with conjunctions, such as *and, or,* or *but*. For example: *Sherman went to the laboratory, and then he went back home*. Commas are used when you are listing several items in a series. For example: *Cindy plays soccer, basketball, handball, racquetball, pinball, and squash*. They are also used in dates, to separate a year from a day of the month. For example: *January 1, 2009*.

Quotation marks (" ") are most commonly used to enclose the exact words of a speaker. For example: *"Do you want to go to the dentist?" asked Ricky*. Ricky's exact words are *"Do you want to go to the dentist?"* so the quotation marks should appear around those words. Now read this sentence. *"I am going to the dentist," said Ricky*. The spoken words *"I am going to the dentist"* would normally end in a period. Because these words are in a quotation, the period should be replaced with a comma, inside the quotation marks. The words *said Ricky* follow them, and are not in quotation marks. If that statement were at the end of the sentence, the statement would end with a period, inside the quotation marks. What's the mistake in this sentence? *"I turned the air conditioner off because my toes were numb." said Jaime*. The period after *numb* needs to be replaced with a comma.

Thinking It Through 1

Read the following sentences. Write them correctly on the lines provided. If the sentence is correct, write "correct as is."

1. Angelina likes to read poetry, fables, and, science, fiction novels.

_____

HINT Commas are used after each item in a list.

2. "Shania, are you going to the movies tonight? she asked."

_____

HINT Remember, quotation marks go around the words a speaker says.

3. Yes I, would like to join you on Thursday.

_____

4. Bicycles, skateboards, and scooters are very popular in school.

_____

5. Last month she forgot, her keys and was locked out of the house.

_____

6. I was thinking of going to the beach what, do you think?

_____

7. Ice cream, popsicles, and, frozen, yogurt are good treats in the summer.

_____

8. On July 8, 2010, my brother John got married.

_____

Quotation marks will appear elsewhere in your writing and in the books you read. Quotation marks are also used around the titles of:

- articles
- short stories
- poems
- chapters in books
- songs

This means that you would use quotation marks when referring to the name of any of these types of writing. Look at the examples below.

> I read an article entitled "Retracing the Path" in today's newspaper.

> My favorite poem is "Hiawatha."

> They all sang "Ding Dong, the Witch Is Dead" together.

> Open your books to Chapter 4, "Algae and You."

Titles of longer written works are italicized or underlined. In a printed text, or a paper you write on a computer, titles should be italicized. When writing by hand or using a typewriter, you underline anything that would normally be in italics. Longer written works include: books, full-length plays, films, and periodicals.

> *Chitty Chitty Bang Bang* is my older sister's favorite movie.

> My brother's school performed the play *Romeo and Juliet*.

> *Movies Monthly* printed a review of *Anchor in the Sea*, the movie based on the novel *Mysterious Lights below the Bering Sea*.

Thinking It Through 2

Read the following sentences. Write them correctly on the lines provided. If the sentence is correct, write "correct as is."

1. In class, we read the short poem *Laughter Never Fades*.

_____

HINT Only titles of longer works, like novels, should be italicized.

2. "Electronics Monthly" and "Pet Fashion" were two magazines in the doctor's office.

_____

HINT Unlike magazine titles, articles from magazines should be placed in quotation marks.

3. Evelyn's mom wrote a book called *Bakers at Dawn*.

_____

4. "The Tempest" is William Shakespeare's best play.

_____

5. The new issue of "Gourmet Today" had a great article called "How to Cook Squash."

_____

6. His favorite poem in the book *The Pictures* is _Birds in the Morning_.

_____

7. Felicia's band wrote a song called "The Sun Falls Down" about the novel *Winter Sunset*.

_____

8. My brother wrote an article called _Painting Landscapes_ in the latest issue of "Movies Today" about the movie "Desert Skies Forever."

_____

Lesson Practice

This passage contains mistakes. Use the Reading Guide to help you find the mistakes.

Reading Guide

Commas are used in many different ways. How are commas being used in paragraph 1?

Book titles can be underlined or italicized. How are the book titles treated in this passage?

Rachel Carson

(1) Marine biologist Rachel Carson helped make people aware of the environment. (2) She once wrote, "The more clearly we can focus our attention on the wonders and realities of the universe about us, the less taste we shall have for destruction." (3) She was, a poet, conservationist, and, author. (4) In her lifetime, she published several pamphlets on natural resources and conservation. (5) She enchanted people with her books about the ocean. (6) Her first book was titled "*Under the Sea-Wind.*" (7) Her second book about the ocean is *The Sea Around Us.*

(8) Carson was disturbed by the use of chemical pesticides after World War II. (9) She wanted to warn the public about the long-term effects of the pesticides. (10) In 1962 she wrote the book Silent Spring. (11) It's about poisonous, chemicals, and pesticides, used on farms to kill pests. (12) She saw birds dying in her hometown where these chemicals were used. (13) "*Silent Spring*" showed how wildlife and the planet were harmed because of certain, chemicals, and pesticides.

(14) Carson had the knowledge of a scientist. (15) She also had poetic writing abilities. (16) She used these skills to urge the government to make stricter rules for using chemicals and pesticides. (17) Most of the chemicals she was concerned about have now been banned.

Answer the following questions.

1. Which is the correct way to punctuate sentence 3?

    A. She was a poet conservationist and, author

    B. She was, a poet, conservationist and author.

    C. She was a poet, conservationist, and author.

    D. She was a poet, conservationist, and, author.

2. Which is the correct way to punctuate sentence 6?

    A. Her first book was titled "Under the Sea-Wind."

    B. Her first book was titled *Under the Sea-Wind.*

    C. Her first book was titled "*Under the Sea-Wind.*"

    D. Her first book was titled "Under the Sea-Wind."

3. Which is the correct way to write sentence 10?

    A. In 1962 she wrote the book, Silent Spring.

    B. In 1962 she wrote the book "Silent Spring."

    C. In 1962, she wrote the book "Silent Spring."

    D. In 1962, she wrote the book *Silent Spring.*

4. Which sentence is correctly punctuated?

    A. It's about poisonous chemicals and pesticides used on farms to kill pests.

    B. It's about poisonous chemicals, and pesticides, used on farms to kill pests.

    C. It's about poisonous chemicals, and pesticides used on farms to kill pests.

    D. It's about poisonous, chemicals, and pesticides used on farms to kill pests.

5. Rewrite the following sentence, correcting any errors.

    "*Silent Spring*" showed how wildlife and the planet were harmed because of certain, chemicals, and pesticides.

    _____

    _____

The following questions do not relate to a passage.

6. Choose all the sentences that are correctly punctuated. There is more than one correct choice listed below.

   A. My dad was born on August 29 1965.

   B. Yes, I'd like to go to the park with you.

   C. No I don't want to go to see that movie this weekend.

   D. Karen saw poultry, horses, cows, and rabbits at the state fair.

   E. His favorite sports to play were tennis hockey soccer and basketball.

   F. My brother likes mustard on his hamburgers, but I prefer ketchup.

---

7. Read the following paragraphs from a story written by a student.

   "Can we go to the fair this weekend?" asked Ralph.

   "No, I don't think we can," said Mom. "We have your sister's birthday party on Saturday and your grandparents' anniversary dinner on Sunday."

   But I really want to go, said Ralph.

   "I'm sorry. It's not going to work," said Mom.

   Underline the sentence that is NOT punctuated correctly. Write the sentence correctly below.

   _____

   _____

   _____

8. The following paragraph is from a student's essay about his weekend. Read the paragraph. Then rewrite it, revising it to correct errors.

This weekend was a busy weekend. First we had my sister's birthday party. She just turned five, so the theme of the party was pink and princesses There were princess plates princess napkins and even a princess cake. My mom made a pink punch and we put up pink balloons to decorate the house. My sister wore a pink, fluffy dress with a tiara on her head. Then, "on Sunday we went my grandparent's house to celebrate their forty-fifth wedding anniversary." Luckily, there were no pink princesses at this party! When they brought out the cake my sister said, "You should have gotten a princess cake." Mine was cuter than yours. Everyone laughed.

_____

_____

_____

_____

_____

_____

_____

_____

_____

_____

_____

_____

_____

_____

_____

_____

_____

25 Grammar and Usage

Getting the Idea

A **verb** is a word that shows action, how two things are connected, or a state of being. Verb **tense** is the time when the action takes place. **Past tense:** The action has already happened. *We traveled*. **Present tense:** The action is happening right now. *We travel*. **Future tense:** The action is going to happen. *We will travel*.

The **perfect tense** shows action already completed. This tense is formed with the appropriate tense of the verb *to have*, plus the past tense of the verb.

Present Perfect: Present tense of *to have* plus past tense of a verb. *Lucy has traveled*.

Past Perfect: Past tense of *to have* plus past tense of a verb. *Lucy had traveled*.

Future Perfect: Future tense of *to have* plus past tense of a verb. *Lucy will have traveled*.

When writing, it is very important to make verb tenses agree. If a writer shifts tense for no reason, this can confuse the reader.

Conjunctions are words that connect two words or thoughts in a sentence. Some common conjunctions are *and*, *or*, *either*, *neither*, *nor*, *but*, *for*, *so*, and *yet*. Use conjunctions to connect adjectives, phrases, and main clauses.

A **preposition** is a word that links nouns, called *objects*, to other words in a sentence. Some common prepositions are: *above*, *by*, *in*, *to*, *after*, *for*, *of*, *through*, *around*, *from*, *on*, and *with*. Together, the preposition and the object form a **Prepositional phrases**. Prepositional phrases describe nouns or verbs. They often indicate directions, or describe motion more precisely. (Bring me the book <u>on the table</u>.)

An **interjection** is a word or phrase that shows strong feeling. Interjections are sometimes set off from the rest of the sentence by an exclamation point. (Wow!)

Thinking It Through 1

Read the following sentences. Write them correctly on the lines provided. If the sentence is correct, write "correct as is."

1. They will have baked a dozen cookies last week.

_____

> **HINT** In the future perfect tense, action is completed in relation to the future.

2. Wyatt wanted to walk the dog and he had to finish his homework first.

_____

> **HINT** How does the conjunction connect the two sentences? Are the two verbs in the sentence the same tense?

3. We will have sleep well after we have hiked for hours.

_____

4. She had played basketball with her teammates already that day.

_____

5. Whoa you're driving too quickly.

_____

6. They after dinner watch a movie.

_____

7. Alex walked his dog over the block.

_____

8. Carefully carried the heavy box, making sure it did not fall.

_____

An **independent clause** is a phrase with a subject and predicate. It can stand alone. For example: *Jeannie jogs every day*. A **simple sentence** has one subject and at least one predicate. In the sentence "The popsicle melts quickly," *popsicle* is the subject and *melts* is the verb. The predicate is *melts quickly*.

Sometimes writers create a **run-on sentences**—long sentences that should really be two or more sentences. For example, "A lever is a simple machine levers can be used to help lift objects" runs two thoughts together. Change a run-on sentence into two simple sentences: *A lever is a simple machine. Levers can be used to help lift objects*. You could also add a conjunction to join the parts of the sentence: *A lever is a simple machine which can be used to help lift objects.*

Sometimes, you may find a **sentence fragment**, a sentence missing a subject or a verb which does not express a complete thought. Either add words to complete the sentence or combine the fragment with another sentence. "Under the dark sky" does not express a complete thought. Correct a sentence fragment by adding a subject and a predicate, like this: *They wandered under the dark sky*.

You can also combine a sentence fragment with another sentence, using a comma and a conjunction: *They wandered under the dark sky, and then they slowly went home*.

Another way is to rephrase the thoughts by fitting them into one sentence. For example: *The box of cereal in the cupboard. It was full this morning, but now it is empty*. "The box of cereal in the cupboard" is a sentence fragment. Here is one way to rephrase it: *The box of cereal in the cupboard was full this morning, but now it is empty*.

Sometimes several small complete sentences may occur next to each other. These sentences may make sense by themselves, but they have a choppy rhythm. To make them read more smoothly, combine them with appropriate punctuation and conjunctions. Be sure that the new sentence has the same essential meaning as the originals.

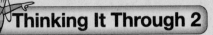

Thinking It Through 2

Read the following sentences. Write them correctly on the lines provided. If the sentence is correct, write "correct as is."

1. Gina and Gabby hurriedly unwrapped the popsicles Gina likes cherry-flavored popsicles.

_____

HINT A run-on sentence expresses more than one complete thought.

2. Thomas and Janet baked different muffins. Blueberry, bran, and raspberry.

_____

HINT You can combine a fragment with a complete sentence by replacing the period in the complete sentence with a comma and adding a conjunction.

3. Covered in sweat, he ran around the track under the blazing sun.

_____

4. The energetic boys and girls in the playground.

_____

5. Roman and Ben went camping. They camped by the lake. There were a lot of mosquitoes at the lake.

_____

6. Letitia walked to the store. While she was there, she bought eggs, milk, and lettuce.

_____

7. Arturo and Crystal stayed up all night. Watched a scary movie.

_____

8. While Angel and Carol looked in the garage, Darius went through the kitchen looking for the missing keys the keys belonged to Angel's mom.

_____

This passage contains mistakes. Use the Reading Guide to help you find the mistakes.

Reading Guide

Remember, perfect tenses show action already completed.

Morgan's Gas Mask

(1) Garrett Morgan was the son of a freed slave and was one of the first African American inventors. (2) In 1912, Morgan will have invented a breathing device. (3) It was first called "Morgan's Safety Hood" yet was later known as a gas mask. (4) The Safety Hood consisted of a hood worn over the head and two tubes. (5) The first tube allowed the user to breathe in clean air. (6) The second tube allowed the user to exhaled out of the hood. (7) Once a person put on the gas mask, he or she would be safe from deadly smoke or chemicals in the air.

(8) In 1916, a violent explosion had happened in a tunnel that will have been dug under Lake Erie. (9) Workers were trapped in the tunnel and had begun choking on smoke and dust and somebody had heard about Morgan's Safety Hood. (10) They called Morgan to help. (11) Morgan became an instant hero, because he saved so many lives. (12) Everyone was amazed by the gas mask. (13) Fire departments around the world began to use masks during rescue efforts. (14) The U.S. Army began to provide gas masks. (15) To soldiers to keep safe during wartime.

(16) Morgan also helped invent the traffic signal. (17) He patented a three-armed signal. (18) Had a caution signal much like the yellow light in traffic signals that we have today. (19) Morgan was highly honored for his contributions.

Answer the following questions.

1. Which sentence from the passage is NOT written correctly?

   A. sentence 1

   B. sentence 2

   C. sentence 4

   D. sentence 5

2. Which conjunction should replace yet in sentence 3?

   A. so

   B. for

   C. but

   D. and

3. Which sentence is a fragment?

   A. sentence 10

   B. sentence 12

   C. sentence 13

   D. sentence 15

4. What is the best way to correct sentence 9?

   A. Workers were trapped in the tunnel and had begun choking on smoke and dust. Somebody had heard about Morgan's Safety Hood.

   B. Workers were trapped in the tunnel and had begun choking on smoke and dust but somebody had heard about Morgan's Safety Hood.

   C. Workers were trapped in the tunnel. Workers had begun choking on smoke. Workers had begun choking on dust. Somebody had heard about Morgan's Safety Hood.

   D. Workers were trapped inside the tunnel and had begun choking around the smoke and dust but somebody had heard about Morgan's Safety Hood.

5. Combine the following sentences.

   He patented a three-armed signal. Had a caution signal much like the yellow light in traffic signals that we have today.

   _____

   _____

   _____

   _____

The following questions do not relate to a passage.

6. A student is writing a report about blizzards. Read this paragraph from the report and the directions that follow.

> A blizzard is a winter storm. It _____ when strong winds are combined with falling snow. This reduces the visibility so that it is very difficult to see.

The student needs to complete the second sentence using the correct verb tense. Which word BEST completes the sentence?

A. occur

B. occurs

C. occurred

D. has occurred

---

7. The following paragraph is from a student's report about a trip. Read the paragraph. Then rewrite it, completing the blanks with conjunctions, prepositions, or interjections.

> This weekend we went to Lake Superior _____ we could see the Tall Ships Festival. Nine different sailing ships that were traditionally rigged with many masts came _____ the harbor. After seeing them, I can imagine what it was like to live _____ the time of Ferdinand Magellan or Christopher Columbus. It was cold and windy the day we went, _____ I didn't mind at all. "_____!" I said. "These are spectacular ships!"

_____

_____

_____

_____

_____

_____

_____

_____

_____

8. Choose all of the sentences that are written correctly. There is more than one correct choice listed below.

   A. A book without a cover.

   B. Cautiously crept to the closed door.

   C. She brushed her teeth then she went straight to bed.

   D. Every day the brothers left for school at the same time.

   E. He wanted to go to the amusement park, but he didn't have any money.

   F. The team went out for ice cream cones the shop was closed so they went home instead.

9. These sentences were written by a student. Read the sentences and the directions that follow.

| During the summer. We like to swim at the high school pool. We like to swim in the lake. |
| During the summer we like to swim at the high school pool, but we also like to swim in the lake. |
| During the summer we like to swim. At the high school pool and at the lake. |

Part A

Circle the sentence that is written correctly.

Part B

Explain why the sentence you chose in Part A is correct and why the others are incorrect. Write your response below.

_____

_____

_____

_____

_____

26 Determining Word Meanings

Getting the Idea

If you find a word you don't know, you can always check for context clues. **Context clues** are words or phrases surrounding an unknown word that give hints about its meaning. The way a word is used in a sentence may also be a context clue. Consider this example:

> My friend Joy loves playing squash. I often see her heading for the indoor courts, racquet in hand.

The passage says that Joy loves "playing squash." From context clues, it is clear that squash is a game, because people play games. The next sentence says that squash involves "courts" and a "racquet." These two words are connected with sports.

Here are five different kinds of context clues.

- **definition** The author explains the word's meaning.

  > Jill's old computer is *obsolete*. It is no longer useful.

- **antonym** The author gives an example to show the opposite meaning of a word.

  > The story didn't make sense, and the ideas seemed confused. There wasn't a single *lucid* thought in it.

- **synonym** The author gives another word that has a similar meaning to the unknown word.

  > The trees were heavily covered with *foliage*, or leaves.

- **restatement** A restatement clue sums up an idea.

  > Lake George was *halcyon* that morning. Not a single movement rippled its surface.

- **example** The author provides specific examples of the unknown word.

  > Dinner included many *delicacies*, such as squab, truffles, oysters, and escargot.

As always, you can check the meaning of unfamiliar words in the dictionary. This will help you to be sure you have used context clues correctly.

Multiple-meaning words are words that are spelled the same but have more than one meaning. The word *cut*, for example, can mean "to slice something into pieces." It can also mean "a wound or an injury." When you come across a word with multiple meanings, use context clues to figure out the right definition. Read this sentence.

> A winter storm was blowing snow everywhere.

A storm can be a very dramatic weather event ("The storm went on all afternoon"). Or it can be a verb, meaning to attack suddenly and ferociously ("The army stormed the dark castle, knowing they were deciding their fate"). Look at the clues. The storm is described as being a winter storm. The sentence also mentions snow, so we know the word *storm* has something to do with weather. You can guess that the first definition of *storm* is used here.

Some multiple-meaning words are spelled the same but are pronounced differently. These words are called **homographs**. Read this sentence.

> If you address a letter to the wrong address, it will probably not get there.

The first *address* is a verb, or action word, that means "to mark with a destination." When you say this word aloud, the stress is on the second syllable. The second *address* is a noun that means "a specific location." The stress on this word is on the first syllable.

Another way to tell the definition of a multiple-meaning word is to look at how the word is used. Is the word a verb (an action word)? Is it a noun (a person, place, or thing)? Is it an adjective (a descriptive word)? Choose the usage that makes the most sense in the sentence.

Thinking It Through

Read the following paragraph, and then answer the questions that follow.

To stop the spread of <u>infectious</u> diseases, doctors recommend that sick people cover their mouths when they sneeze. If people don't cover their mouths, they spread their germs and give other people their cold.

What does the word <u>infectious</u> mean? Which words from the paragraph help you figure out the meaning of <u>infectious</u>?

_____

_____

_____

_____

HINT Reread the paragraph. Think about how the word is used here.

 **DISCUSS** Use the word *infectious* in a new sentence. Share your sentence in a group.

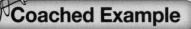

Coached Example

Read the passage and answer the questions.

I was walking downtown with my mother when we found two little birds on the sidewalk. They must have <u>plummeted</u> from their nests, but when we looked up all we saw were tall buildings. I wanted to bring them home, but my mother refused. "No, we don't know how to take care of birds," she said.

I <u>beseeched</u> her until she finally agreed. On our way home, we passed by the pet shop and stopped to buy some bird food. Surprisingly, my mother was much more interested in feeding the birds than I was. She helped nurse them back to health by feeding them and keeping them warm. We brought them downtown and released them in a park near the place where we had found them.

---

1. The word <u>plummeted</u> means

   A. flew.

   B. fell.

   C. rose.

   D. looked.

   HINT Look at the words and sentences around *plummeted*. Which of the choices could replace *plummeted*?

2. Which phrase from the passage helps you figure out the meaning of <u>beseeched</u>?

   A. "until she finally agreed"

   B. "'know how to take care of birds'"

   C. "to buy some bird food"

   D. "my mother was much more interested"

   HINT How is *beseeched* being used in the sentence? Which of the choices helps you figure out how *beseeched* is being used?

Lesson Practice

Use the Reading Guide to help you understand the passage.

Reading Guide

What are some other words that sound like the underlined word in paragraph 2?

Think about how the underlined words are used in the passage. Are there other words you could replace them with that make sense?

As you read, remember that the words near an unfamiliar word can help you find its meaning.

Navajo Code Talkers

The Navajo Tribe is located in the Southwest United States. This tribe has a language that is unwritten, meaning it has no alphabet or symbols. It's only spoken on Navajo lands. But, during World War II, this language helped the United States win the war.

The Japanese are very skilled at breaking codes and were able to <u>break</u> all of the secret military codes that the U.S. Army had. There was a desperate need for a new code so that the United States could organize attacks and move troops. Navajo tribesmen were trained and sent to the Pacific to help in war efforts.

The first twenty-nine Navajo recruits started military training in California in May 1942. The recruits <u>fabricated</u> a code that could not be broken. They created a dictionary, and they invented words for military terms. The codes were not written. They were memorized. The recruits could receive a message in twenty seconds without error. These messages were <u>disseminated</u>, or circulated, over the telephones and radios. By 1945, there were over five hundred Navajo Marines serving in the war, and over three-quarters of them were trained as code talkers.

These codes were <u>classified</u> as secret, because the military continued to use them. So when the Navajo Code Talkers returned home from the war, their invented codes and heroic acts could not be celebrated. Years later, the codes were declassified, and some of the Navajo Code Talkers could receive the recognition that they deserved.

Answer the following questions.

1. The word <u>break</u> means

   A. to ruin.

   B. to figure out.

   C. to hurt.

   D. to plan.

2. Which phrase from the passage helps you figure out the meaning of <u>fabricated</u>?

   A. "could not be broken"

   B. "were trained and sent"

   C. "They created"

   D. "codes were not written"

3. Which phrase from the passage helps you figure out the meaning of <u>disseminated</u>?

   A. "or circulated"

   B. "over five hundred Navajo Marines"

   C. "from the war"

   D. "could receive the recognition"

4. The word <u>classified</u> means

   A. required to be kept.

   B. allowed to be told.

   C. written down.

   D. withheld from the public.

5. Rewrite the last sentence of the passage in your own words.

   _____

   _____

   _____

   _____

   _____

The following questions do not relate to a passage.

6. Read the sentence or sentences in each answer choice. Then match each underlined word to its closest definition on the right.

A. The teacher <u>emphasized</u> the main idea of the story by highlighting the topic sentence.

1. emotional

2. devoted

B. She was <u>fatigued</u> after climbing up the mountainside. She didn't think she could take one more step.

3. relieved

4. stressed

C. He wiped a tear from his eye after looking at old family photos. He was feeling <u>sentimental</u>.

5. tired

6. unwell

7. A student is writing a report about her family vacation. Read this paragraph from the report and the directions that follow.

> **This summer my family went camping. First, we set up our tent. Next, my brother and I <u>collected</u> fallen twigs and branches to use for our evening campfire. Then we hiked five miles in the woods. When we got back we were exhausted and ready to eat dinner.**

Which of the words below has a similar meaning to the underlined word?

A. gathered

B. discovered

C. established

D. traced

---

8. Read the following sentences and the directions that follow.

> **The girl did not want to be a <u>burden</u> to her basketball team. She knew it was a problem to have a player who couldn't run fast, so she quit.**

Part A

Circle the context clues that provide hints to the meaning of the underlined word.

Part B

What type of context clues does the author provide to give hints to the meaning of the underlined word?

A. definition, synonym, restatement

B. antonym, example, synonym

C. synonym, antonym, restatement

D. restatement, example, synonym

E. example, definition, antonym

Lesson

27 Reading in the Content Areas

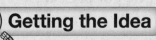 **Getting the Idea**

When you read, you need to pay attention to what type of words are used. The language, or words, you read change depending on the subject. For example, you might notice that the words used in this book are different than the words used in your science and social studies books. Each subject uses words that have meanings that are special to that subject. You will come across many words that you won't know. Sometimes, you will come across a word you do know being used differently than what you've read before. That's because sometimes the same word may have different meanings.

Think about the word *state*. When you read science texts, the word *state* stands for a condition or stage in the physical being of something. But, when you read social studies texts, the word *state* can mean a territory or a political organization. The same word can have different uses and meanings.

Read these two passages.

Axis Grids

You encounter axis grids more often than you might think. An axis grid is a chart with at least one horizontal line and one vertical line in it. The horizontal line, which runs from left to right, is the *x*-axis. The vertical line is called the *y*-axis. Axis grids are very important in geometry. They also show up in other forms of mathematics. You see axis grids all the time in everyday life. For instance, the next time you see a table in a textbook, look at how it is set up. The heads along the top run along the imaginary *x*-axis, while the information in the side column could form a *y*-axis.

The Axis Powers

The term "Axis Powers" was used during World War II. It referred to Germany, Italy, and Japan, the three main countries at war during that time. They made a series of agreements with each other that guaranteed they would help to protect and support each other throughout the conflict. Their enemies were the Allied Powers: the Soviet Union, China, the United States, Great Britain, and France, among other countries.

The two passages are very different in their subjects. They also use identical terms differently. The first passage is about grids in mathematics. The second passage is a social studies text about World War II. The word *axis* is used differently in the passages. In the first passage, the word *axis* refers to a line on a grid. In the second passage, *axis* refers to a group of countries united during a world war.

Since nonfiction texts do not have plots, what keeps you going through the text? A **transition** is a word that helps you go from one sentence or paragraph to the next, showing some relationship between the two. Transitional words are most commonly used to indicate:

- additional information—*also, besides, furthermore, in addition, again.*

- that the following sentence or paragraph is the result of the previous sentence or paragraph—*accordingly, consequently, therefore, thus, as a result.*

- a summary or restatement of the preceding material—*in short, in summary, all in all.*

- a contrast or comparison to the previous sentence or paragraph—*instead, yet, but, however, still, nevertheless.*

- a sequence of events—*next, then, later, earlier, meanwhile, simultaneously.*

Purpose	Sample Sentence
to provide additional information	The test was too hard. *Furthermore*, we didn't have enough time.
to indicate the following sentence or paragraph is the result of the previous sentence or paragraph	I failed my English test. *Therefore*, I must repeat the course.
to give a summary or restatement of the preceding material	The car broke down, we lost our luggage, and the hotel was overbooked. *All in all*, the vacation was a disaster.
to make a contrast or comparison to the previous sentence or paragraph	I don't want to have chicken for dinner. *Instead*, I'd prefer roast beef.
to clarify a sequence of events	First, you need to spread peanut butter on one slice of bread. *Next*, you spread some jam on the other slice.

Thinking It Through

Read the following paragraph, and then answer the questions that follow.

Modern dance is very hard to define. Many types of dancing fall under the name of modern dance. Some modern dance movements use very diverse elements. They take techniques from Native American, African, and South American dances. Still, other modern dance movements use bits and pieces from ballet and theater.

How is the word <u>elements</u> used in the paragraph? Which words from the paragraph help you figure out the meaning of <u>elements</u>?

_____

_____

_____

HINT   Sometimes, words have different meanings in different contexts. Reread the paragraph. What is the paragraph mainly about?

 DISCUSS   Share your answers with a partner.

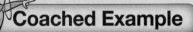

Coached Example

Read the passage and answer the questions.

It took a long time before "The New York Stock Exchange" got its name. Over two hundred hundred years ago, in 1792, it was called the "Buttonwood Agreement." Men used to <u>trade</u> under a huge sycamore tree that they often called the buttonwood tree. In 1817, the organization was given the name "New York Stock and Exchange Board." The group of New York brokers moved to a building on Wall Street. In the 1830s–1860s, trading increased as America expanded. More money was spent on <u>infrastructure</u>; America was building railroads, canals, and turnpikes all over the country.

In 1863, the "New York Stock and Exchange Board" was changed to "The New York Stock Exchange." This is the name it still has. In 1903, the organization moved into a specially designed building on Broad Street where trading is still done today.

---

1. In paragraph 1, the word <u>trade</u> means

   A. a career.

   B. to exchange, buy, or sell.

   C. a custom.

   D. a publication.

    How is the word being used in the paragraph? Is it a verb or a noun?

2. Which phrase from the passage helps you figure out the meaning of <u>infrastructure</u>?

   A. "as America expanded"

   B. "money was spent"

   C. "railroads, canals, and turnpikes"

   D. "trading increased"

   HINT Look at the words and sentences around *infrastructure*. Are specific examples of the unknown word provided?

Lesson Practice

Use the Reading Guide to help you understand the passage.

Reading Guide

Different subjects use different terms. Which words in the passage could only be used in a science passage?

Think about the different meanings of the word *frequency*.

Which transition word could you use to begin sentence 6 of paragraph 3?

Sound Waves

When you throw a stone into a pond, there is a ripple effect. The ripples begin from where the stone initially fell, and the ripples grow continuously until they practically disappear. <u>Sound</u> works in a very similar manner. When you hear a person talking, a dog barking, or a police siren, you hear sound.

Sound is a kind of energy that moves through matter as waves. All sounds are made when something is <u>vibrating</u>. To vibrate means to move back and forth very fast. Vibrations cause air particles to move. The vibrations within air particles are called "sound waves." Sound moves as waves, but the waves are not like water waves.

Think about what happens when someone moves a guitar string. The string vibrates. Each time the string moves, it bumps against nearby air molecules. These molecules <u>bump</u> against other molecules. The string moves back and forth. It bumps molecules over and over. This causes the air molecules to move out in waves.

If vibrations are fast, you will hear high notes, and if they are slow, you will hear low notes. This type of vibration is often called a <u>frequency</u>.

Sound waves travel faster in water than they do in air. For example, a whale can hear a sound from another whale when they're nearly one hundred miles apart.

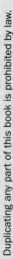

Answer the following questions.

1. In paragraph 1, the word <u>sound</u> means

    A. free from flaw or defect.

    B. undisturbed.

    C. to make known.

    D. something observed by the sense of hearing.

2. Which phrase from the passage helps you figure out the meaning of <u>vibrating</u>?

    A. "moves through matter"

    B. "to move back and forth"

    C. "a kind of energy"

    D. "sounds are made"

3. According to the passage, <u>bump</u> means

    A. swelling.

    B. to proceed.

    C. to collide with.

    D. to encounter an obstacle.

4. Which word BEST fits the beginning of the first sentence in paragraph 4?

    A. Accordingly

    B. All in all

    C. Instead

    D. Besides

5. Which sentence from the passage helps you figure out the meaning of <u>frequency</u>?

    _____

    _____

    _____

    _____

    _____

The following questions do not relate to a passage.

6. Read the sentence in each answer choice. Then match the underlined word in the sentence to its closest definition on the right.

A. English colonists signed the Mayflower Compact, a written document with the rules and regulations that they would follow, before leaving the ship and settling in Plymouth.

1. combination

2. condense

3. problem

B. The recycling center used a machine to compact the aluminum cans to make room for more.

4. communication

5. agreement

C. The main character of the novel used an odd expression when he spoke to the excited crowd gathered around him. I didn't understand what it meant.

6. phrase

D. An expression in math does not include an answer. For example, 4 + 5 is an expression, while 4 + 5 = 9 is an equation.

7. A student is writing a report about eating a nutritious, healthy meal. Read this paragraph from the report and the directions that follow.

> **It is important to make healthy food choices when preparing meals. There are different food groups: fruits, vegetables, grains, proteins, and dairy. To have a healthy diet you need something from each group each day. _____, according to the United States Department of Agriculture, you don't need to eat the same amount from each group. For example, you need three cups of dairy a day, but only 1 ½ cups of fruit a day.**

The student needs to complete the fourth sentence with a transition. What word BEST completes the fourth sentence?

A. Besides

B. However

C. Instead

D. Next

8. A student is writing a report about hamsters. Read this paragraph from the report and the directions that follow.

> **A lot of people have hamsters for pets, but having a hamster is a lot of responsibility. You need to feed it every day and make sure its water bottle is full. Once a week, you have to clean its cage with soap and water. You should also change the shavings, or bedding, once a week. It's important that you always close the cage properly. You don't want your hamster getting out!**

The student needs to complete the paragraph with one more sentence. Which sentence BEST completes the paragraph?

A. Besides, a hamster is easier to take care of than a dog or cat.

B. In addition, hamsters are not a lot of work.

C. Furthermore, a hamster is a great pet.

D. Therefore, there is a lot to consider before you get a hamster.

28 Root Words and Affixes

Getting the Idea

A **root** is the basic word that another word is made from. A root gives a word its main meaning. Many roots come from Latin or Greek. A **base word** is a part of a longer word that can stand on its own. We often call base words **root words**.

An **affix** is a special group of letters that is added before or after a root. A **prefix** is an affix added at the beginning of a root word. A **suffix** is an affix added at the end of a root word. When you understand how affixes change the meaning of a root word, you can figure out what the new word means. To find a root word, look for the "hidden" word that gives the main word its meaning. Sometimes you can see the entire word hidden inside, and other times it may be missing a letter. For example, the -e at the end of a word is often dropped when a suffix is added. Be careful, though. Not every hidden word is the root word. Look at the chart below.

Word	Meaning	Root	Meaning
distribute	hand out	trib	pay
describe	tell what something looks like	scrib	write
infamous	having a very bad reputation	fam	glory
memorize	learn something by heart	memor	mindful
formative	important to development	forma	make

Each prefix or suffix has its own meaning. When you add the affix to the root word, the meaning of the new word is a combination of the meanings of the root and the affix together. Look at the charts on the next page to see some common prefixes and suffixes.

Prefix	Meaning	Example
anti-	against, the opposite of	antibacterial—defending against bacteria
be-	to make something happen	behold—to put or have something in your line of sight
co-	together	cooperate—to act together
counter-	against	counteract—to act against
dis-	the opposite of, not	discourage—to put down, to not encourage
inter-	between, among	interoffice—between offices
mis-	wrong	misinform—to wrongly inform
non-	without	nontoxic—not toxic, not poisonous
pre-	before	preview—to view before
re-	again	reevaluate—to think about something again
semi-	partly, half	semicircle—a half circle
un-	not	unopened—not yet opened

Suffix	Meaning	Example
-able, -ible	able	edible—able to be eaten
-ation	act or process	imagination—the act of imagining something
-er, -or	one who does	teacher—one who teaches
-er	more	brighter—more bright
-est	most	funniest—most funny
-ful	full	mindful—full of awareness
-ian	from, relating to	Italian—a person from Italy
-ic	consisting of, relating to	Icelandic—relating to Iceland
-ion	act of doing something	election—act of electing someone
-less	without	clueless—without a clue
-ly	in a certain way	loudly—in a loud way
-ment	state of doing something	engagement—state of being engaged
-ous	full of something	mysterious—full of mystery
-ward	in a direction	downward—in a down direction

Thinking It Through

Read the following paragraph, and then answer the questions that follow.

Yoga was once thought of as a specialized Eastern practice. Today, however, yoga is practiced by millions of people in the United States alone. Practicing yoga helps many people reduce stress in their lives. People are also realizing the health benefits of yoga. From lowering blood pressure to reducing pain from spinal <u>misalignment</u>, yoga does wonders for the body.

What is the root word in <u>misalignment</u>? How do the prefix and suffix change the meaning of the word?

_____

_____

_____

_____

HINT Sometimes you can see the entire word hidden inside a word with affixes.

 **DISCUSS** With a partner, think of three words with the prefix *mis-* (for example: *mismanage*) and three words with the suffix *-ment* (for example: *treatment*). What do the words mean? Share your ideas with the class.

Coached Example

Read the passage and answer the questions.

There is a redwood tree so big that you can drive right through it! When people visit The Redwood National and State Parks in Northern California, they often say things like: amazing! incredible! <u>unbelievable</u>! Imagine a 35-story building in your town, and that is how tall some redwood trees are. The redwood seed is no bigger than a tiny tomato seed, and yet the trees can grow up to 367 feet high and 22 feet wide. They can live up to 2,000 years; most live up to 600 years. According to the U.S. National Park Service, the ancestors of today's coastal redwoods grew in the Jurassic Era. (The Jurassic Era was 160 million years ago.) These trees live long because they are very near to the coast. This keeps them safe from fire and drought because of the moisture coming off of the Pacific Ocean. They are also free from <u>infection</u> and insects because of the wood's composition.

---

1. What is the root word in <u>unbelievable</u>?

   A. lie

   B. able

   C. believe

   D. un

   HINT Remember, to find a root, look for the "hidden" word that gives the main word its meaning.

2. What is the suffix in <u>infection</u>?

   A. infect

   B. in

   C. ection

   D. ion

   HINT The suffix is the end part of a word.

Lesson Practice

Use the Reading Guide to help you understand the passage.

Reading Guide

What is the root word of *lovely*? How does the suffix change the word?

Look at the prefix in *international*. What does this prefix mean?

What is the suffix in the word *remarkable*?

Neighborhood Friends

Sarah lived in a <u>lovely</u> town near the beach. The house next door was a vacation home. Visitors would often come and stay a couple of nights, then leave. But sometimes there was a family with kids. Because no other kids lived on her street, Sarah often felt <u>disconnected</u>, and she hoped that the people next door would have a little girl or boy her age so she could have a playmate.

She had had many playmates in the past. Her playmates came from all over the state; there had even been <u>international</u> visitors. Last summer, a family from France stayed for a whole month. Sarah showed Jacques and Isabelle all of her favorite places in town. They went swimming in the ocean, went to the tide pools, and ate ice cream at the boardwalk. Sarah had many pen pals and friends to keep in touch with. She came to the <u>realization</u> that she couldn't wait until she was old enough to travel, so she could go visit them all!

Last weekend, she saw new people arrive, so she went in the driveway and waited to see if there were any children her age. The family didn't have any kids. Instead, she <u>befriended</u> a big black dog with curly hair. The dog approached her, wagging its tail.

The dog's name was Henry. Sarah and Henry took walks, played ball, and even had a tea party! It was too bad that they couldn't be pen pals because Sarah and the dog had the most <u>remarkable</u> time together! Henry's owners said they would come back next year, so she would have to wait.

Answer the following questions.

1. What is the root word in underlined disconnected?

   A. disc

   B. disconnect

   C. connect

   D. connected

2. In the word underlined international, the prefix underlined inter- means

   A. before.

   B. again.

   C. together.

   D. among.

3. In the word underlined realization, the suffix underlined -tion means

   A. act or process.

   B. able.

   C. most.

   D. without.

4. The word underlined befriended means

   A. to become friends again.

   B. to have made friends.

   C. to be friendly.

   D. to not have friends.

5. What is the root of underlined remarkable?

   _____

   _____

   _____

   _____

   _____

The following questions do not relate to a passage.

6. Below are three sentences. Some sentences contain words with prefixes and suffixes.

Sam drove to the store to buy milk, bread, and butter for dinner.
Jessica made a commitment to work at the fair on Saturday afternoon.
Kate reconsidered her answers on the test; she was unsure if they were correct.

Part A

Circle the words that have prefixes. Underline the words that have suffixes.

Part B

Below, write the words with prefixes or suffixes you selected in Part A. Break each word into its parts and tell what the word means.

_____

_____

_____

_____

7. Read these sentences and the question that follows.

The teacher wanted to move the desks into a different order. She wanted to _____ the desks.

Which word BEST completes the sentence?

A. arrangement

B. arranger

C. prearrange

D. rearrange

8. Read the sentence or sentences in each answer choice. Then match the underlined word in the sentence to its closest definition on the right.

A. She was <u>disheartened</u> after hearing the news that her team didn't win the competition.

1. teamwork

2. restrain

B. The group used <u>cooperation</u> to finish the project. The members couldn't do it alone.

3. irresponsible

C. Their classmate behaved in a <u>thoughtless</u> manner, putting them all in danger.

4. discouraged

5. praise

6. thorough

29 Idioms, Adages, and Proverbs

Getting the Idea

Literary devices are tools the author uses to make his or her writing interesting and enjoyable to read. One common tool is figurative language. Idioms, adages, and proverbs, like other types of figurative language, have a different or deeper meaning than the literal, or actual, meaning.

An **idiom** is a common figurative phrase. The words of an idiom mean something entirely different from what they seem to mean. For example, "Jenny is on the fence about going to the beach or the movies" does not mean Jenny is actually sitting *on a fence*. It means she has not made up her mind. The expression *on the fence* is an idiom meaning "undecided." Read the following example.

> When Jill left, she broke Jack's heart.

Jill did not physically break Jack's heart. Instead, when Jill left, Jack felt very sad and lonely. Here are two more examples.

> I thought that project was easy. It was a piece of cake!

> When I took this job, I bit off more than I could chew.

The actual meaning of the first sentence is that the project was as enjoyable to do as eating a piece of cake. In the second sentence, "bit off more than I could chew" means taking on more work than I could handle.

To understand idioms and figurative phrases, consider the context of a word or phrase. If a phrase seems impossible or silly and does not make sense as it is written, the writer probably means something else.

A **proverb** is a simple and concrete saying popularly known and repeated. Proverbs often express advice based on common sense or practical experience. *Bad news travels fast* and *better late than never* are proverbs that you have probably heard before. They differ from idioms in that their meaning is literal—they mean exactly what they say.

Some proverbs are used metaphorically. For example, *a chain is no stronger than its weakest link.* The meaning is literal, but it is often applied to people or situations.

> The basketball team's poor shooting will hurt them in the playoffs, because a chain is no stronger than its weakest link.

Proverbs are phrases that represent some advice or commonly believed fact. In this case, the proverb means that everyone has to play equally well for good performance in the playoffs.

An **adage** is a saying that has been popularly accepted over a long period of time. It expresses a truth or insight. For example: *Where there's smoke, there's fire.* Adages may be interesting observations, practical or ethical guidelines, or comments on life. Adages are very similar to proverbs. In fact, the two are often mistaken for each other. Look at the chart below to see some other examples of proverbs and adages.

Examples of Proverbs and Adages
Actions speak louder than words.
A leopard cannot change its spots.
Birds of a feather flock together.
He can't see the forest for the trees.
Every rose has its thorn.
Great minds think alike.
Honesty is the best policy.
It's no use crying over spilt milk.
One man's trash is another man's treasure.
Slow and steady wins the race.
You can't teach an old dog new tricks.

Thinking It Through

Read the following paragraph, and then answer the questions that follow.

Before the discovery of the Rosetta Stone in Egypt in 1799, people could not understand the meaning of Egyptian hieroglyphics. They couldn't make heads or tails out of them. The symbols did not make any sense. The Rosetta Stone allowed scholars to translate the hieroglyphics into Greek. From the Greek, scholars could then translate into other languages.

Which sentence contains an idiom? What does the idiom mean?

_____

_____

_____

_____

 Idioms do not mean what you usually think the words mean. Reread the paragraph and see which words do not mean exactly what they say.

DISCUSS Which words in the paragraph helped you understand the meaning of the idiom? How else could the sentence have been written? Present your ideas in a group.

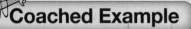

Coached Example

Read the passage and answer the questions.

When you're on a bumper car ride at the amusement park, things may seem out of hand. All the crashing and bumping can get a bit crazy at times. Actually, though, the bumper cars are a great way to learn about physics. Your car has an electric pole extending from the back of your car and up to an electric grid in the ceiling. Electric energy travels down to your car and turns into kinetic energy, which causes movement. And that's where Isaac Newton comes in. He came up with a law of motion. Bumper cars follow that law, believe it or not.

According to Newton's third law of motion, when two objects interact, there is an action and a reaction. The action happens when one object crashes into another. The second object goes in the opposite direction of the first object. This is the reaction.

So, think about what happens when someone bumps into your bumper car. Your car goes in the opposite direction of the person that hit you, and it travels with the same amount of force. A lot of people <u>get a kick</u> out of this ride, but now you know the science of how it works!

---

1. Which sentence from the passage contains an idiom?

    A. "When you're on a bumper car ride at the amusement park, things may seem out of hand."

    B. "This is the reaction."

    C. "The action happens when one object crashes into another."

    D. "He came up with a law of motion."

    HINT Idioms mean something entirely different from what the individual words in the phrase mean.

2. What does <u>get a kick</u> mean?

    A. to kick somebody

    B. to be kicked by somebody

    C. to have a bad time

    D. to have a good time

    HINT Remember, to understand idioms, think about the context.

Lesson Practice

Use the Reading Guide to help you understand the passage.

Reading Guide

Idioms have a different meaning than the words suggest. Which phrases in the passage have a different meaning than the individual words?

Proverbs and adages express a truth or insight. What truth or insight does the last sentence express?

Teaching Kyle

This summer, I taught my little brother Kyle to swim. Kyle was so afraid at first that he would just sit on a step in the shallow end of the pool and cry. Meanwhile, I would be in the deep end encouraging him to come toward me. But he would just sit there and cry until he was blue in the face. My dad always says, "Patience is a virtue." I tried to be as patient as possible as I waited for him to stop crying. I started to wonder if I was <u>not cut out for teaching</u>.

I paddled around some myself, so he could see how fun swimming was. It felt like pulling teeth, but I really wanted him to try. Kyle continued to just sit on his safe little step. I didn't want to force him off it. <u>Better safe than sorry</u>, right?

Kyle sat on his step and watched the other kids swimming and laughing. I crossed my arms and sighed; <u>I made my bed, now I had to lie in it</u>. Finally, I asked, "Do you want me to hold you in the deep part?" Kyle choked on his tears and immediately stopped crying. He nodded his head.

I took him down to the deeper end of the pool. Kyle seemed to enjoy watching the older kids dive off the diving board. I told him, "You'll be able to do that one day. But, you have to learn to walk before you can run."

Answer the following questions.

1. Which sentence from the passage contains an idiom?

    A. "Meanwhile, I would be in the deep end encouraging him to come toward me."

    B. "But he would just sit there and cry until he was blue in the face."

    C. "Kyle continued to just sit on his safe little step."

    D. "I didn't want to force him off it."

2. What does <u>not cut out for teaching</u> mean?

    A. not allowed to teach

    B. not able to cut

    C. not able to teach

    D. made to teach

3. Which sentence from the passage contains a proverb?

    A. "This summer, I taught my little brother Kyle to swim."

    B. "'My dad always says, 'Patience is a virtue.'"

    C. "Kyle choked on his tears and immediately stopped crying."

    D. "I took him down to the deeper end of the pool."

4. What does <u>better safe than sorry</u> mean?

    A. It's better to be nice to other people.

    B. It's better to do what you want.

    C. It's better to be safe than feeling sad.

    D. It's better to be too careful than to be careless and regret it later.

5. What does <u>I made my bed, now I had to lie in it</u> mean in paragraph 3?

    _____

    _____

    _____

    _____

    _____

    _____

    _____

The following questions do not relate to a passage.

6. Read the sentence in each answer choice. Then match the idiom to its meaning on the right.

A. | She let the cat out of the bag. |

B. | She hit the nail on the head. |

C. | She hit the books. |

1. | She has too much work. |

2. | She told the secret. |

3. | She was right. |

4. | She needs to be careful. |

5. | She studied hard. |

6. | She cheated. |

7. The following paragraphs are from a student's story. Read these paragraphs from the story and the directions that follow.

"Where are my sunglasses?" Mom asked.

"They are as plain as the nose on your face," I said, and laughed.

"Very funny," Mom said. "They cost me an arm and a leg. Now, spill the beans! Where are they?"

I pointed to the top of her head.

Part A

Underline the figurative language in the paragraphs.

Part B

Write the meaning of each phrase you underlined in Part A on the lines below.

_____

_____

_____

_____

8. A student is writing an essay about his grandfather. Read the paragraphs and the directions that follow.

My grandpa had never before used a computer. "They're just too complicated for someone like me," he said. "I'll never figure out how to use one."

"I can teach you how to use it," I said.

He said, "I don't think so. _____."

The student needs to fill in the blank line with an adage. Which adage BEST fits the essay?

A. Slow and steady wins the race.

B. Birds of feather flock together.

C. You can't teach an old dog new tricks.

D. Don't count your chickens before they hatch.

30 Word Relationships

Getting the Idea

Writers choose words with care. Some writers use simple language and short sentences. Some writers use specific language and longer sentences. There are many different ways to say the same thing. A writer has to have a large **vocabulary**, or set of words he or she knows how to use when writing. A good vocabulary helps a writer express ideas and actions clearly.

Synonyms are words that have the same, or almost the same, meaning. For example, the words *speedy* and *quickly* are synonyms because they both mean that something moves fast. The chart below lists some common synonyms.

Word	Synonyms
little	tiny, small
big	huge, large
laugh	chuckle, giggle
wet	damp, moist, soaked
silly	ridiculous, crazy
smart	clever, intelligent
pretty	beautiful, gorgeous
rich	wealthy, well-off

Antonyms are words that have the opposite meaning, such as *hot* and *cold*. For words to be antonyms, it is not enough for them to have different meanings—they must have opposite meanings. For example, the words *table* and *chair* are often used as a pair, and they have different meanings. They are not opposites, however, so they cannot be antonyms. The chart on the next page lists some common antonyms.

Word	Antonym
ugly	beautiful
tall	short
inside	outside
asleep	awake
difficult	easy
old	young
happy	sad
broken	fixed

Identifying synonyms and antonyms can help you build your vocabulary and teach you relationships between words. Synonyms teach you different ways to say the same thing. For example, three synonyms for *sad* are *gloomy, miserable,* and *heartbroken*. These words mean almost the same thing as *sad*, but there are slight differences between them. Writers often choose between synonyms to show such differences. *Heartbroken* expresses greater unhappiness than the word *sad*. In learning synonyms, you will find that words have different shades of meaning. You will find that certain words are more suggestive. They hint or imply certain feelings or ideas that other words do not.

Recognizing and understanding synonyms and antonyms can help readers understand passages with unfamiliar words or phrases. At the same time, understanding synonyms and antonyms can help writers express their thoughts and ideas more precisely.

Thinking It Through

Read the following paragraph, and then answer the questions that follow.

Surfing is one of the <u>oldest</u> sports practiced on the planet. It involves riding a board along breaking waves by the shore. Early surfboards were very <u>large</u>. Today, surfboards are smaller and lighter. Surfers lie on their stomach and paddle out to the breaking waves. When a tall wave approaches, surfers stand on their boards and ride the wave.

What is an antonym for <u>oldest</u>? What are synonyms for <u>large</u>?

_____

_____

_____

_____

 What word means the opposite of *oldest*? Which words could replace *large*?

DISCUSS Discuss your answers with a partner. Then find other words in the paragraph, such as *early*, *smaller*, *lighter*, and *tall*, and come up with synonyms or antonyms for them. Share your ideas in a group.

Coached Example

Read the passage and answer the questions.

There was once a cat named Snowflake. When she was a kitten, she sat at the windowsill and tried to catch the snowflakes coming down. Snowflake lived in a tall apartment building. Consequently, she never went outside, because there wasn't a yard or patio for her to go out and play. She often sat looking out the window, rain or shine. Snowflake wasn't <u>distracted</u> by other animal life like other dogs or cats, because she was too far from the sidewalk to even notice them. Sometimes, the chirping of a bird or the squirrels playing in the tall trees caught her eye.

When Snowflake had to move, she was sad and excited. The new house was much larger than the old apartment, and it had a yard. The first week at the new house gave Snowflake plenty of surprises. She played in the flowerbeds and was <u>startled</u> by the barking dog next door. Next, she was attacked by another cat. Then, she got fleas. Now, when she sits by the window, she sees her enemy cats outside and doesn't know what to do. Poor Snowflake wants to be back in her old apartment!

---

1. What is a synonym for <u>distracted</u>?

  A. focused

  B. known

  C. bothered

  D. confused

> **HINT** Synonyms are words that have the same, or almost the same, meaning. Which of the answer choices could fit in the sentence?

2. The word <u>startled</u> means the opposite of

  A. calmed.

  B. spooked.

  C. amazed.

  D. surprised.

> **HINT** Remember, for this question, it is not enough for words to have different meanings. They must have opposite meanings.

Lesson Practice

Use the Reading Guide to help you understand the passage.

Reading Guide

Which words have the same meaning as *poor*?

Which word means the opposite of *famous*?

Remember that synonyms may have different shades of meaning.

Louis Armstrong

Louis Armstrong was born in 1901 in New Orleans, Louisiana. He grew up in a <u>poor</u> family. He was only seven years old when he started playing music. For money, he sang on the streets and played music for funerals, among other <u>odd</u> jobs. He played in bands that had different jazz styles. The jazz scene of New Orleans inspired this gifted musician. Armstrong enhanced his musical skills as he gathered and cooperated with other talented musicians. Armstrong was jazz great King Oliver's apprentice. He researched with Oliver and learned from him.

When Armstrong moved to New York City, he was an up-and-coming jazz musician. But, America was suffering from the Great Depression. Amazingly, it was during this time that Armstrong became world famous.

Millions of people were jobless; Americans everywhere had to <u>struggle</u> to survive. In 1932, only 10 million records in the country were sold. But, only seven years later, in 1939, 50 million records were sold. The jump in sales was caused by "swing," which was a new kind of jazz. Swing music <u>made</u> people want to dance and uplifted people's spirits during hard times. Because Armstrong played swing and helped to make it <u>famous</u>, he became very successful during this period.

Answer the following questions.

1. What is a synonym for <u>odd</u>?

   A. unusual   C. unpaired

   B. alone   D. unremarkable

2. Read the following sentence from paragraph 1.

   > **Armstrong enhanced his musical skills as he gathered and cooperated with other talented musicians.**

   Which of the following sentences would better match the rest of the passage?

   A. Armstrong enhanced his musical skills as he organized and played with other musicians.

   B. Armstrong improved his musical skills as he met and participated with others.

   C. Armstrong improved his musical skills as he met and played with other talented musicians.

   D. Armstrong enhanced his skills as he encountered and played with other talented musicians.

3. The word <u>struggle</u> means the opposite of

   A. labor.

   B. relax.

   C. work hard.

   D. play.

4. Which of the following words does NOT have a similar meaning to <u>made</u>, as used in the passage?

   A. caused

   B. asked

   C. encouraged

   D. discouraged

5. Read the following sentences from the passage.

   > **Armstrong was jazz great King Oliver's apprentice. He researched with Oliver and learned from him.**

   Rewrite the sentences, using synonyms to better match the rest of the passage.

   _____

The following questions do not relate to a passage.

6. A student is writing a report about a family meal. Read this paragraph from the report and the directions that follow.

> On Sunday we worked together to make a family feast. We had turkey, mashed potatoes, and corn. The turkey was my favorite; it was <u>good</u>. Everyone else must have enjoyed it, too, because there was none left.

Choose all the words with similar meanings that could be used to replace the underlined word. There is more than one correct choice listed below.

A. acceptable   D. excellent

B. tasty   E. satisfactory

C. delicious   F. unsavory

7. Read the paragraph below.

> Mrs. Williams loudly declared her excitement about her upcoming vacation hiking in the mountains. She <u>suppressed</u> her enthusiasm around her neighbor, who had broken her leg and wasn't able to go on the trip. But around her family, Mrs. Williams revealed her true feelings. She proclaimed, "I can't wait to go!"

Part A

Circle the antonyms of the underlined word.

Part B

Explain the meanings of the antonyms to support your answer in Part A.

_____

_____

_____

_____

8. Read the sentence in each answer choice. Then match the underlined word in the sentence to its antonym on the right.

A. | The wait to pay for our purchase was <u>prolonged</u> due to the long lines.

1. tired

2. lengthy

B. | He had an <u>ambitious</u> goal of one day becoming president of the United States.

3. modest

C. | She was <u>weary</u> from all of the homework she had to do after being sick for so long.

4. shortened

5. challenging

6. energetic

4 Cumulative Assessment

The following passage contains mistakes. Read the passage and answer the questions that follow.

Home Run Champion

(1) Tom's room had three bookshelfs. (2) They were filled with many of the things you would find in any ten-year-old boy's room. (3) Tom had books, baseballs, and model, cars. (4) Tom also had several trophys for, soccer, tennis, and football. (5) What he didn't have was a trophy for the most home runs. (6) Tom wanted that trophy badly. (7) He knew that where there's a will, there's a way.

(8) Each day after school he went to the batting cage to practice. (9) He hit ball after ball forcefully. (10) Now, here he was in the final game of the season. (11) Tom just need to hit one home run to beat the record. (12) At his first turn at bat, Tom marched to the plate with <u>determination</u>. (13) He thought he saw the perfect pitch. (14) "Wait for it! He coached himself." (15) As it zoomed toward the plate, Tom kept his eyes on the ball. (16) He controlled his movements.

(17) The ball went high. (18) Straight into the outfield. (19) "Please don't catch it!" he hoped as he rounded the bases. (20) As Tom headed home, the second-base player wound up to throw the ball to the catcher. (21) Tom ran faster than he thought he could. (22) His heart was pounding in his chest. (23) He slid onto the plate as the umpire yelled "Safe!" (24) Tom had finally acheived his goal.

1. Which sentence from the passage does NOT have a spelling error?

   A. Tom's room had three bookshelfs.

   B. Tom also had several trophys for, soccer, tennis, and football.

   C. Tom wanted that trophy badly.

   D. Tom had finally acheived his goal.

2. Which sentence from the passage is punctuated correctly?

   A. Tom had books, baseballs, and model, cars.

   B. Tom also had several trophys for, soccer, tennis, and football.

   C. "Wait for it! He coached himself."

   D. At his first turn at bat, Tom marched to the plate with determination.

3. Which sentence from the passage contains a proverb?

   A. Tom wanted that trophy badly.

   B. He knew that where there's a will, there's a way.

   C. He hit ball after ball forcefully.

   D. He controlled his movements.

4. Which of the following sentences contains a preposition?

   A. He thought he saw the perfect pitch.

   B. The ball went high.

   C. His heart was pounding in his chest.

   D. Tom ran faster than he thought he could.

5. In sentence 12, the word determination means

   A. firm intention.

   B. direction.

   C. not sure.

   D. uncertainty.

6. Which is the BEST way to combine sentences 17 and 18? Write it below.

   The ball went high. Straight into the outfield.

The following passage contains mistakes. Read the passage and answer the questions that follow.

Being an Inuit

(1) My name is Buniq, which means "sweet daughter" in the Inuit language. (2) Some people call Inuit people Eskimos, but I just call them family. (3) We live in the southern part of Alaska on the Alaskan peninsula. (4) I love being an Inuit.

(5) We are known for our artwork especially our, beautiful, stone, carvings. (6) I love walking through the village and seeing everyone's creations. (7) Mr. James Houston visited our village in the 1940s and taught my people the art of <u>printmaking</u>. (8) Some people in our village make nature prints. (9) People think Alaska is bare and covered with snow all the time. (10) However in the spring the fields are, filled with tiny wildflowers. (11) Even winter gives ideas, with icicles drooping from pines, and hares leaving paw prints as they hurdle across the snow.

(12) I am also an artist. (13) I work with my mother, Nukka. (14) She makes beautiful nature prints and I had wrote poems to go with them. (15) We <u>recently</u> published a book called *A Walk with the Inuit*. (16) I am planning a trip to the museum in, Albany New York to share my book at an exhibit of Inuit art.

7. Which phrase from the passage helps you figure out the meaning of <u>printmaking</u>?

    A. "walking through the village"

    B. "Alaska is bare"

    C. "make nature prints"

    D. "hares leaving paw prints"

8. What is the root word in <u>recently</u>?

    A. cent

    B. rec

    C. ly

    D. recent

9. Read this sentence from the passage.

    She makes beautiful nature prints and I had wrote poems to go with them.

    Which of the following is written correctly?

    A. She makes beautiful nature prints, and I had write poems to go with them.

    B. She makes beautiful nature prints, and I write poems to go with them.

    C. She made beautiful nature prints, and I had written poems to go with them.

    D. She made beautiful nature prints, and I had write poems to go with them.

10. Which of the following sentences contains a conjunction?

    A. sentence 1

    B. sentence 2

    C. sentence 3

    D. sentence 5

11. Which sentence from the passage is punctuated correctly?

    A. We are known for our artwork especially our, beautiful, stone, carvings.

    B. However in the spring the fields are, filled with tiny wildflowers.

    C. I work with my mother, Nukka.

    D. I am planning a trip to the museum in, Albany New York to share my book at an exhibit of Inuit art.

12. Read the following sentence from paragraph 2.

Even winter gives ideas, with icicles drooping from pines and hares leaving paw prints as they hurdle across the snow.

Rewrite the sentence using synonyms to better match the rest of the passage.

_____

_____

_____

_____

_____

_____

_____

_____

Glossary

adage a saying that has been popularly accepted over a long period of time

affix a group of letters that is added before or after a root

alliteration the repetition of consonant sounds at the beginnings of words

analyze to think deeply about what you read

antonym a word that has the opposite meaning of another word

atlas a book of maps

base word a part of a longer word that can stand on its own

bibliography a listing of the resources used for a written project

capitalization the use of capital letters at the beginning of sentences and certain kinds of words

cause the reason something happens

chapter section of a book

character any person or creature that takes part in the action of a story

climax the point in a story at which the conflict of the story is addressed by the main character(s)

comma (,) a punctuation mark used in lists, with conjunctions, between clauses, after an introductory word or phrase, and to set off a direct address

compare to identify ways that multiple things are alike

conclusion the final paragraph in an essay

conflict the struggle or problem faced by the characters in a story

conjunction a word that connects two or more words or sentences

context clues words in a sentence or paragraph that help you figure out the meaning of an unfamiliar word

contrast to identify ways that multiple things are different

definition the literal meaning of a word

detail a piece of information in literature, such as a name, an action, or a description

dialect the way a person who lives in a specific geographical area might speak

dialogue conversations that characters have with each other

dictionary a book that lists words alphabetically, tells how to pronounce them, and gives their definitions

draft one of the first versions of a writer's work

drama a type of literature written to be performed onstage by actors

editing correcting and changing a text in order to improve it

effect a result of a cause

encyclopedia a book or set of books that gives facts about many topics

evidence information that supports a claim in a text, such as statistics and survey results

example a piece of information that demonstrates or illustrates a broader word or concept

exclamation point (!) punctuation used to show excitement or emotion, placed at the end of a sentence

exposition introduces the reader to the characters and the setting early in a story

fact something that can be proven to be true

fiction a work of literature, such as a story or a novel, that is made up

figurative language descriptive language that is not used literally and creates an image in the reader's mind

first person a way of telling a story from the point of view of *I* or *we*

future perfect a form of the perfect tense made by combining the future tense of *to have* with the past tense form of a verb

future tense a form of a verb that describes actions that have not happened yet

generalization a broad statement based on specific facts and examples

graphic organizer a tool that helps to organize ideas and can be used to visually illustrate ideas

homographs two words that look alike but have different meanings

idiom a kind of figurative language that would not make sense if taken literally

independent clause a phrase that has a subject and verb and can stand alone as its own sentence

inference an educated guess about a passage based on details in the passage, prior knowledge, and common sense

informational writing writing that tells the reader about something, gives facts, or explains something

interjection a word or phrase that shows strong feeling

interpret to consider an aspect of a literary work to better understand its meaning

introduction the opening section or paragraph of an essay or a report

lines words spoken by the actors in a drama

literature written works such as short stories, novels, poems, and plays

main idea what the passage is mostly about

metaphor figurative language that makes a direct comparison between two things or ideas

motivation the reason a character does a certain thing or acts a certain way

multiple-meaning words words that are spelled the same but have more than one meaning

narrative writing writing that tells a story

narrator the character who tells a story

online directory an Internet reference that gives a list of Internet sites related to a topic

opinion a statement that cannot be proven. It communicates someone's feeling or judgment.

outline the plan for an essay or report in list form

paragraph a group of sentences that supports or explains one main idea

paraphrase to express ideas from a text in your own words

past perfect a form of the perfect tense made by combining the past tense of *to have* with the past tense of a verb

past tense a form of a verb used to describe actions that have already happened

perfect tense a form of a verb used to describe actions that have already been completed

period (.) a punctuation mark used to end a sentence that is a statement or command

periodical a publication, such as a newspaper, magazine, or brochure, that is released daily, weekly, monthly, or yearly

persuasive writing writing that tries to convince readers to do something or think a certain way

plot the events that happen in a story

poetry writing broken into lines or stanzas, often with rhyme and rhythm

point of view the position from which a story is told; also the attitude or perspective of the author

prefix a group of letters added to the beginning of a root word

preposition a word that links objects (generally nouns or pronouns) to other words in a sentence

prepositional phrase a phrase containing a preposition and an object

present perfect a form of the perfect tense made by combining the present tense of *to have* with the past participle of a verb

present tense a form of a verb used to describe actions or events happening currently

prior knowledge knowledge you have before you read a text, which is used to make inferences about the text

proofreading the process of reading your writing and looking for errors in grammar, spelling, and structure

proper noun a capitalized word that names a particular person, place, or thing

proverb a simple and concrete saying popularly known and repeated

punctuation marks that tell the reader when to pause, when a sentence ends, or what kind of sentence he or she is reading

quotation marks (" ") punctuation marks used around direct dialogue and certain titles

reference materials books or Web sites that contain particular kinds of information

relevant evidence information in a piece of persuasive writing that is related to its issue and supports its position

research the use of sources, such as books, newspapers, and the Internet, to find information

resolution the part of the story when the problems are solved and the story ends

resource any material that will help a writer find information

restatement when used as a context clue, a statement that sums up an idea

revise to make corrections and changes in a draft

root the most basic part of a word, often from Latin or Greek

root word the basic word part that another word is made of, when an affix is added

run-on sentence a long sentence that expresses two complete thoughts and should really be two sentences

sentence fragment a sentence that is missing a subject or a predicate and does not express a complete thought

sequence the order in which things happen in a text

setting the location and time in which a story takes place

simile figurative language that compares two things using *like* or *as*

simple sentence a sentence with one subject and at least one predicate

spelling using the correct arrangement of letters when writing a word

stanza a group of lines in a poem

suffix letters added to the end of a root word that change the meaning of the word

summary/summarize/summarizing a brief retelling of a passage in your own words; to briefly restate a text in your own words, including only the main ideas and the most important details

supporting details information that helps to prove or describe the main idea

syllable the smallest unit of sound in a word that contains at least a vowel or a vowel and consonant

synonym a word that means the same or almost the same as another word

tense the form of a verb that tells you when the action takes place

textbook a reference material that contains extensive information on subjects studied in schools

theme the central idea or meaning of a story

third person a way of telling a story from the point of view of someone who is not involved in the story

third-person limited a point of view in which *he* and *she* are used, and readers learn little about all characters' thoughts

third-person omniscient a point of view in which *he* and *she* are used, and readers learn much about all characters' thoughts

topic sentence a sentence that tells the main idea of a paragraph

trait a quality that is part of a character's personality

transition a word that links ideas in a text

verb a word that expresses action, a relationship between two things, or a state of being

verse a line of a poem or song

vocabulary words an author chooses when writing

Notes